한국의 토익 수험자 여러분께,

토익 시험은 세계적인 직무 영어능력 평가 시험으로, 지난 40여 년간 비즈니스 현장에서 필요한 영어능력 평가의 기준을 제시해 왔습니다. 토익 시험 및 토익스피킹, 토익라이팅 시험은 세계에서 가장 널리 통용되는 영어능력 검증 시험으로, 160여 개국 14,000여 기관이 토익 성적을 의사결정에 활용하고 있습니다.

YBM은 한국의 토익 시험을 주관하는 ETS 독점 계약사입니다.

ETS는 한국 수험자들의 효과적인 토익 학습을 돕고자 YBM을 통하여 'ETS 토익 공식 교재'를 독점 출간하고 있습니다. 또한 'ETS 토익 공식 교재' 시리즈에 기출문항을 제공해 한국의 다른 교재들에 수록된 기출을 복제하거나 변형한 문항으로 인하여 발생할 수 있는 수험자들의 혼동을 방지하고 있습니다.

복제 및 변형 문항들은 토익 시험의 출제의도를 벗어날 수 있기 때문에 기출문항을 수록한 'ETS 토익 공식 교재'만큼 시험에 잘 대비할 수 없습니다.

'ETS 토익 공식 교재'를 통하여 수험자 여러분의 영어 소통을 위한 노력에 큰 성취가 있기를 바랍니다.

감사합니다.

Dear TOEIC Test Takers in Korea,

The TOEIC program is the global leader in English-language assessment for the workplace. It has set the standard for assessing English-language skills needed in the workplace for more than 40 years. The TOEIC tests are the most widely used English language assessments around the world, with 14,000+ organizations across more than 160 countries trusting TOEIC scores to make decisions.

YBM is the ETS Country Master Distributor for the TOEIC program in Korea and so is the exclusive distributor for TOEIC Korea.

To support effective learning for TOEIC test-takers in Korea, ETS has authorized YBM to publish the only Official TOEIC prep books in Korea. These books contain actual TOEIC items to help prevent confusion among Korean test-takers that might be caused by other prep book publishers' use of reproduced or paraphrased items.

Reproduced or paraphrased items may fail to reflect the intent of actual TOEIC items and so will not prepare test-takers as well as the actual items contained in the ETS TOEIC Official prep books published by YBM.

We hope that these ETS TOEIC Official prep books enable you, as test-takers, to achieve great success in your efforts to communicate effectively in English.

Thank you.

입문부터 실전까지 수준별 학습을 통해 최단기 목표점수 달성!

ETS TOEIC® 공식수험서
스마트 학습 지원

www.ybmbooks.com에서도 무료 MP3를 다운로드 받을 수 있습니다.

ETS 토익 모바일 학습 플랫폼!
ETS 토익기출 수험서 어플

구글플레이　　앱스토어

교재 학습 지원	• 교재 해설 강의
	• LC 음원 MP3
	• 교재/부록 모의고사 채점 분석
	• 단어 암기장
부가 서비스	• 데일리 학습(토익 기출문제 풀이)
	• 토익 최신 경향 무료 특강
	• 토익 타이머
모의고사 결과 분석	• 파트별/문항별 정답률
	• 파트별/유형별 취약점 리포트
	• 전체 응시자 점수 분포도

ETS 토익 학습 전용 온라인 커뮤티니!
ETS TOEIC® Book 공식카페

etstoeicbook.co.kr

강사진의 학습 지원	토익 대표강사들의 학습 지원과 멘토링
교재 학습관 운영	교재별 학습게시판을 통해 무료 동영상 강의 등 학습 지원
학습 콘텐츠 제공	토익 학습 콘텐츠와 정기시험 예비특강 업데이트

토익,

실력과 점수를 한 번에!
출제기관이 만든
진짜 문제로 승부하라!

왜
출제기관에서
만든 문제여야
할까요?

2,300명의
시험개발 전문가!

교육, 심리, 통계, 인문학, 사회학 등
2,300여 명의 전문 연구원이 모인 ETS.
토익 한 세트가 완성되려면 문제 설계 및 집필,
내용 검토, 문항의 공정성 및 타당성 검증,
난이도 조정, 모의시험 등 15단계의 개발공정에서
수많은 전문가의 손을 거쳐야 합니다.

2,300

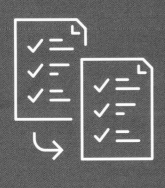

싱크로율 100%

ETS TOEIC 교재의 모든 예문과 문항 및 해설은
100% ETS TOEIC 정기시험 개발부서에서 개발
및 검수되었습니다.
그러므로 사진, LC 음원, 문항 유형 및 난이도 등
모든 면에서 실제 시험과 싱크로율 100%입니다.

100%

최고의 정기시험
적중률!

기출 문항을 변형한 복제 문항이 아닌,
ETS 토익 출제팀이 만든 원본 문항 100%로,
시중의 어느 교재와도 비교할 수 없는 압도적으로
높은 적중률을 보장합니다.

최고의 적중률!

토익 정기시험 기출종합서 LC

발행인	허문호
발행처	YBM
편집	허유정
디자인	DOTS
마케팅	정연철, 박천산, 고영노, 김동진, 박찬경, 김윤하
초판발행	2021년 11월 8일
5쇄 발행	2024년 12월 5일
신고일자	1964년 3월 28일
신고번호	제 1964-000003호
주소	서울시 종로구 종로 104
전화	(02) 2000-0515 [구입문의] / (02) 2000-0429 [내용문의]
팩스	(02) 2285-1523
홈페이지	www.ybmbooks.com

ISBN 978-89-17-23860-0

*toeic.

LC 토익 정기 시험 기출종합서

PREFACE

Dear test taker,

Here is a test preparation book created to help you succeed in using English as a tool for communication both in Korea and around the world.

This book will provide you with practical steps that you can take right now to improve your English proficiency and your TOEIC® test score. Now more than ever, your TOEIC score is a respected professional credential and an indicator of how well you can use English in a wide variety of situations to get the job done. As always, your TOEIC score is recognized globally as evidence of your English-language proficiency.

With the ETS TOEIC® Official Prep Book, you can make sure you have the best and most thorough preparation for the TOEIC® test. This book contains test questions that have appeared in actual TOEIC® tests, as well as test questions that were developed separately by the same specialists who write the TOEIC® test. It will enable you to master key points of the test at a rapid pace by studying and practicing with actual TOEIC® questions.

The ETS TOEIC® Official Prep Book includes the following key features.
· Questions from actual TOEIC tests
· Analyses of the TOEIC question types and preparation strategies
· Detailed explanations for learners
· The same voice actors that you will hear in an ETS test administration

Use the ETS TOEIC® Official Prep Book to help you prepare to use English in an ever-globalizing workplace. You will become familiar with the test, including the new test tasks, content, and format. These learning materials have been carefully crafted to help you advance in proficiency and gain a score report that will show the world what you know and what you can do.

출제기관이 만든
국내 유일 **토익 시험 대비서!**

기본기부터 실전까지 가장 빠르고 효과적으로 도달하는 방법, 이 한 권에 모두 담았습니다!

독점제공	**출제기관**이 제공하는 **기출문제 독점** 수록!
유일무이	정기시험 음원과 **동일한 성우 녹음!**
최신경향	토익 기출문제로 **정확한 최신 경향 분석!**
국내최고	정기시험과 동일한 수준의 **ETS 개발 문항!**

목차

PART 3

PART 4

WHAT IS THE TOEIC?

TOEIC은 어떤 시험인가요?

Test of English for International Communication (국제적 의사소통을 위한 영어 시험)의 약자로서,
영어가 모국어가 아닌 사람들이 일상생활 또는 비즈니스 현장에서 꼭 필요한 실용적 영어 구사 능력을 갖추었는가를
평가하는 시험이다.

■ 시험 구성

구성	Part		내용	문항수	시간	배점
듣기(LC)	1		사진 묘사	6	45분	495점
	2		질의 & 응답	25		
	3		짧은 대화	39		
	4		짧은 담화	30		
읽기(RC)	5		단문 빈칸 채우기 (문법 / 어휘)	30	75분	495점
	6		장문 빈칸 채우기	16		
	7	독해	단일 지문	29		
			이중 지문	10		
			삼중 지문	15		
Total	7 Parts			200문항	120분	990점

■ TOEIC 접수는 어떻게 하나요?

TOEIC 접수는 한국 토익 위원회 사이트(www.toeic.co.kr)에서 온라인 상으로만 접수가 가능하다. 사이트에서 매월 자세한 접수일정과 시험 일정 등의 구체적 정보 확인이 가능하니, 미리 일정을 확인하여 접수하도록 한다.

■ **시험장에 반드시 가져가야 할 준비물은요?**

신분증 규정 신분증만 가능
(주민등록증, 운전면허증, 기간 만료 전의 여권, 공무원증 등)

필기구 연필, 지우개 (볼펜이나 사인펜은 사용 금지)

■ **시험은 어떻게 진행되나요?**

09:20	입실 (09:50 이후는 입실 불가)
09:30 - 09:45	답안지 작성에 관한 오리엔테이션
09:45 - 09:50	휴식
09:50 - 10:05	신분증 확인
10:05 - 10:10	문제지 배부 및 파본 확인
10:10 - 10:55	듣기 평가 (Listening Test)
10:55 - 12:10	독해 평가 (Reading Test)

■ **TOEIC 성적 확인은 어떻게 하죠?**

시험일로부터 약 10-11일 후, 인터넷과 ARS(060-800-0515)로 성적을 확인할 수 있다. TOEIC 성적표는 우편이나 온라인으로 발급 받을 수 있다(시험 접수시, 양자 택일). 우편으로 발급 받을 경우는 성적 발표 후 대략 일주일이 소요되며, 온라인 발급을 선택하면 유효기간 내에 홈페이지에서 본인이 직접 1회에 한해 무료 출력할 수 있다. TOEIC 성적은 시험일로부터 2년간 유효하다.

■ **TOEIC은 몇 점 만점인가요?**

TOEIC 점수는 듣기 영역(LC) 점수, 읽기 영역(RC) 점수, 그리고 이 두 영역을 합계한 전체 점수 세 부분으로 구성된다. 각 부분의 점수는 5점 단위이며, 5점에서 495점에 걸쳐 주어지고, 전체 점수는 10점에서 990점까지이며, 만점은 990점이다. TOEIC 성적은 각 문제 유형의 난이도에 따른 점수 환산표에 의해 결정된다.

학습 스케줄

4 주 완성
학습 플랜

단기간에 토익을
마스터하고자 하는
중급 학습자

8 주 완성
학습 플랜

차근차근 토익을
마스터 하고자 하는
초중급 학습자

4 주 완성 학습 플랜

1주	☐ **Day 1** Part 1 Chapter 01 Unit 01~02	☐ **Day 2** Part 1 Chapter 01 Unit 03~04	☐ **Day 3** Part 1 Chapter 02 Unit 05~06	☐ **Day 4** Part 1 Chapter 02 Unit 07~08	☐ **Day 5** Part 1 Actual Test Part 2 Chapter 01 Unit 01~02
2주	☐ **Day 6** Part 2 Chapter 01 Unit 03~06	☐ **Day 7** Part 2 Chapter 02 Unit 07~10	☐ **Day 8** Part 2 Chapter 02 Unit 11~14	☐ **Day 9** Part 2 Actual Test Part 1, 2 복습	☐ **Day 10** Part 3 Chapter 01 Unit 01~04
3주	☐ **Day 11** Part 3 Chapter 01 Unit 05~08	☐ **Day 12** Part 3 Chapter 02 Unit 09~10	☐ **Day 13** Part 3 Chapter 02 Unit 11~12	☐ **Day 14** Part 3 Actual Test Part 4 Chapter 01 Unit 01~04	☐ **Day 15** Part 4 Chapter 01 Unit 05~08
4주	☐ **Day 16** Part 4 Chapter 02 Unit 09~10	☐ **Day 17** Part 4 Chapter 02 Unit 11~12	☐ **Day 18** Part 4 Chapter 02 Unit 13~15	☐ **Day 19** Part 4 Actual Test Part 3, 4 복습	☐ **Day 20** ETS Final Test 전체 복습

8 주 완성 학습 플랜

1주	☐ **Day 1** Part 1 Chapter 01 Unit 01~02	☐ **Day 2** Part 1 Chapter 01 Unit 03~04	☐ **Day 3** Part 1 Chapter 02 Unit 05~06	☐ **Day 4** Part 1 Chapter 02 Unit 07~08	☐ **Day 5** Part 1 Actual Test Part 1 복습
2주	☐ **Day 6** Part 2 Chapter 01 Unit 01~02	☐ **Day 7** Part 2 Chapter 01 Unit 03~04	☐ **Day 8** Part 2 Chapter 01 Unit 05~06	☐ **Day 9** Part 2 Chapter 02 Unit 07~08	☐ **Day 10** Part 2 Chapter 02 Unit 09~10
3주	☐ **Day 11** Part 2 Chapter 02 Unit 11~12	☐ **Day 12** Part 2 Chapter 02 Unit 13~14	☐ **Day 13** Part 2 Actual Test Part 2 복습	☐ **Day 14** Part 3 Chapter 01 Unit 01~02	☐ **Day 15** Part 3 Chapter 01 Unit 03~04
4주	☐ **Day 16** Part 3 Chapter 01 Unit 05~06	☐ **Day 17** Part 3 Chapter 01 Unit 07	☐ **Day 18** Part 3 Chapter 01 Unit 08	☐ **Day 19** Part 3 Chapter 02 Unit 09	☐ **Day 20** Part 3 Chapter 02 Unit 10
5주	☐ **Day 21** Part 3 Chapter 02 Unit 11	☐ **Day 22** Part 3 Chapter 02 Unit 12	☐ **Day 23** Part 3 Actual Test Part 3 복습	☐ **Day 24** Part 4 Chapter 01 Unit 01~02	☐ **Day 25** Part 4 Chapter 01 Unit 03~04
6주	☐ **Day 26** Part 4 Chapter 01 Unit 05~06	☐ **Day 27** Part 4 Chapter 01 Unit 07	☐ **Day 28** Part 4 Chapter 01 Unit 08	☐ **Day 29** Part 4 Chapter 02 Unit 09	☐ **Day 30** Part 4 Chapter 02 Unit 10
7주	☐ **Day 31** Part 4 Chapter 02 Unit 11	☐ **Day 32** Part 4 Chapter 02 Unit 12	☐ **Day 33** Part 4 Chapter 02 Unit 13	☐ **Day 34** Part 4 Chapter 02 Unit 14	☐ **Day 35** Part 4 Chapter 02 Unit 15
8주	☐ **Day 36** Part 4 Actual Test Part 4 복습	☐ **Day 37** Part 1, 2 복습	☐ **Day 38** Part 3 복습	☐ **Day 39** Part 4 복습	☐ **Day 40** ETS Final Test 최종 점검

점수 환산표 및 산출법

점수 환산표
이 책에 수록된 Final Test를 풀고 난 후, 맞은 개수를 세어 점수를 환산해 보세요.

LISTENING Raw Score (맞은 개수)	LISTENING Scaled Score (환산 점수)	READING Raw Score (맞은 개수)	READING Scaled Score (환산 점수)
96 – 100	475 – 495	96 – 100	460 – 495
91 – 95	435 – 495	91 – 95	425 – 490
86 – 90	405 – 470	86 – 90	400 – 465
81 – 85	370 – 450	81 – 85	375 – 440
76 – 80	345 – 420	76 – 80	340 – 415
71 – 75	320 – 390	71 – 75	310 – 390
66 – 70	290 – 360	66 – 70	285 – 370
61 – 65	265 – 335	61 – 65	255 – 340
56 – 60	240 – 310	56 – 60	230 – 310
51 – 55	215 – 280	51 – 55	200 – 275
46 – 50	190 – 255	46 – 50	170 – 245
41 – 45	160 – 230	41 – 45	140 – 215
36 – 40	130 – 205	36 – 40	115 – 180
31 – 35	105 – 175	31 – 35	95 – 150
26 – 30	85 – 145	26 – 30	75 – 120
21 – 25	60 – 115	21 – 25	60 – 95
16 – 20	30 – 90	16 – 20	45 – 75
11 – 15	5 – 70	11 – 15	30 – 55
6 – 10	5 – 60	6 – 10	10 – 40
1 – 5	5 – 50	1 – 5	5 – 30
0	5 – 35	0	5 – 15

점수 산출 방법

아래의 방식으로 점수를 산출할 수 있다.

STEP 1

자신의 답안을 수록된 정답과 대조하여 채점한다. 각 Section의 맞은 개수가 본인의 Section별 '실제 점수 (통계 처리하기 전의 점수, raw score)'이다. Listening Test와 Reading Test의 정답 수를 세어, 자신의 실제 점수를 아래의 해당란에 기록한다.

	맞은 개수	환산 점수대
LISTENING		
READING		
총점		

Section별 실제 점수가 그대로 Section별 TOEIC 점수가 되는 것은 아니다. TOEIC은 시행할 때마다 별도로 특정한 통계 처리 방법을 사용하며 이러한 실제 점수를 환산 점수(converted[scaled] score)로 전환하게 된다. 이렇게 전환함으로써, 매번 시행될 때마다 문제는 달라지지만 그 점수가 갖는 의미는 같아지게 된다. 예를 들어 어느 한 시험에서 총점 550점의 성적으로 받는 실력이라면 다른 시험에서도 거의 550점대의 성적을 받게 되는 것이다.

▼

STEP 2

실제 점수를 위 표에 기록한 후 왼쪽 페이지의 점수 환산표를 보도록 한다. TOEIC이 시행될 때마다 대개 이와 비슷한 형태의 표가 작성되는데, 여기 제시된 환산표는 본 교재에 수록된 Test용으로 개발된 것이다. 이 표를 사용하여 자신의 실제 점수를 환산 점수로 전환하도록 한다. 즉, 예를 들어 Listening Test의 실제 정답 수가 61~65개이면 환산 점수는 265점에서 335점 사이가 된다. 여기서 실제 정답 수가 61개이면 환산 점수가 265점이고, 65개이면 환산 점수가 335점 임을 의미하는 것은 아니다. 본 책의 Test를 위해 작성된 이 점수 환산표가 자신의 영어 실력이 어느 정도인지 대략적으로 파악하는 데 도움이 되긴 하지만, 이 표가 실제 TOEIC 성적 산출에 그대로 사용된 적은 없다는 사실을 밝혀 둔다.

미국식 발음 VS. 영국식 발음

❶ 모음

🎧 P0_01

o의 발음

미국식 영어에서는 /ɑ/ [아], 영국식 영어에서는 /ɒ/ [오]에 가깝게 발음된다.

예	미국식 발음	영국식 발음
job	[잡]	[좁]
doctor	[닥터r]	[독터]

예	미국식 발음	영국식 발음
stock	[스딱]	[스톡]
possible	[파써블]	[포써블]

a의 발음

미국식 영어에서는 /æ/ [애], 영국식 영어에서는 /ɑ/ [아]에 가깝게 발음된다.

예	미국식 발음	영국식 발음
staff	[스태f]	[스타f]
advance	[어드밴스]	[어드반스]

예	미국식 발음	영국식 발음
morale	[머랠]	[머랄]
behalf	[비해f]	[비하f]

i, ei의 발음

미국식 영어에서는 /i/ [이]나 /ə/ [어], 영국식 영어에서는 /aɪ/ [아이]에 가깝게 발음된다.

예	미국식 발음	영국식 발음
either	[이더r]	[아이더]
direction	[더렉션]	[다이렉션]

예	미국식 발음	영국식 발음
mobile	[모우블]	[머우바일]
fragile	[f래절]	[f래자일]

PRACTICE   다음 문장을 잘 듣고 빈칸을 채우세요. (녹음은 미국식, 영국식 두 번 들려 줍니다.)   🎧 P0_02

1. I'm sorry, but that _____ phone is out of _____.   죄송하지만, 그 핸드폰은 재고가 없습니다.

2. You don't have to book the tickets in _____.   사전에 표를 예약할 필요는 없습니다.

3. Positive feedback would help improve _____ among the _____

   긍정적인 피드백은 직원 간 사기를 높이는 데 도움이 될 것이다

4. Let me _____ someone for _____.   제가 누군가에게 길을 물어보겠습니다.

5. You can choose _____ tea or coffee.   차 혹은 커피를 선택하실 수 있습니다.

1. mobile, stock 2. advance 3. morale, staff 4. ask, directions 5. either

토익 리스닝에서는 같은 단어나 문장이라도 화자의 억양에 따라 다르게 들리기 때문에, 미국식 발음과 영국식
발음의 차이를 알고 청취 시 이를 구분하여 이해하는 것이 중요하다.

❷ 자음

 P0_03

r의 발음

발음 기호 상 /r/이 자음 앞이나 음절 끝에 위치할 경우, 미국식 영어에서는 혀를 약간 굴려 /r/을 발음하고,
영국식 영어에서는 이를 생략한다.

예	미국식 발음	영국식 발음	예	미국식 발음	영국식 발음
award	[어워rㄷ]	[어워드]	**airport**	[에어r포rㅌ]	[에어포트]
manager	[매니저r]	[매니저]	**department**	[디파r트먼트]	[디파트먼트]

t의 발음

발음 기호 상 /t/가 모음 사이나 /l/, /m/, /n/ 앞에 위치할 경우, 미국식 영어에서는 부드러운 /d/나 /r/에
가까운 소리로 발음하고, 영국식 영어에서는 그대로 발음한다.

예	미국식 발음	영국식 발음	예	미국식 발음	영국식 발음
quality	[퀄러디]	[퀄러티]	**written**	[뤼든]	[뤼튼]
bottom	[바럼]	[보텀]	**bottle**	[바를]	[보틀]

그러나 미국식 영어에서도 /t/의 앞 음절에 강세가 없으면 /t/가 발음된다. 예) guitar [기타]

nt의 발음

발음 기호 상 /t/가 /n/ 뒤에 위치할 경우, 미국식 영어에서는 묵음 처리하고, 영국식 영어에서는 그대로 발음한다.

예	미국식 발음	영국식 발음	예	미국식 발음	영국식 발음
interview	[이너r뷰]	[인터뷰]	**advantage**	[어드배니지]	[어드반티지]
percentage	[퍼r세니지]	[퍼센티지]	**international**	[이너내셔널]	[인터내셔널]

PRACTICE   다음 문장을 잘 듣고 빈칸을 채우세요. (녹음은 미국식, 영국식 두 번 들려 줍니다.) P0_04

1. A special _____ will be given to the editorial _____   편집부가 특별상을 받을 것이다.

2. The hiring _____ read all the _____ of recommendation before the
_____.   인사 부장은 면접 전에 모든 추천서를 다 읽었다.

3. The publication date is _____ on the _____ of the first page.
발행일이 첫 페이지 하단에 적혀 있다.

4. Our dishes are made with high _____ ingredients.   저희 요리는 고급 재료로 만들어집니다.

5. The university has the highest _____ of _____ students in the region.
그 대학교는 해당 지역에서 국제 학생의 비율이 가장 높다.

---

1. award, department 2. manager, letters, interview 3. written, bottom 4. quality 5. percentage, international

PART
1

사진 묘사

LC

PART 1

사진 묘사
PHOTOGRAPHS

사진을 가장 적절히 설명한 보기를 선택하는 유형으로, 총 6문항이 출제된다. 사람 및 사물의 동작이나 상태, 배경 등을 묘사하는 문장이 나온다.

기본 풀이 전략

P1_01

문제지

STEP 01 문제 듣기 전에 사진 파악하기

등장 인물: 여자 1명
동작/자세/상태: writing, sitting, wearing a headscarf
주변 사물: paper, pen, mobile phone, chair
장소/배경: room, wall

음원

Number 1. Look at the picture marked number 1 in your test book.

(A) She's answering her phone.
(B) She's tying her headscarf.
(C) She's writing on some paper.
(D) She's moving some chairs.

STEP 02 오답 소거하며 정답 찾기

(A) X 전화를 받고 있는 모습이 아니다.
(B) X 스카프를 묶고 있는 모습이 아니다.
(C) O 펜으로 종이 위에 무언가를 쓰고 있다.
(D) X 의자를 옮기는 모습이 아니다.

최신 출제 경향

① **사진 유형**   인물 등장 사진이 주를 이루며, 사물/풍경 사진은 보통 후반에 1~2문항 정도 출제된다.

② **사진 장소**   실내 업무 및 실외 작업 장소의 비중이 높고, 상점, 거리, 공원 등 다양한 장소도 등장한다.

③ **정답의 시제와 태**   현재 진행 시제(be + -ing)가 가장 많이 사용되며, 현재 완료 수동태(have + been + p.p.)와 단순 현재 수동태(be + p.p.)도 자주 나온다.

④ **보기의 구성**   인물 묘사 보기만 있는 문제 〉 인물 묘사, 사물 묘사 보기가 섞인 문제 〉 사물/풍경 묘사 보기만 있는 문제 순으로 많이 출제된다.

1 사진에 없는 사람 / 사물 언급

사진에 없는 사물이나 사람 어휘에 주의한다.

오답　He's pulling **a cart**.　남자가 카트를 끌고 있다.

정답　He's rowing a boat.　남자가 노를 젓고 있다.

2 잘못된 동작 / 상태 묘사

인물 묘사에서 자주 등장하는 오답 유형으로, 동작이나 상태를 혼동시키거나 잘못 묘사한 동사 어휘가 나온다.

오답　She's **putting on** a jacket.
　　　여자가 재킷을 입고 있다.

정답　She's picking up a notebook.
　　　여자가 공책을 집어 들고 있다.

3 잘못된 위치 묘사

위치만 틀리게 묘사하여 오답을 유도하는 경우가 있으므로, 끝까지 확실하게 듣는다.

오답　A guitar is leaning **against a bookshelf**.
　　　기타 한 대가 책장에 기대어 세워져 있다.

정답　Stacks of paper have been left on a desk.
　　　종이 더미가 책상에 놓여 있다.

4 혼동 어휘 사용

유사 발음, 다의어 등을 이용해 순간적인 혼동을 유도하는 오답이 등장한다.

오답　She's **working** on a road.
　　　여자가 도로에서 작업을 하고 있다.

정답　She's pushing a bicycle.
　　　여자가 자전거를 밀고 있다.

❶ 1인 등장 사진

 출제공식

1 한 사람의 동작이나 상태를 be + -ing 형태로 묘사하는 경우가 대부분이다.

2 인물의 동작, 상태, 자세, 시선 등을 묘사하는 동사를 정확히 듣고 답을 가려내야 한다.

3 인물 중심 사진이라도 사물 묘사가 정답이 될 수 있으므로, 보기에 사람 주어와 사물 주어가 섞여 나올 때 유의해야 한다. 사물 주어가 들리면 해당 대상으로 시선을 옮긴다.

✏️ **풀이 전략 | 사람의 주요 동작이나 상태를 우선적으로 파악** 🎧 P1_02

해당 인물의 동작 및 상태를 먼저 확인한 후, 동작을 당하는 대상과 주요 사물의 위치를 파악한다.

정답 He **is talking** on the phone.
남자가 전화 통화를 하고 있다.

오답 He **is setting up** a computer.
남자가 컴퓨터를 설치하고 있다.

Possible Answers

A man **is seated** at a desk.
남자가 책상에 앉아 있다.

A clock **is hanging** on a wall.
벽에 시계가 걸려 있다.

만점 전략 동작 표현과 상태 표현을 확실히 구분한다.

wearing vs. **putting/trying on**
입은 상태　　　 입는 동작

O wearing a T-shirt
X putting on a T-shirt

riding vs. **getting on**
탄 상태　　　 타려는 동작

O riding a horse
X getting on a horse

ETS CHECK-UP 🎧 P1_03 정답 및 해설 p.2

1.

(A)　　(B)　　(C)　　(D)

2.

(A)　　(B)　　(C)　　(D)

❷ 2인 이상 등장 사진

출제공식

1 사진에 등장하는 인물들의 공통/상호 동작이나 한 명의 두드러지는 개별 동작/상태를 be + -ing로 묘사하는 정답이 자주 출제된다.

2 보기에 1인 주어, 복수 주어, 사물 주어 모두 나올 수 있다는 점을 염두에 둔다.

3 다수의 사람이 있는 사진에는 workers, spectators, crowd 등의 주어가 나오기도 한다.

✏️ 풀이 전략 | 사람들의 공통/상호 동작, 눈에 띄는 개별 동작이나 상태 파악　🎧 P1_04

복수 주어가 나오면 공통/상호 동작에, 1인 주어가 나오면 개별 동작이나 상태에 집중한다.

정답　The woman **is standing** behind the counter. 여자가 카운터 뒤에 서 있다.

오답　The man **is speaking** to an audience.
남자가 청중에게 말하고 있다.

Possible Answers

Some people **are facing** each other.
사람들이 서로 마주보고 있다.

Two counters **have been placed** side by side.
카운터 두 개가 나란히 놓여 있다.

만점 전략　〈사물 주어 + 현재진행 수동태(be + being + p.p.)〉로 인물의 행동을 묘사할 수 있다.

A wheelchair **is being pushed**.
= One of the women **is pushing** a wheelchair. (밀고 있는 모습)

A piece of equipment **is being examined**.
= They **are examining** a piece of equipment. (살펴보는 모습)

ETS CHECK-UP　🎧 P1_05 정답 및 해설 p. 2

1.

(A)　(B)　(C)　(D)

2.

(A)　(B)　(C)　(D)

🎧 P1_06

손 동작 묘사

holding a container 용기를 들고 있다
grabbing a book from a shelf 선반에서 책을 집어 꺼내고 있다
grasping the handle 손잡이를 잡고 있다
carrying a tray with food 음식이 든 쟁반을 나르고 있다
moving a chair 의자를 나르고 있다
loading a cart 카트에 짐을 싣고 있다
unloading a truck 트럭에서 짐을 내리고 있다
lifting a wooden plank 나무 판자를 들어올리고 있다
picking up a bag 가방을 집어 들고 있다
putting away some tools 도구를 치우고 있다
putting together a shelf 선반을 조립하고 있다
opening a drawer 서랍을 열고 있다
tying his shoe 신발끈을 매고 있다
wrapping (up) a box 상자를 포장하고 있다
packing some merchandise 상품을 포장하고 있다
unpacking a suitcase 여행가방에 든 짐을 풀고 있다
securing some equipment 장비를 고정시키고 있다

hanging (up) some posters 포스터를 걸고 있다
folding a newspaper 신문을 접고 있다
rolling up his sleeves 소매를 말아 올리고 있다
buttoning up her coat 코트의 단추를 채우고 있다
unzipping her jacket 재킷 지퍼를 내리고 있다
stacking some boxes 상자들을 쌓고 있다
reaching into a cabinet 캐비닛 안으로 손을 뻗고 있다
reaching for a telephone 전화기를 잡으려고 손을 뻗고 있다
extending her arm 팔을 뻗고 있다
pointing at a screen 스크린을 가리키고 있다
adjusting some blinds 블라인드를 조정하고 있다
handing a bag to a customer 고객에게 가방을 건네고 있다
handing[passing] out some flyers 전단을 나누어 주고 있다
shaking hands 악수하고 있다
sweeping a walkway 보도를 쓸고 있다
mopping the floor 바닥을 닦고 있다
wiping (off) a counter 카운터를 닦고 있다

발 동작 묘사

going up/down the stairs 계단을 오르고/내려오고 있다
walking up/down a hill 언덕을 오르고/내려오고 있다
climbing up/down some steps 계단을 오르고/내려오고 있다
stepping onto/off the bus 버스에 타다/버스에서 내리다

walking toward a doorway 출입구를 향해 걷고 있다
strolling along a beach 해안을 따라 걷고 있다
approaching an entrance 입구 쪽으로 다가가고 있다
passing through a storage area 창고를 가로질러 가고 있다

착용 동작/상태 묘사

동작
putting on a sweater 스웨터를 입는 중이다
trying on a pair of shoes 신발을 신어 보고 있다
removing[taking off] his hat 모자를 벗고 있다

상태
wearing a jacket 재킷을 입고 있다
wearing glasses 안경을 쓰고 있다
wearing a backpack 가방을 메고 있다

시선/자세 묘사

시선
watching a film 영화를 보고 있다
looking[staring/gazing] out the window 창 밖을 보고 있다
looking at a notebook 공책을 보고 있다
reviewing a document 서류를 검토하고 있다
studying the menu 메뉴를 살펴보고 있다
checking his phone 휴대전화를 보고 있다
examining some merchandise 상품을 살펴보고 있다
inspecting a car 차량을 살펴보고 있다
facing each other 서로 마주보고 있다

자세
sitting on a bench 벤치에 앉아 있다
be seated at the table 테이블에 앉아 있다
standing side by side 나란히 서 있다
lying on the grass 잔디에 누워 있다
bending over[down] 몸을 구부리고[숙이고] 있다
leaning over a sink 싱크대로 몸을 구부리고 있다
leaning against a windowsill 창턱에 기대고 있다
holding onto a railing 난간을 잡고 있다
kneeling down 무릎을 꿇고 있다

LISTENING **PRACTICE**

🎧 P1_07 정답 및 해설 p.3

STEP 01 먼저 녹음을 들으면서 문제를 푸세요.　**STEP 02** 다시 들으면서 빈칸을 채우세요.

1.

(A)　　(B)　　(C)　　(D)

(A) She's _____.
(B) She's _____.
(C) She's _____.
(D) She's _____.

| POSSIBLE ANSWERS |
A woman is _____.
Some boxes have _____.

2.

(A)　　(B)　　(C)　　(D)

(A) The man is _____.
(B) The man is _____.
(C) There are _____.
(D) The drawers are _____.

| POSSIBLE ANSWERS |
He is _____.
Some appliances have _____.

3.

(A)　　(B)　　(C)　　(D)

(A) The spokes on a wheel are _____.
(B) A bicycle is _____.
(C) One of the men is _____.
(D) One of the men is _____.

| POSSIBLE ANSWERS |
They are _____.
One of the men is _____.

4.

(A)　　(B)　　(C)　　(D)

(A) They're _____.
(B) A man is _____.
(C) Some beverages are _____.
(D) Some of the people are _____.

| POSSIBLE ANSWERS |
One of the women is _____.
Some of the people are _____.

1.

(A)   (B)   (C)   (D)

2.

(A)   (B)   (C)   (D)

3.

(A)   (B)   (C)   (D)

4.

(A)   (B)   (C)   (D)

5.

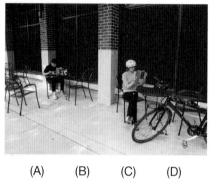

(A)   (B)   (C)   (D)

6.

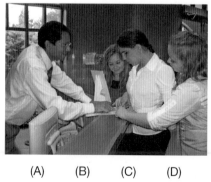

(A)   (B)   (C)   (D)

P1_08 정답 및 해설 p.5

7.

(A)   (B)   (C)   (D)

8.

(A)   (B)   (C)   (D)

9.

(A)   (B)   (C)   (D)

10.

(A)   (B)   (C)   (D)

11.

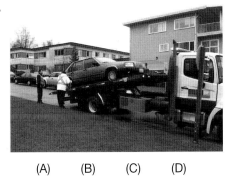

(A)   (B)   (C)   (D)

12.

(A)   (B)   (C)   (D)

사물 사진

출제공식 1 실내에 있는 주요 사물을 be + p.p., have + been + p.p.로 묘사하는 경우가 많다. be동사 + -ing /
형용사구 / 전치사구, 혹은 There is / are + 전치사구를 활용한 보기도 정답으로 출제된다.
2 사물의 위치 및 상태를 잘못 묘사하거나 사진에 없는 사물 / 사람을 언급한 보기가 오답으로 나올
확률이 높다.

✏️ **풀이 전략 | 주요 사물의 상태 및 위치 파악** 🎧 P1_09

사물의 상태나 위치가 정확히 묘사되는지가 중요하므로, 전치사구까지 확실히 듣는다.

정답 A shelf **is full of boxes.**
선반이 상자들로 가득 차 있다.

오답 A bulletin board **is leaning against a chair.** 게시판이 의자에 기대어 있다.

Possible Answers
There is a lamp **on the desk.**
책상 위에 램프가 있다.

Some files **have been arranged on a shelf.**
파일들이 선반 위에 정리되어 있다.

만점 전략 사물의 상태를 표현하는 주요 동사 형태와 예외 사항을 알아둔다.

주요 동사 형태

① 수동태(be + p.p.), 현재 완료 수동태(have + been + p.p.)
Containers have been stacked on top of each other.
= Containers are stacked on top of each other.

② 현재 진행(be + -ing)
Some items are hanging from the ceiling.

③ There + be동사 + 전치사구
There are bottles in a display case.

예외 사항

be + being + p.p.는 주로 사람의 동작을 나타내므로
사물 사진에서는 오답일 확률이 높다. 하지만 일부 동사는
be + being + p.p.로 상태를 묘사할 수도 있다.

Some shirts are being displayed. (진열된 모습)
Files are being stored on shelves. (보관된 모습)
Shadows are being cast on the ground.
(드리운 모습)

ETS CHECK-UP 🎧 P1_10 정답 및 해설 p.9

1.

(A) (B) (C) (D)

2.

(A) (B) (C) (D)

❹ 풍경 사진

출제공식
1 실외 풍경이나 주요 사물을 다양한 동사 형태로 묘사하는 유형으로, 출제 빈도가 낮은 편이다.
2 인물 중심 사진에서는 잘 사용되지 않는 단순 현재 시제가 정답으로 출제되기도 한다.
3 사진에 없는 사람 / 사물을 언급하거나 be + being + p.p.로 사람의 동작을 묘사한 오답이 자주
나온다.

✏️ **풀이 전략 | 전체적인 풍경 및 눈에 띄는 사물의 구도 파악**　🎧 P1_11

배경이 되는 장소, 주요 사물 및 구조물의 구도를 확인한 후, 주어가 들리면 해당 대상에 집중한다.

정답　Columns **line a walkway**.
기둥들이 보도를 따라 줄지어 서 있다.

오답　Leaves **are being swept** out of a road.
나뭇잎들이 길 밖으로 쓸려지고 있다.

Possible Answers
The benches **are unoccupied**.
벤치들이 비어 있다.

There are grassy areas **beside the path**.
길 옆에 풀밭이 있다.

만점 전략 풍경 사진에 특화된 어휘와 동사 형태를 알아둔다.

풍경 사진에 특화된 어휘

① 도로, 길, 다리 등과 관련된 동사
run / lead / wind : 길이 나 있다 / ~로 이어지다 / 굽이치다
extend : 뻗어 있다
cross / span : 가로지르다 / 걸쳐 있다

② 건물 및 주변 풍경과 관련된 동사
overlook / face : 내려보다 / 마주보다[향하다]
surround : 둘러싸다

풍경 사진에 특화된 동사 형태

① 단순 현재
The path leads to the entrance.
A fence surrounds a field.

② 현재 진행(be + -ing)
Trees are lining a street.
Some buildings are facing a parking area.

ETS CHECK-UP　🎧 P1_12 정답 및 해설 p.9

1.

(A)　　(B)　　(C)　　(D)

2.

(A)　　(B)　　(C)　　(D)

사물 묘사

식물 / 화분 / 과일

Some plants are hanging from the ceiling.
식물들이 천장에 매달려 있다.

A seating area is decorated with potted plants.
좌석 구역이 화분들로 장식되어 있다.

A vase of flowers has been set on the dining table.
꽃병이 식탁 위에 놓여 있다.

A basket has been filled with fruit.
바구니가 과일로 가득 차 있다.

상자 / 짐 / 선반 / 카트

Some boxes have been stored on a rack.
상자들이 선반에 보관되어 있다.

Containers are stacked in the corner.
용기들이 구석에 쌓여 있다.

Some suitcases are lined up on a conveyor belt.
여행 가방들이 컨베이어벨트에 정렬되어 있다.

Some packages have been left on a cart.
소포들이 카트에 놓여 있다.

A cabinet is stocked with supplies.
캐비닛이 물품으로 채워져 있다.

책 / 그림 / 사진

Books have been piled on a television.
책들이 텔레비전 위에 쌓여 있다.

Some magazines are arranged on shelves.
잡지 몇 권이 선반 위에 정돈되어 있다.

Some artwork has been mounted[hung] on a wall.
예술작품이 벽에 걸려 있다.

Some paintings have been placed next to a door.
그림들이 문 옆에 자리잡고 있다.

가구 / 인테리어

A table has been positioned between two chairs.
테이블이 두 개의 의자 사이에 있다.

A mirror is propped[leaning] against the wall.
거울이 벽에 기대어져 있다.

Lighting fixtures are attached to the ceiling.
조명 기구들이 천장에 부착되어 있다.

A rug[carpet] is laid out on the floor.
양탄자가 바닥에 깔려 있다.

Some blinds have been closed[pulled down].
블라인드가 닫혀[내려져] 있다.

풍경 묘사

공원 / 물가

A fence surrounds a field.
울타리가 들판을 둘러싸고 있다.

A path winds through a garden.
정원에 길이 구불구불 나 있다.

A chair is situated on the grass.
의자가 풀밭 위에 있다.

Some trees have been planted along a walkway.
나무 몇 그루가 도보를 따라 심어져 있다.

The chairs are shaded by umbrellas.
의자들이 파라솔에 그늘져 있다.

Several boats are docked in a harbor.
배 몇 척이 항구에 정박해 있다.

A ship is tied to a pier.
배 한 척이 부두에 묶여 있다.

Some of the boats are floating in the water.
배들 중 몇 척이 물에 떠 있다.

A bridge spans[crosses over] the river.
다리가 강을 가로지르고 있다.

Some buildings are reflected in the water.
건물들이 물에 비치고 있다.

도로 / 차량 / 건물

Cars are traveling in the same direction.
차들이 같은 방향으로 이동하고 있다.

A truck is being driven down the road.
트럭 한 대가 길을 따라 운행되고 있다.

A bus is waiting at a traffic light.
버스 한 대가 신호등에서 대기하고 있다.

A train is stopped at a platform.
기차 한 대가 플랫폼에 서 있다.

Vehicles are parked on the side of a road.
차량들이 길 한 편에 주차되어 있다.

A row of lampposts lines the street.
가로등들이 거리를 따라 늘어서 있다.

Some stairs lead to a building.
계단이 건물로 이어져 있다.

There is a balcony overlooking a garden.
정원이 내려다 보이는 발코니가 있다.

A building is casting a shadow across the street.
건물이 거리에 그림자를 드리우고 있다.

Some buildings are located near a hill.
언덕 근처에 건물이 몇 채 있다.

LISTENING **PRACTICE**

♪ ♭ P1_14 정답 및 해설 p. 10

먼저 녹음을 들으면서 문제를 푸세요.   **STEP 02** 다시 들으면서 빈칸을 채우세요.

1.

(A)   (B)   (C)   (D)

(A) Clocks have _____.
(B) The clocks are _____.
(C) Clocks are _____.
(D) The clocks have _____.

| POSSIBLE ANSWERS |

The clocks are _____.
Clocks have _____.

2.

(A)   (B)   (C)   (D)

(A) Some people are _____.
(B) Some workers are _____.
(C) Some vehicles have _____.
(D) Some banners have _____.

| POSSIBLE ANSWERS |

A building _____.
Some vehicles are _____.

3.

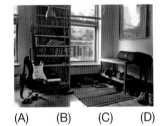

(A)   (B)   (C)   (D)

(A) An instrument case is _____.
(B) A bookcase is _____.
(C) Some shoes are _____.
(D) A rug is _____.

| POSSIBLE ANSWERS |

A picture is _____.
Some books are _____.

4.

(A)   (B)   (C)   (D)

(A) Some boats are _____.
(B) _____ from a dock.
(C) One of the boats is _____.
(D) A sail has been _____.

| POSSIBLE ANSWERS |

Some boats have _____.
There are _____.

1.

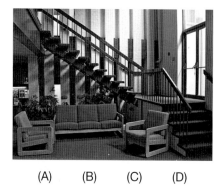

(A)   (B)   (C)   (D)

2.

(A)   (B)   (C)   (D)

3.

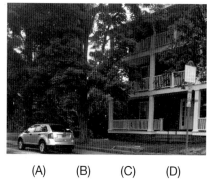

(A)   (B)   (C)   (D)

4.

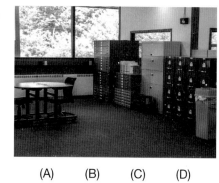

(A)   (B)   (C)   (D)

5.

(A)   (B)   (C)   (D)

6.

(A)   (B)   (C)   (D)

7.

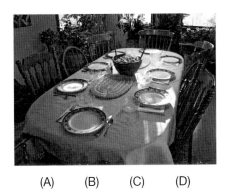

(A)　　　(B)　　　(C)　　　(D)

8.

(A)　　　(B)　　　(C)　　　(D)

9.

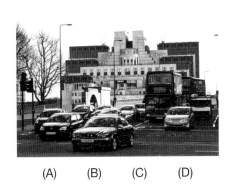

(A)　　　(B)　　　(C)　　　(D)

10.

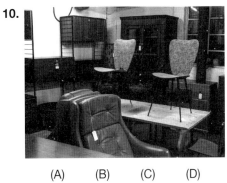

(A)　　　(B)　　　(C)　　　(D)

11.

(A)　　　(B)　　　(C)　　　(D)

12.

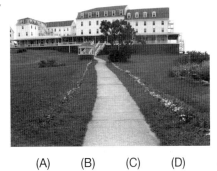

(A)　　　(B)　　　(C)　　　(D)

❺ 실내 업무 장소 빈출 상황

🎧 P1_16

● **사무실** | 서류 검토/작성, 동료 간 대화, 전화 통화, 사무 기기 및 용품 사용 등

The woman is taking notes by hand.
여자가 손으로 메모하고 있다.

A file is being removed from a drawer.
파일 하나가 서랍에서 꺼내지고 있다.

● **회의실/강당** | 회의/토론, 다수를 대상으로 발표, 발표자 경청, 자료 배포/검토 등

People have gathered for a meeting.
사람들이 회의를 위해 모여 있다.

Presenters are seated in front of microphones.
발표자들이 마이크 앞에 앉아 있다.

● **기타 작업 장소** | 창고, 공장, 도서관, 분류실, 실험실 등에서 작업, 관련 기기 및 용품 사용 등

He is operating some factory machinery.
남자가 공장 기계를 작동시키고 있다.

She is reaching into the cabinet.
여자가 수납장 안으로 손을 뻗고 있다.

ETS CHECK-UP

🎧 P1_17 정답 및 해설 p. 16

1.

(A)　　(B)　　(C)　　(D)

2.

(A)　　(B)　　(C)　　(D)

ETS X-FILE | 실내 업무 장소 빈출 표현

♪ ♭ P1_18

실내 업무 장소

사무실

talking on the phone 통화를 하고 있다

taking notes 메모하고 있다

working at a computer 컴퓨터로 작업하고 있다

typing on a keyboard 키보드를 치고 있다

using some office equipment 사무기기를 사용하고 있다

installing a photocopier 복사기를 설치하고 있다

putting paper in a copy machine
복사기에 종이를 넣고 있다

copying a document 서류를 복사하고 있다

sorting papers 서류를 분류하고 있다

arranging materials on the table
테이블 위 자료를 정리하고 있다

filing a document 문서를 파일로 철하고 있다

placing binders in a cabinet 캐비닛에 바인더를 넣고 있다

posting a notice on a bulletin board
게시판에 공지를 붙이고 있다

consulting a manual 설명서를 찾아보고 있다

securing a box with tape 테이프로 상자를 단단히 봉하고 있다

회의실

have[be] gathered for a meeting 회의하려고 모여 있다

greeting each other 서로 인사하고 있다

exchanging business cards 명함을 교환하고 있다

be seated in a circle 둥글게 앉아 있다

distributing[passing around] papers 서류를 나눠주고 있다

reading[reviewing] a document 서류를 읽고 있다

writing notes on a board 칠판에 적고 있다

cleaning[erasing] a whiteboard 흰 칠판을 닦고 있다

pointing to a chart 차트를 가리키고 있다

chatting in a conference room
회의실에서 이야기하고 있다

addressing meeting participants
회의 참가자들에게 말하고 있다

강의실 / 강당

entering an auditorium 강당에 들어가고 있다

setting up a podium 연단을 설치하고 있다

lining up chairs 의자를 일렬로 배열하고 있다

sitting in rows 여러 줄로 앉아 있다

giving[making] a presentation 발표하고 있다

attending a presentation 프레젠테이션에 참석하고 있다

giving[delivering] a lecture 강의를 하고 있다

listening to a speaker 발표자의 말을 경청하고 있다

speaking into a microphone 마이크에 대고 말하고 있다

raising their hands 손을 들고 있다

Some seats are unoccupied. 좌석 일부가 비어 있다.

작업실 / 실험실

inspecting some power lines 전선을 점검하고 있다

plugging in a computer 컴퓨터의 전원을 연결하고 있다

unplugging a power cord 플러그를 뽑고 있다

operating a machine 기계를 작동하고 있다

pushing[pressing] a button 버튼을 누르고 있다

packing items into boxes 물품을 상자에 넣고 있다

moving a piece of furniture 가구 한 점을 옮기고 있다

measuring a cabinet 캐비닛 치수를 재고 있다

assembling some shelving units
선반 세트를 조립하고 있다

A tool box is lying on a counter.
공구 상자가 작업대에 놓여 있다.

Some tools are spread[laid] out on a table.
장비가 테이블 위에 널려 있나.

using a microscope 현미경을 사용하고 있다

working with some laboratory equipment
실험 장비를 가지고 일하고 있다

wearing a lab coat 실험실 가운을 입고 있다

서점 / 도서관

walking between bookcases 책장 사이를 걷고 있다

reading a magazine 잡지를 읽고 있다

reaching for a book 책을 향해 손을 뻗고 있다

taking[removing] a book from a shelf
선반에서 책을 꺼내고 있다

borrowing[checking out] some books
책을 대출하고 있다

organizing books on a bookcase
책꽂이의 책들을 정리하고 있다

arranging books on a cart 카트의 책들을 정돈하고 있다

Shelves are filled with books. 선반이 책들로 가득 차 있다.

Books are on display in a library.
도서관에 책들이 전시되어 있다.

병원 / 호텔 / 은행 / 우체국

waiting in a lobby 로비에서 기다리고 있다

seated in a waiting area 대기실에 앉아 있다

organizing a reception area 접수 구역을 정돈하고 있다

having a conversation 대화를 나누고 있다

filling out a form 양식을 작성하고 있다

working behind the counter 카운터 뒤에서 일하고 있다

be stationed at a service window
서비스 창구에 있다

examining a patient 환자를 진찰하고 있다

loading some luggage into a cart
카트에 짐을 싣고 있다

P1_19 정답 및 해설 p. 16

STEP 01 먼저 녹음을 들으면서 문제를 푸세요.   **STEP 02** 다시 들으면서 빈칸을 채우세요.

1.

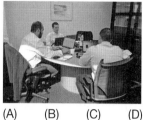

(A)   (B)   (C)   (D)

(A) They're _____.
(B) They're _____.
(C) One of the men is _____.
(D) One of the men is _____.

| POSSIBLE ANSWERS |
They're _____.
Some people are _____.

2.

(A)   (B)   (C)   (D)

(A) The position of a microphone is _____.
(B) The woman's _____.
(C) A pair of headphones has _____.
(D) The woman's _____.

| POSSIBLE ANSWERS |
The woman is _____.
A woman is _____.

3.

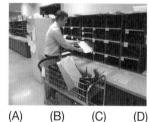

(A)   (B)   (C)   (D)

(A) A man is _____.
(B) Labels have _____.
(C) A man is _____.
(D) Some newspapers have _____.

| POSSIBLE ANSWERS |
Some items have _____.
He's _____.

4.

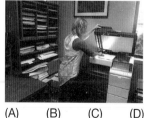

(A)   (B)   (C)   (D)

(A) She's _____.
(B) She's _____.
(C) She's _____.
(D) She's _____.

| POSSIBLE ANSWERS |
A woman is _____.
Some shelves are _____.

ETS **TEST**

♪ ♭ P1_20 정답 및 해설 p. 18

1.

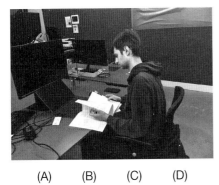

(A)   (B)   (C)   (D)

2.

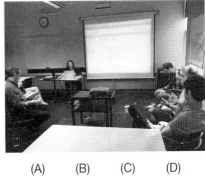

(A)   (B)   (C)   (D)

3.

(A)   (B)   (C)   (D)

4.

(A)   (B)   (C)   (D)

5.

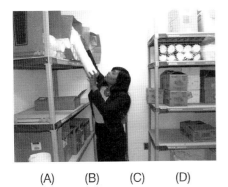

(A)   (B)   (C)   (D)

6.

(A)   (B)   (C)   (D)

❻ 실외 작업/교통 관련 장소 빈출 상황

● **공사장/작업장** | 건물 및 도로 공사, 수리 작업, 중장비 사용, 자재 운반 등

The people are working on a house.
사람들이 집을 수리하고 있다.

Some cargo is being transported on a forklift.
화물이 지게차로 운반되고 있다.

● **건물 주변/정원** | 건물 주변 청소 및 조경 작업, 경작 등

A man is clearing off the street.
남자가 거리를 청소하고 있다.

The man is watering some plants.
남자가 식물에 물을 주고 있다.

● **교통 관련 장소** | 도로 위 차량, 통행하는 사람들, 승강장, 공항 내/외부, 항구 등

Pedestrians are crossing the road.
보행자들이 길을 건너가고 있다.

A vehicle has stopped on the street.
차량 한 대가 길에 멈춰 서 있다.

ETS CHECK-UP

P1_22 정답 및 해설 p.20

1.

(A)　　(B)　　(C)　　(D)

2.

(A)　　(B)　　(C)　　(D)

ETS X-FILE | 실외 작업 / 교통 관련 장소 빈출 표현

P1_23

실외 작업/교통 관련 장소

공사 작업

be under construction 공사 중이다
wearing safety helmets 안전모를 쓰고 있다
fastening their helmets 헬멧을 조이고 있다
be stacked in a pile 무더기로 쌓여 있다
erecting[setting up] scaffolding 비계를 세우고 있다
drilling a hole 드릴로 구멍을 내고 있다
hammering a nail 못을 박고 있다
climbing a ladder 사다리에 오르고 있다
pouring cement into a container
시멘트를 용기에 붓고 있다
repairing the roof of the house 집의 지붕을 수리하고 있다
replacing some tiles 타일을 교체하고 있다
pushing a wheelbarrow 수레를 밀고 있다
working on the power lines 전선 작업을 하고 있다
adjusting a wire 전선을 조정하고 있다
A ladder is propped[leaning] against the building. 사다리가 건물에 기대어져 있다.
A cart has been left next to a pile of bricks.
카트가 벽돌 더미 옆에 놓여 있다.
Some construction work is being carried out.
공사 작업이 진행되고 있다.

도로 / 보도 작업

painting lines on a road
도로에 선을 그리고 있다
paving a walkway with bricks 보도를 벽돌로 포장하고 있다
A lamppost is being fixed. 가로등이 수리되고 있다.
A walkway is divided by a railing.
보도가 난간으로 분리되어 있다.
The road is closed for construction.
공사로 도로가 폐쇄되었다.
A pedestrian walkway is being resurfaced.
보행자 통로가 재포장되고 있다.

정원 / 경작

planting flowers 꽃을 심고 있다
trimming some bushes 관목을 다듬고 있다
cutting the grass 잔디를 깎고 있다
mowing the lawn 기계로 잔디를 깎고 있다
using a lawn mower 잔디 깎는 기계를 사용하고 있다
watering some plants 식물에 물을 주고 있다
raking leaves 갈퀴로 낙엽을 모으고 있다
using[working with] a shovel 삽으로 작업하고 있다
carrying a bucket 양동이를 나르고 있다
placing tools in a crate
나무상자에 공구를 넣고 있다

승강장 / 역 / 공항 / 항구

waiting at a platform 승강장에서 기다리고 있다
standing in line 줄 서 있다
boarding a bus 버스에 올라타고 있다
getting into a truck 트럭에 올라타고 있다
getting out of a vehicle 차에서 내리고 있다
exiting a bus 버스에서 내리고 있다
stepping down from a train 기차에서 내리고 있다
checking tickets on a train 기차에서 표를 검사하고 있다
storing luggage above their seats
좌석 위에 짐을 보관하고 있다
stowing[putting] her luggage in the overhead compartment 머리 위 짐칸에 짐을 넣고 있다
approaching the platform 승강장으로 들어오고 있다
departing from a station 역에서 출발하고 있다
taking off from a runway 활주로에서 이륙하고 있다
landing at the airport 공항에 착륙하고 있다
backing a car into a garage 차고에 차를 후진해서 넣고 있다
A bicycle is chained to a pole.
자전거가 기둥에 체인으로 묶여 있다.
There is a railing beside the railroad tracks.
철로 옆에 난간이 있다.

차량 관련 작업

pumping fuel into a car 차에 주유하고 있다
working on a vehicle 차를 수리하고 있다
checking an engine 엔진을 점검하고 있다
changing a tire 타이어를 교체하고 있다
loading some materials onto a truck
트럭에 물품들을 싣고 있다
unloading supplies from a truck
트럭에서 물품들을 내리고 있다
transporting a load of bricks 벽돌을 한 짐 운반하고 있다
being transported on a forklift 지게차로 운반되고 있다

도로 / 교통

be stuck in traffic 차가 밀려 갇히다
be stopped at an intersection 교차로에 서 있다
waiting at a traffic light 신호가 바뀌기를 기다리고 있다
driving down the road 도로에서 운전하고 있다
heading in the same direction 같은 방향으로 가고 있다
traveling in opposite directions
반대 방향으로 이동하고 있다
driving across the bridge 다리를 건너고 있다
being towed 견인되고 있다
crossing the road[street] 길을 건너고 있다
directing traffic 교통정리를 하고 있다

STEP 01 먼저 녹음을 들으면서 문제를 푸세요.　**STEP 02** 다시 들으면서 빈칸을 채우세요.

1.

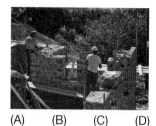

(A)　(B)　(C)　(D)

(A) The men are _____.
(B) The men are _____.
(C) The men are _____.
(D) The men are _____.

| POSSIBLE ANSWERS |
A man is _____.
A building is _____.

2.

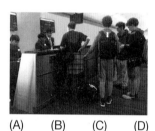

(A)　(B)　(C)　(D)

(A) Some people are _____.
(B) Some people are _____.
(C) One of the men is _____.
(D) One of the women is _____.

| POSSIBLE ANSWERS |
Some people are _____.
One of the men is _____.

3.

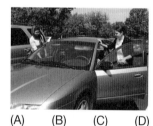

(A)　(B)　(C)　(D)

(A) Some women are _____.
(B) Some women are _____.
(C) A woman is _____.
(D) A woman is _____.

| POSSIBLE ANSWERS |
A car door has _____.
One of the women is _____.

4.

(A)　(B)　(C)　(D)

(A) He's _____.
(B) He's _____.
(C) A brick chimney is _____.
(D) A broom has _____.

| POSSIBLE ANSWERS |
A man is _____.
The man is _____.

ETS TEST

🎧 P1_25 정답 및 해설 p. 22

1.

(A)　　(B)　　(C)　　(D)

2.

(A)　　(B)　　(C)　　(D)

3.

(A)　　(B)　　(C)　　(D)

4.

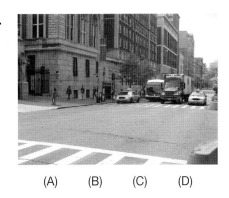

(A)　　(B)　　(C)　　(D)

5.

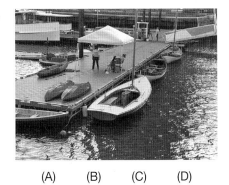

(A)　　(B)　　(C)　　(D)

6.

(A)　　(B)　　(C)　　(D)

❼ 쇼핑/여가 관련 장소 빈출 상황

● **쇼핑 장소 |** 상점/시장 구경, 제품 선택/착용, 계산대, 진열된 상품 등

A woman is checking her appearance in a mirror. 여자가 거울로 자신의 모습을 살펴보고 있다.

A man is selecting an item from a display.
남자가 진열대에서 물건을 고르고 있다.

● **실외 여가 장소 |** 공원/해변 산책, 운동, 휴식, 스포츠 경기, 거리 공연 등

Some people are riding bicycles by the water. 사람들이 물가에서 자전거를 타고 있다.

Spectators have filled the stadium.
관중들이 경기장을 채웠다.

● **실내 여가 장소 |** 미술 작품 감상, 그림 그리기, 실내 공연 관람 등

They are looking at some artwork on the wall. 사람들이 벽에 걸린 작품을 보고 있다.

An audience is seated in rows.
청중이 줄지어 앉아 있다.

ETS CHECK-UP

🎧 P1_27 정답 및 해설 p.24

1.

(A)   (B)   (C)   (D)

2.

(A)   (B)   (C)   (D)

ETS X-FILE | 쇼핑 / 여가 관련 장소 빈출 표현

P1_28

쇼핑 / 여가 관련 장소

상점 / 시장

stocking shelves 선반에 물건을 채우고 있다
arranging a display 진열품을 배열하고 있다
hanging a jacket on a rack 옷걸이에 재킷을 걸고 있다
putting away their display items 진열품들을 치우고 있다
folding some clothing 옷을 개고 있다
shopping in an open-air market 노천 시장에서 장을 보고 있다
looking at a store window 가게 진열창을 보고 있다
examining goods on display 진열된 상품을 살펴보고 있다
browsing in a store 가게 안을 둘러보고 있다
showing customers an item 손님들에게 물건을 보여주고 있다
reaching for some merchandise
상품을 집으려고 손을 뻗고 있다
assisting some customers 손님들을 도와주고 있다
wrapping a product 상품을 포장하고 있다
trying on a hat 모자를 써보고 있다
looking at his reflection in a mirror
거울에 비친 모습을 보고 있다
pushing a cart 카트를 밀고 있다
selecting some groceries 식료품을 고르고 있다
weighing an item on a scale 저울에 물건의 무게를 재고 있다
purchasing a beverage 음료를 구입하고 있다
standing by a checkout counter
계산대 주위에서 기다리고 있다
handing a card to the cashier 카드를 계산원에게 건네고 있다
paying for a purchase 구매품을 계산하고 있다
looking through a bag 가방 안을 들여다보고 있다
Merchandise is being displayed in a store
window. 상품이 가게 진열창에 진열되어 있다.
Some produce has been put in a shopping cart.
농산물이 쇼핑 카트 안에 놓여 있다.
Baskets have been piled near the entrance.
바구니들이 입구 근처에 쌓여 있다.
Beverages have been lined up in a display case.
음료수가 진열장에 나란히 진열되어 있다.

운동

jogging along the shore 해안을 따라 조깅을 하고 있다
exercising[working out] in a gym
체육관에서 운동을 하고 있다
running up a ramp 경사로를 뛰어 올라가고 있다
skating in a park 공원에서 스케이트를 타고 있다
hiking through a forest 숲에서 하이킹을 하고 있다
Cyclists are riding down the street.
도로에서 자전거를 타고 있다.

공원 / 해변

lying on the beach 해변에 누워 있다
resting[relaxing] by a tree 나무 옆에서 쉬고 있다
be gathered near a fountain 분수대 주위에 모여 있다
strolling on a path 오솔길을 거닐고 있다
walking into a garden area 정원 구역으로 걸어가고 있다
A walkway is lined with benches.
보도에 벤치가 줄 지어 있다.
taking a boat ride 배를 타고 있다
paddling kayaks 카약의 노를 젓고 있다
rowing a boat 노를 젓고 있다
sailing in the ocean 바다에서 항해하고 있다
holding an oar 노를 잡고 있다
swimming in a lake 호수에서 수영을 하고 있다
diving off a pier 부두에서 다이빙을 하고 있다
fishing from a dock 부두에서 낚시를 하고 있다
holding a fishing rod[pole] 낚싯대를 쥐고 있다

공연 / 전시

performing on a stage 무대에서 공연하고 있다
bowing to an audience 관중에게 인사하고 있다
watching an outdoor performance
야외 공연을 보고 있다
playing musical instruments 악기를 연주하고 있다
entertaining an audience 관객을 즐겁게 해주고 있다
clapping for performers 공연자들에게 박수를 보내고 있다
applauding the performance
공연에 박수 갈채를 보내고 있다
dancing in a parade 퍼레이드에서 춤을 추고 있다
marching in a plaza 광장에서 행진하고 있다
viewing a sculpture 조각품을 보고 있다
looking at some artwork 예술 작품을 보고 있다
attending an art exhibit 전시회에 참석하고 있다
Paintings are being hung on the wall.
그림들이 벽에 걸려 있다.

기타 취미생활

arranging flowers in a vase 꽃병에 꽃꽂이를 하고 있다
drawing[painting] on a large canvas
큰 캔버스에 그림을 그리고 있다
working on a drawing 그림을 그리고 있다
taking a photograph 사진을 찍고 있다
framing a photograph 사진을 액자에 끼우고 있다
posing for a picture 사진을 찍기 위해 포즈를 취하고 있다

🎧 P1_29 정답 및 해설 p.25

STEP 01 먼저 녹음을 들으면서 문제를 푸세요.   **STEP 02** 다시 들으면서 빈칸을 채우세요.

1.

(A)   (B)   (C)   (D)

(A) The woman is _____.
(B) The woman is _____.
(C) The woman is _____.
(D) The woman and man _____.

| POSSIBLE ANSWERS |
She's _____.
The woman is _____.

2.

(A)   (B)   (C)   (D)

(A) The women are _____.
(B) The women are _____.
(C) One woman is _____.
(D) One woman is _____.

| POSSIBLE ANSWERS |
A woman is _____.
One woman is _____.

3.

(A)   (B)   (C)   (D)

(A) A customer is _____.
(B) The cashier is _____.
(C) A customer is _____.
(D) The cashier is _____.

| POSSIBLE ANSWERS |
There is _____.
A customer is _____.

4.

(A)   (B)   (C)   (D)

(A) Some women are _____.
(B) Some women are _____.
(C) Some women are _____.
(D) Some women are _____.

| POSSIBLE ANSWERS |
One of the women is _____.
_____ on a wall.

ETS TEST

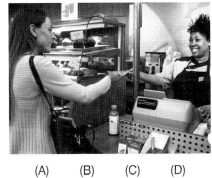

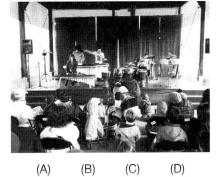

P1_30 정답 및 해설 p.26

1.

(A)   (B)   (C)   (D)

2.

(A)   (B)   (C)   (D)

3.

(A)   (B)   (C)   (D)

4.

(A)   (B)   (C)   (D)

5.

(A)   (B)   (C)   (D)

6.

(A)   (B)   (C)   (D)

⑧ 식사/가사 관련 장소 빈출 상황

● 식당/카페 | 메뉴 확인, 식사, 서빙, 세팅된 테이블, 계산대, 음식 진열장 등

Some men are looking at menus.
남자들이 메뉴를 보고 있다.

The tables have been prepared for a meal.
테이블이 식사를 위해 차려져 있다.

● 주방 | 요리, 재료 배합, 설거지, 조리대 청소, 주방 용품 사용 등

A man is cooking in a kitchen.
남자가 주방에서 요리를 하고 있다.

A tray is being put into an oven.
쟁반이 오븐에 들어가고 있다.

● 가정집 | 청소 등의 집안일, 가구 나르기, 집 주변 가꾸기, 집 내부 모습 등

A woman is carrying a chair.
여자가 의자를 나르고 있다.

A rug is lying in front of a door.
깔개가 문 앞에 놓여 있다.

ETS CHECK-UP

P1_32 정답 및 해설 p.28

1.

(A)   (B)   (C)   (D)

2.

(A)   (B)   (C)   (D)

ETS X-FILE | 식사 / 가사 관련 장소 빈출 표현

P1_33

식사 / 가사 관련 장소

주문 / 식사

opening / closing the menus 메뉴판을 펼치고 있다 / 접고 있다
reading[looking at, studying] the menu 메뉴를 보고 있다
pointing at a menu 메뉴를 손가락으로 가리키고 있다
picking up a menu 메뉴를 들어올리고 있다
ordering a meal 식사를 주문하고 있다
taking an order 주문을 받고 있다
writing down an order 주문을 적고 있다
having[eating] a meal 식사하고 있다
dining by the water 물가에서 식사를 하고 있다
drinking from a cup / bottle 컵 / 병에 있는 물을 마시고 있다
sipping from a coffee mug 머그잔으로 커피를 마시고 있다

요리 / 서빙

preparing[cooking] a meal 음식을 준비하고 있다
chopping vegetables 채소를 잘게 썰고 있다
grilling some food 음식을 그릴에 굽고 있다
removing baked goods from the oven
오븐에서 빵을 꺼내고 있다
pouring a beverage into a glass 음료를 잔에 따르고 있다
stirring a pot 냄비를 젓고 있다
spreading out a tablecloth 식탁보를 펼치고 있다
setting the table 상을 차리고 있다
filling a cup 컵을 채우고 있다
holding a serving tray 쟁반을 들고 있다
passing a plate of food 음식이 담긴 접시를 건네고 있다
being brought to the diners 식사 손님에게 제공되고 있다
serving refreshments 다과를 제공하고 있다
cleaning[wiping off] the table 식탁을 닦고 있다
being cleared from the counter 카운터에서 치워지고 있다

식당 / 카페 / 주방 묘사

being displayed in a glass case
유리 진열장에 진열되어 있다
Glasses have been stored in a cupboard.
유리잔들이 찬장에 보관되어 있다.
There are dishes on the table. 테이블에 요리가 있다.
Dishes are stacked on a counter.
접시가 조리대에 쌓여 있다.
A table is empty. 테이블이 비어 있다.
Some seats are unoccupied. 일부 좌석이 비어 있다.
A table has been set[prepared] for a meal.
테이블이 식사를 위해 차려져 있다.

가사 활동

sewing a garment 옷을 꿰매고 있다
folding a shirt 셔츠를 개고 있다
ironing some clothing 옷을 다림질하고 있다
arranging pillows 베개를 정돈하고 있다
opening a window 창문을 열고 있다
vacuuming the floor 바닥을 진공청소기로 청소하고 있다
sweeping with a broom 빗자루로 쓸고 있다
mopping the floor 바닥을 대걸레로 닦고 있다
cleaning the carpet 카펫을 청소하고 있다
wiping a kitchen stove 레인지를 닦고 있다
dusting the furniture 가구의 먼지를 닦고 있다
emptying a trash can 쓰레기통을 비우고 있다
hanging a picture on a wall 벽에 사진을 걸고 있다
moving some flowerpots 꽃화분을 옮기고 있다
washing pans in a sink 싱크대에서 프라이팬을 씻고 있다
standing on a stool 등받이 없는 의자에 올라가 있다
decorating a wall 벽면을 꾸미고 있다
placing flowers in a vase 화병에 꽃을 꽂고 있다

가정집 묘사

be set on a mattress 매트리스 위에 놓여 있다
have been placed on the counter 조리대에 놓여 있다
have been fastened to the ceiling 천장에 고정되어 있다
hanging over a doorway 출입구 위에 걸려 있다
be positioned along a wall 벽을 따라 놓여 있다
be located on both sides of a fireplace
벽난로 양쪽에 놓여 있다
have been pushed to one side of the room
방 한쪽으로 밀려나 있다
The door has been left open. 문이 열려 있다.
Water is flowing from a tap.
수도꼭지에서 물이 흐르고 있다.
There's a sofa on a patio. 테라스에 소파가 있다.
The armchairs are facing the paintings.
안락의자가 그림 쪽을 향해 있다.
Some lights are suspended from the ceiling.
천장에 조명이 매달려 있다.
A plant is sitting on a windowsill.
식물이 창문턱에 놓여 있다.
The floor is partially covered by a rug.
바닥 일부분이 양탄자로 덮여 있다.

LISTENING **PRACTICE**

🎧 P1_34 정답 및 해설 p.29

STEP 01 먼저 녹음을 들으면서 문제를 푸세요.　**STEP 02** 다시 들으면서 빈칸을 채우세요.

1.

(A)　(B)　(C)　(D)

(A) They're _____.
(B) They're _____.
(C) They're _____.
(D) They're _____.

| POSSIBLE ANSWERS |
They're _____.
Some pictures have _____.

2.

(A)　(B)　(C)　(D)

(A) The man is _____.
(B) The man is _____.
(C) One of the women is _____.
(D) One of the women is _____.

| POSSIBLE ANSWERS |
The women are _____.
There are _____.

3.

(A)　(B)　(C)　(D)

(A) She's _____.
(B) She's _____.
(C) She's _____.
(D) She's _____.

| POSSIBLE ANSWERS |
Coffee is _____.
Tables have _____.

4.

(A)　(B)　(C)　(D)

(A) A bucket is _____.
(B) The man is _____.
(C) A door frame is _____.
(D) Paint is _____.

| POSSIBLE ANSWERS |
The wall is _____.
A man is _____.

ETS TEST

🎧 P1_35 정답 및 해설 p.30

1.

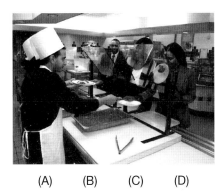

(A)   (B)   (C)   (D)

2.

(A)   (B)   (C)   (D)

3.

(A)   (B)   (C)   (D)

4.

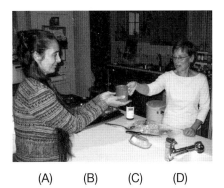

(A)   (B)   (C)   (D)

5.

(A)   (B)   (C)   (D)

6.

(A)   (B)   (C)   (D)

LISTENING TEST

In the Listening test, you will be asked to demonstrate how well you understand spoken English. The entire Listening test will last approximately 45 minutes. There are four parts, and directions are given for each part. You must mark your answers on the separate answer sheet. Do not write your answers in your test book.

PART 1

Directions: For each question in this part, you will hear four statements about a picture in your test book. When you hear the statements, you must select the one statement that best describes what you see in the picture. Then find the number of the question on your answer sheet and mark your answer. The statements will not be printed in your test book and will be spoken only one time.

Statement (C), "They're sitting at a table," is the best description of the picture, so you should select answer (C) and mark it on your answer sheet.

1.

2.

Go on to the next page

3.

4.

5.

6.

PART
2

질의 & 응답

LC

PART 2

질의 & 응답
QUESTION - RESPONSE

무료인강

질문 혹은 서술문과 3개의 보기를 들은 후 가장 적절한 응답을 선택하는 유형으로, 총 25문항이 출제된다.

기본 풀이 전략

🎧 P2_01

문제지

음원

7. Mark your answer on your answer sheet.

다른 파트와 달리 파트 2에서는 문제지에 아무것도 주어지지 않는다.

Number 7.
M Why is the light still not working?

W (A) No, he's still on vacation.
(B) The electrician wasn't able to fix it.
(C) I thought so, too.

STEP.01 질문 파악하기

질문 유형: 의문사 vs. 비의문사 확인
키워드: 의문사, 주어, 동사에 집중

STEP 02 오답 소거하며 정답 찾기

(A) X 의문사 의문문에 Yes / No로 응답할 수 없다.
(B) O Because를 생략하고 이유를 설명한 정답이다.
(C) X 상대방의 의견에 동의하는 대답이다.

최신 출제 경향

① 의문사 의문문 출제 비율

과거에는 의문사 의문문이 평균 50퍼센트 이상을 차지하였으나, 최근에는 그 이하로 출제된다.

② 비의문사 의문문 및 평서문 출제 비율

제안·요청 의문문, 부가 의문문, 그리고 평서문의 출제 비중이 높아지고 있다. 응답을 예측하기 어려운 평서문이 예전보다 많이 출제되기 때문에 난이도가 높아졌다고 할 수 있다.

③ 다양해진 응답 패턴

질문에 직접적인 답변을 주지 않고 우회적/간접적으로 답하는 경우가 많아지고 있다. 따라서 다양한 응답 패턴을 미리 익혀두는 것이 좋다.

질문	Where should I put these product samples? 이 제품 샘플들을 어디에 놓을까요?
직접적 응답	On the desk over there. 저쪽에 있는 책상 위예요.
우회적 응답	Let me make some space in the cabinet. 제가 캐비닛에 공간을 좀 만들어 볼게요.
'모른다' 응답	Try asking Ms. Diaz. 디아즈 씨에게 물어보세요.
제3의 응답	Oh, I thought we handed them all out earlier. 아, 전 우리가 아까 전부 나누어 줬다고 생각했는데요.
되묻는 응답	How many of them are there? 몇 개 있나요?

파트 2에서는 기본적으로 질문의 키워드를 정확히 파악하고 가장 적절한 응답을 선택하는 것이 중요하나, 다만 아래와 같은 대표적인 오답 유형을 알아두면 소거하는 데 도움이 될 수 있다.

❶ 의문사 의문문에 Yes / No로 시작하는 응답

Who, What, When 등으로 시작해 특정 정보를 묻는 의문사 의문문에는 Yes, Okay와 같은 긍정 응답이나 No, Not at all과 같은 부정 응답을 할 수 없다.

Q **Who** do you think is better qualified for the position? 누가 그 자리에 더 적합하다고 생각하세요?
오답 **Yes,** he was just hired. 네, 그는 막 고용되었어요.
정답 I like them both. 저는 둘 다 마음에 듭니다.

❷ 다른 의문사에 적합한 답변을 활용한 응답

질문에 사용된 의문사 대신 다른 의문사가 들어갔다면 정답이 될 수 있는 보기가 오답으로 나오기도 한다. 질문의 키워드를 명확히 기억하고 있어야 이러한 오답을 피해갈 수 있다.

Q **Where** are we meeting with the clients tomorrow? 내일 의뢰인들과 어디에서 회의하나요?
오답 **At ten o'clock.** 오전 10시에요. (의문사가 When이면 가능)
정답 Actually, they just canceled. 사실 그들이 방금 취소했어요.

❸ 유사 발음, 반복 어휘, 파생어를 활용한 응답

질문에서 들린 단어와 발음이 동일하거나 유사한 단어, 혹은 파생어를 포함한 오답이 종종 등장한다. 하지만 이러한 보기가 간혹 정답이 될 수도 있으니 무조건 소거하는 일은 없도록 한다.

Q How many people are coming to the reception **tonight**? 오늘 밤 사람들이 얼마나 환영회에 오나요?
오답 I don't have time **tonight**. 저는 오늘 밤 시간이 없어요.
정답 There could be a hundred. 백 명은 될 겁니다.

❹ 연상 가능한 어휘를 활용한 응답

질문에 쓰인 특정 단어에서 연상되는 어휘가 오답 보기에 활용되기도 한다. 다만 응답 패턴이 다양해진 만큼 정답에도 쓰일 가능성이 충분히 있기 때문에, 응답을 듣기 전에 질문을 정확히 파악하는 데 중점을 두도록 한다.

Q When can I look at the **apartment**? 제가 언제 아파트를 볼 수 있죠?
오답 It has two **bedrooms**. 침실이 두 개 있습니다.
정답 Anytime tomorrow afternoon. 내일 오후 아무 때나요.

의문사 의문문

❶ Who 의문문

출제공식
1 어떤 행위의 주체나 특정 업무를 담당하는 사람을 묻는 문제가 자주 출제된다.
2 이름으로 답하는 경우가 많지만, 직위, 부서 / 회사명, 부정대명사 등으로도 답할 수도 있다.
우회적으로 본인임을 암시하거나 모른다는 것을 드러내며 해당 정보를 확인할 수 있는 곳 / 방법을
알려주는 응답도 종종 나온다.

✏️ 빈출 질문 & 응답 패턴 🎧 P2_02

사람 이름	**Q** Who's in charge of sending out the weekly newsletter? **A** **Esther's** responsible for that.	누가 주간 뉴스레터 발송을 담당하고 있나요? 에스더가 담당해요.
직위 / 직업	**Q** Who will review the budget proposal? **A** **The accounting manager.**	누가 예산안을 검토할 건가요? 경리부장이요.
부서 / 회사명	**Q** Who should I contact about updating this software? **A** Try the **IT department.**	이 소프트웨어 프로그램 업데이트 관련해서 누구에게 연락해야 하죠? IT 부서에 해보세요.
부정 대명사	**Q** Who made the opening remarks at the conference? **A** I think it was **someone** from Eastland University.	누가 학회에서 개회사를 했나요? 이스트랜드 대학교에서 온 사람이었던 것 같아요.
우회적 응답	**Q** Who's going to meet the clients at the train station? **A** **I'm free** this afternoon.	누가 기차역에 고객들을 마중 나갈 건가요? 제가 오늘 오후에 시간이 됩니다.
'모른다' 응답	**Q** Who organized the fund-raising dinner last year? **A** **Steve might know.**	작년에 누가 기금 행사 만찬을 준비했죠? 스티브가 알지도 몰라요.

만점 전략 누구인지 말해주지 않는 "비협조적"인 응답! 오답으로 소거하지 않도록 주의한다.

Q Who was selected as the new graphic designer? 새 그래픽 디자이너로 선발된 사람이 누구인가요?

A1 They are holding interviews tomorrow. 내일 면접 진행한대요. (They = 채용 담당자들)

A2 Didn't Maria tell you? 마리아가 말해주지 않았나요?

ETS CHECK-UP 🎧 P2_03 정답 및 해설 p.35

1.	(A)	(B)	(C)	**4.**	(A)	(B)	(C)
2.	(A)	(B)	(C)	**5.**	(A)	(B)	(C)
3.	(A)	(B)	(C)	**6.**	(A)	(B)	(C)

❷ What/Which 의문문

1 What 의문문은 〈What + 명사〉 형태로 시간, 종류 등을 묻거나 단독으로 쓰여 의견, 할 일, 주제 등 다양한 정보를 묻는다.

2 Which 의문문은 주로 〈Which + 명사〉 형태를 띠며, 뒤에 오는 명사가 핵심포인트가 된다.

3 What/Which 뒤에 오는 명사의 유의어, 하위어, 또는 대명사 one이 포함된 응답이 자주 나온다.

🖊 빈출 질문 & 응답 패턴　　　　　　　　　　　　　　　　🎧 P2_04

시간	**Q** What time does the new-hire orientation begin? **A** It starts **at two.**/**In an hour.**/**Right after lunch.**	신입 사원 오리엔테이션이 몇 시에 시작하나요? 2시에 시작해요. / 1시간 후예요. / 점심 직후예요.
종류	**Q** What kind of business does Mr. Perez manage? **A** He runs a **Mexican restaurant.**	페레즈 씨는 어떤 종류의 사업체를 운영하나요? 멕시칸 음식점을 운영해요.
의견	**Q** What do you think of my article? **A** It seems **well-written.**/**I haven't read it yet.**	제 기사에 대해 어떻게 생각하세요? 잘 작성된 것 같아요. / 아직 안 읽어 봤어요.
할 일	**Q** What should the interns do now? **A** **They can wait in the lobby.**	이제 인턴들은 무엇을 해야 될까요? 로비에서 기다리면 됩니다.
Which 명사	**Q** Which copy machine needs to be repaired? **A** **The one** next to the printer.	어떤 복사기가 수리되어야 하나요? 프린터 옆에 있는 거요.
Which of	**Q** Which of these paintings should I hang on the wall? **A** **Whichever** you want.	이 그림들 중 어느 것을 벽에 걸까요? 당신이 원하는 거요.

만점 전략 다른 관련 정보를 제공하는 제3의 응답과 정보 확인처를 알려주는 응답도 익혀 둔다.

Q　What/Which gate does Flight 234 depart from? 234 항공편이 어느 게이트에서 출발하나요?

A1　Sorry, but it has been canceled. 죄송하지만 그 항공편은 취소되었습니다.

A2　The information will soon appear on the display monitor.
해당 정보는 곧 전광판에 나올 겁니다. (= 직접 확인하세요.)

ETS CHECK-UP　　　　　　　　　　　🎧 P2_05 정답 및 해설 p.36

1.　　(A)　(B)　(C)　　　　**4.**　　(A)　(B)　(C)

2.　　(A)　(B)　(C)　　　　**5.**　　(A)　(B)　(C)

3.　　(A)　(B)　(C)　　　　**6.**　　(A)　(B)　(C)

ETS X-FILE | Who / What / Which 의문문 필수 표현

Who 의문문

직책·신분 어휘

assistant 비서, 부하 직원

board members 임원, 이사진 (= board of directors)

(vice) president (부)사장

committee member 위원

supervisor 관리자, 감독관

department manager 부서장

director 이사, 부장, 감독

colleague 동료 (= coworker)

tenant 세입자 ↔ **landlord** 집주인

real estate agent 부동산 중개인

property manager 부동산 관리인, 관리소장

program coordinator 프로그램 진행자, 기획자

accountant 회계사

financial consultant 재무 상담가

keynote speaker 기조 연설자

사람 이름 포함 응답

John is [in charge of] / [responsible for] that.
존이 담당하고 있어요.

Mr. Yang took care of it. 양 씨가 그 일을 처리했어요.

Rita said she would. 리타가 자기가 하겠다고 했어요.

That's Brenda's job. 그건 브렌다의 직무예요.

I believe it's Ms. Kim. 김 씨로 알고 있어요.

Ms. Hayashi took it over. 하야시 씨가 인계 받았어요.

I'll be going with José. 호세와 함께 갈 거예요.

기타 응답

We take turns. 우리는 교대로 합니다.

No one, yet. 아직 아무도 없습니다.

I'll do it later this afternoon. 제가 이따 오후에 할게요.

I can't remember the person's name.
그 사람 이름이 기억이 안 나요.

Here's the staff schedule. 여기 직원 근무 일정표예요.

What 의문문

시간 / 날짜 질문에 대한 응답

At ten in the morning. 아침 10시요.

I think June twenty first. 6월 21일인 것 같아요.

It's scheduled for nine A.M. 오전 9시로 예정되어 있어요.

I sent you the itinerary. 제가 일정표 보내드렸잖아요.

주제 질문에 대한 응답

The upcoming product launch. 다가오는 제품 출시요.

Last month's sales figures. 지난달 매출액이요.

Promoting businesses on social media.
소셜 미디어에서의 업체 홍보요.

종류 질문에 대한 응답

Comedies, mostly. 주로 코미디 프로그램이요.

I like thrillers. 스릴러를 좋아합니다.

It's chocolate. 초콜릿이에요.

One that sells furniture. 가구를 파는 곳이요.

가격 질문에 대한 응답

It's on sale for 50 dollars. 세일해서 50달러에요.

It depends on the size. 크기에 따라 다릅니다.

It should say on the box. 상자에 써 있을 겁니다.

Is the price tag missing? 가격표가 없나요?

할 일 질문에 대한 응답

Leave it on my desk. 제 책상 위에 두세요.

Can you set up the projector? 프로젝터를 준비해 줄래요?

I already took care of everything.
제가 이미 모든 것을 처리했어요.

의견 / 생각 질문에 대한 응답

It was very informative. 굉장히 유익했어요.

I like how simple it is. 간편해서 좋아요.

He seems well-qualified.
충분한 자격을 갖춘 것으로 보이네요.

Which 의문문

직접적 응답

The one on the right. 오른쪽에 있는 거요.

The one with a yellow tag. 노란색 표가 달린 거요.

The red one parked outside. 밖에 주차된 빨간 거요.

Let's get the latest model. 최신 모델을 사죠.

We'll stay with our current one. 현재 것으로 유지할 거예요

우회적 응답

It doesn't matter to me. 전 상관없어요.

All of them were great. 모두가 좋았어요.

Actually, I didn't buy any. 사실 전 아무것도 사지 않았어요.

They're still conducting interviews.
아직 면접이 진행 중이에요.

LISTENING **PRACTICE**

대화를 듣고 적절한 응답을 고르세요. 다시 듣고 빈칸을 채우세요. (녹음은 두 번씩 들려줍니다.)

1. (A) (B) (C)

_____ the Langdon account?

(A) It's _____.

(B) _____ that.

(C) _____.

| POSSIBLE ANSWERS |

_____ Ms. Taylor.

_____ department.

2. (A) (B) (C)

_____ of car sales this quarter?

(A) Many _____.

(B) We just _____.

(C) The northwest _____.

| POSSIBLE ANSWERS |

I _____ yet.

Mr. Robbins _____.

3. (A) (B) (C)

What was Mr. Kim's group _____ this month?

(A) Sure, I'll _____.

(B) The _____.

(C) _____.

| POSSIBLE ANSWERS |

The _____.

I heard, _____.

4. (A) (B) (C)

Who _____ of assignment changes?

(A) The _____.

(B) Just a _____.

(C) With the _____.

| POSSIBLE ANSWERS |

It _____.

_____ this afternoon.

5. (A) (B) (C)

_____ for the photo shoot?

(A) _____.

(B) In the _____.

(C) _____, too.

| POSSIBLE ANSWERS |

It _____.

The _____.

6. (A) (B) (C)

_____ did you like the best?

(A) I'll _____.

(B) The _____.

(C) There were _____.

| POSSIBLE ANSWERS |

_____ great.

Actually, I _____.

ETS TEST

1. Mark your answer on your answer sheet.   (A) (B) (C)

2. Mark your answer on your answer sheet.   (A) (B) (C)

3. Mark your answer on your answer sheet.   (A) (B) (C)

4. Mark your answer on your answer sheet.   (A) (B) (C)

5. Mark your answer on your answer sheet.   (A) (B) (C)

6. Mark your answer on your answer sheet.   (A) (B) (C)

7. Mark your answer on your answer sheet.   (A) (B) (C)

8. Mark your answer on your answer sheet.   (A) (B) (C)

9. Mark your answer on your answer sheet.   (A) (B) (C)

10. Mark your answer on your answer sheet.   (A) (B) (C)

11. Mark your answer on your answer sheet.   (A) (B) (C)

12. Mark your answer on your answer sheet.   (A) (B) (C)

13. Mark your answer on your answer sheet.   (A) (B) (C)

14. Mark your answer on your answer sheet.   (A)   (B)   (C)

15. Mark your answer on your answer sheet.   (A)   (B)   (C)

16. Mark your answer on your answer sheet.   (A)   (B)   (C)

17. Mark your answer on your answer sheet.   (A)   (B)   (C)

18. Mark your answer on your answer sheet.   (A)   (B)   (C)

19. Mark your answer on your answer sheet.   (A)   (B)   (C)

20. Mark your answer on your answer sheet.   (A)   (B)   (C)

21. Mark your answer on your answer sheet.   (A)   (B)   (C)

22. Mark your answer on your answer sheet.   (A)   (B)   (C)

23. Mark your answer on your answer sheet.   (A)   (B)   (C)

24. Mark your answer on your answer sheet.   (A)   (B)   (C)

25. Mark your answer on your answer sheet.   (A)   (B)   (C)

③ When 의문문

출제공식 1 특정 행위가 발생하는 시점을 묻는 유형으로 매회 꾸준히 출제되는 편이다. 과거, 현재, 미래를 나타내는 여러 가지 형태의 동사가 사용된다.

2 in, on, at, by, before, after 등 시간과 관련된 표현이 들어간 보기가 정답일 가능성이 높다. 확답을 피하며 언제인지 말해줄 수 없는 이유를 설명하는 응답도 종종 나온다.

✎ 빈출 질문 & 응답 패턴　　　　　　　　　　　🎧 P2_09

구체적 시점	**Q** When does the restaurant close on weekdays? **A** Usually at nine o'clock.	그 레스토랑은 주중에 언제 문을 닫나요? 보통 저녁 9시예요.
	Q When is the project expected to be completed? **A** In two months. / Not until the end of this month.	프로젝트가 언제 완료될까요? 2달 뒤에요. / 이번 달 말은 되어야 할 거예요.
모호한 시점	**Q** When are we going to schedule the interviews? **A** After reviewing all the applications.	언제 면접 일정을 잡을 예정인가요? 모든 지원서를 검토한 후에요.
우회적 응답	**Q** When will Ms. Yoshida come back from her holiday? **A** I saw her at the meeting this morning.	요시다 씨는 휴가에서 언제 돌아올 건가요? 오늘 아침 회의에서 봤는데요.
'모른다' 응답	**Q** When are you transferring to the Chicago branch? **A** The schedule is still being arranged.	시카고 지점에 언제 전근을 가나요? 아직 일정이 조정되는 중이에요.
제3의 응답	**Q** When did you paint this beautiful picture? **A** I got it from a gift shop.	이 아름다운 그림을 언제 그렸나요? 선물 가게에서 샀어요.

만점 전략 질문과 시제가 달라도 정답이 될 수 있다.

Q　When are we going to book the venue? 언제 장소를 예약할 건가요?

정답　Lily already made all the arrangements. 릴리가 이미 모든 준비를 해놓았어요. (= 우리가 할 필요 없어요.)

오답　For three days. / Until tomorrow. 3일 동안요. / 내일까지요. (기간 / 지속을 나타내는 오답에 유의!)

ETS CHECK-UP　　　　　　　　　　　🎧 P2_10 정답 및 해설 p. 43

1.	(A)	(B)	(C)		**4.**	(A)	(B)	(C)
2.	(A)	(B)	(C)		**5.**	(A)	(B)	(C)
3.	(A)	(B)	(C)		**6.**	(A)	(B)	(C)

❹ Where 의문문

출제공식

1 주로 장소 및 위치를 묻는 문제가 출제되며, 출처나 관련 정보를 찾을 수 있는 곳을 묻는 질문이 나오기도 한다.

2 in, at, on, next to 등 장소 및 위치를 나타내는 표현이 포함된 보기가 정답일 확률이 높다. 하지만 담당 기관이나 사람을 언급하는 경우도 있으며, 다양한 우회적 응답도 나오는 추세이다.

✏️ **빈출 질문 & 응답 패턴**   🎧 P2_11

장소/ 위치	**Q** Where did you buy this table? **A** **At the antique shop near my place.**	이 탁자 어디에서 샀나요? 제 집 근처에 있는 골동품 상점에서요.
	Q Where do we keep the patient information sheets? **A** **In the top drawer.**	환자 정보 양식을 어디에다 보관하죠? 맨 위 서랍이요.
출처/ 확인처	**Q** Where can I find the complete list of your products? **A** It's **on our Web site.**	귀사의 전 제품 목록을 어디에서 찾을 수 있나요? 저희 웹사이트에 있습니다.
기관/ 사람	**Q** Where should I put this scarf I found in the lobby? **A** You can **leave it with the receptionist.**	로비에서 주운 이 스카프를 어디에 둘까요? 안내원에게 맡기시면 됩니다.
'모른다' 응답	**Q** Where is the main entrance to the hospital? **A** Actually, **I'm new here** as well.	병원 정문이 어디인가요? 사실 저도 여기 처음 온 거예요.
제3의 응답	**Q** Where are we holding the launch party for our new book? **A** **It's been postponed until next month.**	우리의 신간 도서 론칭 파티를 어디서 하나요? 그게 다음 달로 연기되었어요.

만점 전략 우회적 / 제3의 응답과 함께 나오는 장소 / 위치 표현 오답에 유의한다.

Q Where can I get a laptop for remote employees? 원격 근무 직원을 위한 노트북 어디에서 받을 수 있나요?

정답 You need to get approval from your manager first. 먼저 관리자에게 승인을 받아야 합니다.

오답 I'll put the monitor in the storage room. 창고에 모니터를 둘게요. (그럴 듯하게 들리는 장소 표현에 유의!)

ETS CHECK-UP   🎧 P2_12 정답 및 해설 p.45

1.	(A)	(B)	(C)		**4.**	(A)	(B)	(C)
2.	(A)	(B)	(C)		**5.**	(A)	(B)	(C)
3.	(A)	(B)	(C)		**6.**	(A)	(B)	(C)

ETS X-FILE | When / Where 의문문 필수 표현

🎧 P2_13

When 의문문

과거

last year 작년에

the day before yesterday 그저께

since last spring 지난봄 이후로

quite recently 꽤 최근에

earlier this morning 오늘 아까 아침에

I think it was two years ago. 2년 전이었던 것 같아요.

현재

any minute now 지금 당장에라도

every ten minutes 10분마다

every other week[month] 격주[격월]로

every night at nine 매일 밤 9시에

the first Thursday of every month 매월 첫째 주 목요일에

every fourth Tuesday 네 번째 화요일마다

시간 접속사

as soon as I sign the lease 임대차 계약서에 서명하자마자

as soon as you confirm the address
당신이 주소를 확인하자마자

after more tests are completed 더 많은 실험이 완료된 후에

after I finish this paperwork 이 서류작업을 마친 후에

미래

right away 즉각

pretty soon 이제 곧

right after lunch 점심시간 직후에

at three thirty this afternoon 오늘 오후 3시 30분에

anytime before five o'clock 5시 이전이면 아무 때나

by the end of the day 오늘까지, 오늘 안으로

no later than Friday 늦어도 금요일까지

in about a week 약 1주 후에

sometime next week 다음 주 중에

on October fifteenth 10월 15일에

not for another two weeks 2주 후에야

not until January 1월 이후에야

still have a month left 아직 1달이 남은

on the first day of next month 다음 달 첫째 날에

probably at the end of the month
아마도 이달 말에

by eight o'clock at the latest 늦어도 8시까지

at the next marketing meeting
다음 마케팅 회의에서

within twenty-four hours 24시간 내로

Where 의문문

in / at / on / to

in the front[back] row 앞[뒷]줄에

in the file cabinet 파일 캐비닛 안에

in the folder on my desk 책상 위에 있는 폴더에

in the top drawer 첫 번째 서랍에

in the storage area 창고에

in the tenth floor meeting room 10층 회의실에서

at the end of the hall 복도 끝에

at the customer service desk 고객 서비스 창구에서

at the district office 지역 사무실에서

on the bottom shelf 맨 아래 선반에

on the second floor 2층에

on the next block 다음 블록에

on the first page 첫 번째 장에

on the company's Web site 회사 웹사이트 상에

to the address below 아래에 있는 주소로

to the supply room 비품실로

to the airport 공항으로

to the right of the elevator 엘리베이터 오른쪽으로

closer to the city center 시내 중심부에 더 가까이

기타 전치사 / 부사

from the warehouse 창고에서

from a new supplier 새로운 공급처로부터

over there 저쪽에

by the register 계산대 옆에

right next to the university 대학교 바로 옆에

behind the office building 사무실 건물 뒤에

around the corner 모퉁이에

near Fourth Avenue 4번 가 근처에

down the street 길 따라 가다 보면

directly across from the pharmacy 약국 바로 건너편에

somewhere downtown 시내 어딘가

장소 관련 우회적 응답

The same place as last year. 지난해와 같은 장소요.

She went out for lunch. 그녀는 점심 먹으러 나갔습니다.

I'm going that way now. 제가 지금 그쪽으로 가는 길이에요.

Actually, I'm on my way there now.
사실 제가 지금 거기 가는 중이에요.

Well, people are standing in line over there.
음, 사람들이 저기에 줄을 서 있네요.

66

LISTENING **PRACTICE**

◌ P2_14 정답 및 해설 p.46

대화를 듣고 적절한 응답을 고르세요. 다시 듣고 빈칸을 채우세요. (녹음은 두 번씩 들려줍니다.)

1. (A)   (B)   (C)

_____ of the contract?

(A) _____ the United States.

(B) I think my _____.

(C) Yes, the last _____.

| POSSIBLE ANSWERS |

I'll find out _____.

I'd _____ it.

2. (A)   (B)   (C)

When will the current _____?

(A) I'll _____.

(B) _____.

(C) By _____.

| POSSIBLE ANSWERS |

After they _____.

It's probably _____.

3. (A)   (B)   (C)

_____ the new-employee

orientation?

(A) _____ as last year.

(B) In _____.

(C) A _____.

| POSSIBLE ANSWERS |

It _____ will attend.

Let's _____.

4. (A)   (B)   (C)

_____ my medicine?

(A) He _____.

(B) _____.

(C) At _____.

| POSSIBLE ANSWERS |

It _____.

We'll _____.

5. (A)   (B)   (C)

Where will _____?

(A) We're _____.

(B) It's _____.

(C) _____ number five.

| POSSIBLE ANSWERS |

_____ is still deciding.

Our Chinese _____.

6. (A)   (B)   (C)

_____ be published?

(A) _____.

(B) Unfortunately, _____.

(C) Just _____.

| POSSIBLE ANSWERS |

_____.

_____ two weeks.

PART 2 | CHAPTER 01

1. Mark your answer on your answer sheet.   (A)   (B)   (C)

2. Mark your answer on your answer sheet.   (A)   (B)   (C)

3. Mark your answer on your answer sheet.   (A)   (B)   (C)

4. Mark your answer on your answer sheet.   (A)   (B)   (C)

5. Mark your answer on your answer sheet.   (A)   (B)   (C)

6. Mark your answer on your answer sheet.   (A)   (B)   (C)

7. Mark your answer on your answer sheet.   (A)   (B)   (C)

8. Mark your answer on your answer sheet.   (A)   (B)   (C)

9. Mark your answer on your answer sheet.   (A)   (B)   (C)

10. Mark your answer on your answer sheet.   (A)   (B)   (C)

11. Mark your answer on your answer sheet.   (A)   (B)   (C)

12. Mark your answer on your answer sheet.   (A)   (B)   (C)

13. Mark your answer on your answer sheet.   (A)   (B)   (C)

14. Mark your answer on your answer sheet. (A) (B) (C)

15. Mark your answer on your answer sheet. (A) (B) (C)

16. Mark your answer on your answer sheet. (A) (B) (C)

17. Mark your answer on your answer sheet. (A) (B) (C)

18. Mark your answer on your answer sheet. (A) (B) (C)

19. Mark your answer on your answer sheet. (A) (B) (C)

20. Mark your answer on your answer sheet. (A) (B) (C)

21. Mark your answer on your answer sheet. (A) (B) (C)

22. Mark your answer on your answer sheet. (A) (B) (C)

23. Mark your answer on your answer sheet. (A) (B) (C)

24. Mark your answer on your answer sheet. (A) (B) (C)

25. Mark your answer on your answer sheet. (A) (B) (C)

❺ How 의문문

1 〈How + 형용사/부사〉 형태로 수량/가격(many, much), 기간(long), 빈도(often), 시기(soon, late), 거리(far) 등을 묻거나, 단독으로 쓰여 방법, 의견, 상태/상황 등을 묻는 문제가 주로 출제된다.

2 〈How + 형용사/부사〉 질문에는 숫자 표현, 방법/의견 질문에는 직접적인 서술형 답의 비율이 높다. 하지만 정보 확인처를 알려주거나 간접적으로 생각을 드러내는 등 응답 패턴이 다양해지고 있다.

✏️ 빈출 질문 & 응답 패턴   🎧 P2_16

수량/가격	**Q** How many people will attend the marketing seminar? **A** About **fifty.** / You'll have to **ask Mark.**	마케팅 세미나에 몇 명이 참석할 예정인가요? 약 50명이요. / 마크에게 물어보셔야 할 거예요.
기간	**Q** How long does it take to complete this course? **A** **Five to seven months.**	이 과정을 수료하는 데 얼마나 걸리나요? 5개월에서 7개월이요.
빈도	**Q** How often do I have to change my password? **A** At least **once every three months.**	제 비밀번호를 얼마나 자주 바꿔야 하나요? 적어도 세 달에 한 번이요.
방법/수단	**Q** How do I get reimbursed for travel expenses? **A** **The instructions are on the bulletin board.**	출장비를 어떻게 환급 받나요? 게시판에 설명문이 있어요.
의견	**Q** How was your trip to Australia? **A** I had a great time. / It rained every single day.	호주 여행 어땠어요? 즐거운 시간을 보냈어요. / 매일 비가 내렸어요.
상태/상황	**Q** How did the sales presentation go? **A** It went well. / It was Elio who gave the presentation.	제품 설명 프레젠테이션 어떻게 되었나요? 잘 끝났어요. / 발표를 한 건 엘리오였어요.

만점 전략 How 의문문의 다양한 의도(방법·의견 문의 / 걱정 표현 등)를 알아둔다.

Q How are we going to make the project deadline? 프로젝트 마감일을 어떻게 맞추죠? (방법 문의 / 걱정 표현)

정답 Don't worry. I'll ask for an extension. 걱정 마세요. 제가 연장해 달라고 할 겁니다. (걱정 말라며 대안 제시)

오답 For two months. 2개월 동안이요. (〈How + 형용사/부사〉 의문문에 적합한 오답에 유의!)

ETS CHECK-UP   🎧 P2_17 정답 및 해설 p.52

1.	(A)	(B)	(C)		4.	(A)	(B)	(C)
2.	(A)	(B)	(C)		5.	(A)	(B)	(C)
3.	(A)	(B)	(C)		6.	(A)	(B)	(C)

❻ Why 의문문

출제공식

1 원인/이유나 목적을 묻는 질문이 주를 이루며, 'Why isn't / hasn't ~?' 등과 같이 부정 의문문 형태로도 종종 출제된다.

2 Because 혹은 to부정사를 사용하거나, 생략한 채 이유를 설명하는 경우가 대부분이다. 하지만 이유를 설명할 수 없음을 드러내는 응답, 상대방을 정정하는 응답, 되묻는 응답도 나올 수 있다.

✎ 빈출 질문 & 응답 패턴 🎧 P2_18

원인/이유	**Q** Why is the department store closed today? **A** Because it's being renovated.	왜 백화점이 오늘 휴업하나요? 수리되는 중이라서 그래요.
	Q Why was the performance rescheduled for next week? **A** There was a problem with the audio equipment.	왜 공연 일정이 다음 주로 변경되었나요? 음향 장비에 문제가 있었어요.
목적	**Q** Why are you meeting with Ms. Adler this afternoon? **A** To discuss the details of our new project.	왜 오늘 오후에 애들러 씨와 회의하시는 건가요? 새 프로젝트의 세부사항을 논의하기 위해서요.
'모른다' 응답	**Q** Why did our sales decrease last month? **A** Tim is looking into it.	왜 지난달 우리 매출이 감소했죠? 팀이 조사하고 있습니다.
제3의 응답	**Q** Why isn't the conference room set up yet? **A** I thought you were taking care of that.	왜 회의실 준비가 아직 안 되어있죠? 저는 당신이 하는 줄 알고 있었어요.
되묻는 응답	**Q** Why has today's workshop been postponed? **A** Didn't you receive the e-mail about that?	왜 오늘 워크숍이 연기되었나요? 관련 이메일 못 받았나요?

만점 전략 Why 의문문을 불평으로 받아들여 해결 방안을 제시하는 응답이 나오기도 한다.

Q Why are there so many errors in this report? 이 보고서에 오류가 왜 이렇게 많은 건가요?

A1 I'll ask Erica to proofread it. 에리카에게 검수해 달라고 요청할게요.

A2 Do you want me look it over again? 제가 다시 검토할까요?

ETS CHECK-UP 🎧 P2_19 정답 및 해설 p.54

1.	(A)	(B)	(C)		**4.**	(A)	(B)	(C)
2.	(A)	(B)	(C)		**5.**	(A)	(B)	(C)
3.	(A)	(B)	(C)		**6.**	(A)	(B)	(C)

ETS X-FILE | How / Why 의문문 필수 표현

How 의문문

방법 / 수단

in person 직접, 손수 (= personally)

in alphabetical order 알파벳 순으로

in cash 현금으로 ↔ **by credit card** 신용카드로

by the date they were created 생성된 날짜 순으로

by overnight delivery 익일 배송으로

by using social media 소셜 미디어를 활용해서

You can do that online. 온라인으로 할 수 있어요.

You should call the help desk.
업무 지원 센터에 전화해 보세요.

The instructions are on the back of the box.
설명문이 상자 뒤쪽에 있어요.

It should say on the label. 라벨에 쓰여 있을 거예요.

There's a map behind you. 당신 뒤에 지도가 있어요.

Push the button on the side. 측면에 있는 버튼을 누르세요.

의견 / 상태 / 상황

I really enjoyed it. 정말 즐거웠어요.

It went very well. 잘 진행되었어요.

It couldn't have been better. 정말 최고였어요.

It was too crowded. 너무 붐볐어요.

It has a great view. 전망이 아주 좋아요.

It's too close to the kitchen. 당비실하고 너무 가까워요.

The location is perfect. 위치가 완벽해요.

기간 / 빈도 / 시기

for two days 이틀간

more than ten years 10년 이상

the rest of the month 이번 달 남은 기간(동안)

biweekly 격주로(= every two weeks)

once in a while 가끔

at least once a month 최소한 한 달에 한 번

usually just on Saturdays 보통 토요일에만

whenever a new version is released
새로운 버전이 출시될 때마다

at the next meeting 다음 회의 때

It should be ready soon. 곧 준비 될 겁니다.

It won't take long. 오래 걸리지 않을 거예요.

It shouldn't take more than five minutes.
5분 이상 걸리진 않을 거예요.

가격 / 수량

by ten percent 10퍼센트

up to one hundred 100까지

enough for a dozen people 12명에게 충분할 정도로

between ten and twenty dollars 10에서 20달러 사이

thirty euros each 각각 30유로로

It's almost doubled. 거의 두 배가 되었습니다.

We have a party of fifteen coming in.
단체 손님이 15분 오셔요.

Why 의문문

원인 / 이유

because of bad[inclement] weather 악천후 때문에

due to heavy traffic[a traffic jam] 교통 체증 때문에

Because I had to finish a report. 보고서를 끝내야 했어요.

Because the manager is out of the office.
부장님이 사무실에 안 계셔서요.

Because his meeting ran late. 그의 회의가 늦어져서요.

It's being replaced / repaired. 그것은 교체 / 수리 중이에요.

It's under construction. 공사 중이에요.

It's out of ink[paper]. 잉크[종이]가 떨어졌어요.

Maybe it needs to be cleaned. 세척 되어야 하나 봐요.

There's rain in the forecast. 비 예보가 있어요.

The instructor is late. 강사가 늦어서요.

The air conditioner is broken. 에어컨이 고장 났어요.

The delivery's been delayed. 배달이 지연되었어요.

There was a scheduling conflict. 일정이 겹쳤어요.

There are still some problems to resolve.
아직 해결해야 할 문제가 있어요.

목적

for a business trip 출장으로

for a new job 새 직장 때문에

for personal business 개인적인 용무 때문에

for a dentist appointment 치과 예약 때문에

to protect them 그것들을 보호하기 위해

to make some copies 복사를 하기 위해

to renew their contract 그들의 계약을 갱신하기 위해

to lead a seminar 세미나를 진행하기 위해

to expand our client base 우리의 고객층을 넓히기 위해

to display the new merchandise 신상품을 진열하기 위해

to discuss a new project 새로운 프로젝트에 관해 논의하기 위해

to thank us for our hard work
우리의 노고에 대해 감사하기 위해

to accommodate more customers
더 많은 고객을 수용하기 위해

So that more people can attend.
더 많은 사람들이 참석할 수 있도록.

♪ ♭ P2_21 정답 및 해설 p. 55

대화를 듣고 적절한 응답을 고르세요. 다시 듣고 빈칸을 채우세요. (녹음은 두 번씩 들려줍니다.)

1. (A)   (B)   (C)

_____ conference room?

(A) _____ people were coming.

(B) The books _____.

(C) Sure, _____ right away.

| POSSIBLE ANSWERS |

More people _____.

That was _____.

2. (A)   (B)   (C)

_____ the new French restaurant?

(A) _____ at this corner.

(B) About _____.

(C) I'll be _____, actually.

| POSSIBLE ANSWERS |

I _____.

It _____.

3. (A)   (B)   (C)

Why is _____ early tonight?

(A) _____. I already ate.

(B) _____.

(C) At _____.

| POSSIBLE ANSWERS |

Because _____.

To _____ the kitchen.

4. (A)   (B)   (C)

_____ to the awards banquet?

(A) Many _____.

(B) No, _____.

(C) _____.

| POSSIBLE ANSWERS |

Oliver _____.

Here's _____.

5. (A)   (B)   (C)

_____ being rearranged?

(A) I'll _____.

(B) To _____.

(C) _____ floor.

| POSSIBLE ANSWERS |

_____ the new products.

Didn't the manager _____?

6. (A)   (B)   (C)

_____ have a sale?

(A) The bus _____.

(B) _____ during the summer.

(C) Generally, _____.

| POSSIBLE ANSWERS |

I _____.

_____.

1. Mark your answer on your answer sheet.   (A)   (B)   (C)

2. Mark your answer on your answer sheet.   (A)   (B)   (C)

3. Mark your answer on your answer sheet.   (A)   (B)   (C)

4. Mark your answer on your answer sheet.   (A)   (B)   (C)

5. Mark your answer on your answer sheet.   (A)   (B)   (C)

6. Mark your answer on your answer sheet.   (A)   (B)   (C)

7. Mark your answer on your answer sheet.   (A)   (B)   (C)

8. Mark your answer on your answer sheet.   (A)   (B)   (C)

9. Mark your answer on your answer sheet.   (A)   (B)   (C)

10. Mark your answer on your answer sheet.   (A)   (B)   (C)

11. Mark your answer on your answer sheet.   (A)   (B)   (C)

12. Mark your answer on your answer sheet.   (A)   (B)   (C)

13. Mark your answer on your answer sheet.   (A)   (B)   (C)

14. Mark your answer on your answer sheet. (A) (B) (C)

15. Mark your answer on your answer sheet. (A) (B) (C)

16. Mark your answer on your answer sheet. (A) (B) (C)

17. Mark your answer on your answer sheet. (A) (B) (C)

18. Mark your answer on your answer sheet. (A) (B) (C)

19. Mark your answer on your answer sheet. (A) (B) (C)

20. Mark your answer on your answer sheet. (A) (B) (C)

21. Mark your answer on your answer sheet. (A) (B) (C)

22. Mark your answer on your answer sheet. (A) (B) (C)

23. Mark your answer on your answer sheet. (A) (B) (C)

24. Mark your answer on your answer sheet. (A) (B) (C)

25. Mark your answer on your answer sheet. (A) (B) (C)

비의문사 의문문

⑦ Be동사 의문문

출제공식
1 사실 여부, 존재 유무를 묻거나 계획, 상태/상황 등을 확인하는 질문으로, 출제 빈도가 높지는 않은 편이다.
2 Yes/No, Sure와 같은 표현으로 직접적인 답변을 하는 경우가 많다. 하지만 Yes/No를 생략한 응답도 자주 나오며, 확답할 수 없음을 드러내거나 다른 정보를 주는 응답도 종종 출제된다.

✎ 빈출 질문 & 응답 패턴 🎧 P2_23

사실 여부	**Q** Was this hotel renovated recently?	이 호텔이 최근에 개조되었나요?
	A Yes, it took about two months.	네, 약 2달이 걸렸어요.
존재 유무	**Q** Is there a fee to attend the fitness class?	체력 단련 수업에 참석하려면 비용이 드나요?
	A No, it's included in your gym membership.	아니요, 헬스장 회원권에 포함되어 있습니다.
계획/ 예정	**Q** Are you going to sign up for the business webinar?	비즈니스 웨비나에 등록할 계획인가요?
	A I'm too busy this week.	제가 이번 주에는 너무 바빠요.
	Q Is Ms. Romano coming to the reception tonight?	로마노 씨가 오늘 밤 환영회에 오나요?
	A I'm not sure.	잘 모르겠어요.
상태	**Q** Are you ready to go out for shopping?	쇼핑하러 나갈 준비 되었나요?
	A I just realized that my wallet is missing.	제 지갑이 없어진 걸 지금 알았어요.
진행 상황	**Q** Are you still reading the monthly report?	아직도 월례 보고서를 읽는 중인가요?
	A I'm almost done.	거의 다 읽어가요.

만점 전략 Yes/No로 시작하는 보기가 오답일 수 있으니 끝까지 주의 깊게 듣도록 한다.

Q Are there any vacancies on your team? 그쪽 팀에 공석이 있나요?

정답 We'll let you know if one arises. 생기면 알려 드릴게요. (= 지금은 없어요.)

오답 Yes, we're on vacation. 네, 휴가 중이에요. (vacancy-vacation 유사 발음에 유의!)

ETS CHECK-UP
🎧 P2_24 정답 및 해설 p.62

1. (A) (B) (C)   **4.** (A) (B) (C)

2. (A) (B) (C)   **5.** (A) (B) (C)

3. (A) (B) (C)   **6.** (A) (B) (C)

⑧ 부정 의문문

출제공식 1 주로 사실 여부를 확인하는 질문이 출제되며, 제안을 하거나 동의를 구하는 질문이 나오기도 한다. 부정어 뒤에 오는 내용의 키워드를 포착하고 질문의 의도를 파악하는 것이 중요하다.

2 〈Yes / No + 부연 설명〉 형태의 답변과 Yes / No를 함축한 답변이 자주 나온다. 하지만 모른다는 것을 드러내는 응답을 비롯해, 질문의 의도에 따라 다양한 반응이 정답이 될 수도 있다.

✏️ 빈출 질문 & 응답 패턴   🎧 P2_25

Be 부정	**Q** Isn't Jerome <u>going to join</u> the conference call? **A** **No, he called in sick.**	제롬이 전화 회의에 참석하지 않을 건가요? 안 합니다. 아파서 결근한다고 전화 왔어요.
Do 부정	**Q** Don't you <u>have to pick up</u> Ms. Ito at the airport? **A** **Yes, I'll leave soon.**	공항에서 이토 씨를 모셔와야 하지 않나요? 네, 곧 떠날 거예요.
Have 부정	**Q** Hasn't the estimate <u>been revised</u> yet? **A** **I'll check with Amanda.**	아직 견적서가 수정되지 않았나요? 제가 아만다에게 확인해 볼게요.
Will / Should / Can / 부정	**Q** Won't Ellen <u>be speaking</u> at the conference this year? **A** **She'll let us know tomorrow.**	엘렌이 이번 해엔 회의에서 연설하지 않을 건가요? 그녀가 내일 우리에게 말해줄 거예요.
	Q Shouldn't we <u>replace the chairs</u> in our banquet room? **A** **I think they look fine.**	연회실에 있는 의자를 교체해야 하지 않을까요? 전 괜찮아 보이는 것 같은데요.
	Q Can't we <u>use a different supplier</u> for dairy products? **A** **Let's discuss it tomorrow.**	다른 유제품 공급업체를 쓰면 안 될까요? 내일 논의합시다.

만점 전략   부정 의문문의 여러 가지 용도를 알아두면 답변을 예측하는 데 도움이 된다.

<u>Didn't</u> you <u>use my stapler</u> earlier? 아까 제 스테이플러를 사용하지 않았나요? (= 과거 사실 / 물건의 행방 확인하기)

<u>Wasn't</u> yesterday's seminar <u>helpful</u>? 어제 열린 세미나가 도움이 되지 않았나요? (= 의견 / 동의 구하기)

<u>Shouldn't</u> we <u>buy</u> the labels <u>in bulk</u>? 라벨을 대량으로 구입해야 하지 않을까요? (= 제안)

ETS CHECK-UP   🎧 P2_26 정답 및 해설 p.63

1.	(A)	(B)	(C)		**4.**	(A)	(B)	(C)
2.	(A)	(B)	(C)		**5.**	(A)	(B)	(C)
3.	(A)	(B)	(C)		**6.**	(A)	(B)	(C)

ETS X-FILE | 사실 확인 / 정보 제공 불가 응답 필수 표현

사실 확인 / 정보 제공 불가

잘 모른다

I have no idea. 몰라요.

I'm not sure[certain]. 잘 모르겠어요.

Not that I know of. 제가 알기로는 아니에요.

I don't know anything about it.
그것에 대해선 전혀 몰라요.

I'm not in charge of that. 제가 담당하는 게 아니에요.

Mary will[should] know. 메리가 알 거예요.

James has the schedule. 제임스에게 일정표가 있어요.

I was out of the office. 전 사무실에 없었어요.

I just got back from vacation.
휴가 갔다가 이제 막 왔어요.

I'm not from around here. 제가 여기 출신이 아니에요.

I'm new to this area, too. 저도 이 지역엔 처음 왔어요.

I just started working here.
여기서 일 시작한 지 얼마 안돼요.

I'm still looking into that.
아직도 알아보는 중이에요.

I'm not the best person to ask.
저 말고 다른 사람에게 물어보는 게 낫겠어요.

통지 받지 못했다

I haven't been told yet. 아직 들은 바가 없어요.

I haven't been informed[notified]. 통지 받지 못했어요.

He hasn't told us yet. 그가 아직 말하지 않았어요.

That's news to me. 처음 듣는 이야기인데요.

I haven't heard about it.
그것에 대해 전혀 들은 바가 없어요.

확인해 보겠다

Let me look and see. 알아볼게요.

Let me check that for you. 확인해 볼게요.

Let me ask my manager. 점장님께 여쭤 볼게요.

Let me call the supplier. 납품업체에 전화해 볼게요.

I haven't checked. 확인해 보지 않았어요.

I'll find out. 제가 알아볼게요.

I'll let you know soon. 곧 알려 드릴게요.

I'll check the schedule. 제가 일정을 확인해 볼게요.

I'll check with Mr. Park. 박 씨에게 확인해 볼게요.

I'll have a look at their Web site.
그들의 웹사이트를 봐 볼게요.

결정되지 않았다

I'm still considering it. 아직 고려 중이에요.

It's still up in the air. 아직 결정 난 게 아니에요.

I'm still waiting. 여전히 기다리고 있어요.

I'm still thinking about it. 아직 그것에 대해 생각 중이에요.

I haven't made up my mind. 아직 결정하지 못했어요.

We're still deciding. 아직 결정 중이에요.

We will decide tomorrow. 내일 결정할 거예요.

The manager is reviewing it. 매니저가 검토 중입니다.

They haven't made a decision yet.
그들이 아직 결정하지 않았어요.

It hasn't been decided / finalized yet.
아직 결정 / 확정되지 않았어요.

It hasn't been discussed yet. 아직 논의되지 않았어요.

It is still being revised. 아직 계속 수정 중이에요.

It depends on the design. 그건 디자인에 따라 달라요.

It depends on when they start.
그들이 언제 시작할 지에 달렸어요.

It's up to the director to decide.
이사님께서 결정하실 일이에요.

잊었다 / 기억이 나지 않는다

I heard, but I forgot. 들었는데 기억이 나질 않네요.

I forget what it's called. 뭐라고 하는지 잊었어요.

It completely slipped my mind. 까맣게 잊고 있었네요.

I forgot that I lent it to Sam. 샘에게 빌려 준 것을 깜박했어요.

I can't remember it, either. 저도 그게 기억이 나지 않아요.

문의해 보다 / 참고하다

Try asking Mr. Taylor. 테일러 씨에게 문의해 보세요.

Check with Anna. 안나에게 문의해 보세요.

You'd better ask Megumi. 메구미에게 물어보시는 게 나아요.

You'll have to ask the supervisor.
관리자에게 물어봐야 할 거예요.

Go to the reception desk. 접수처로 가보세요.

Refer to your manual. 설명서를 참고해 주세요.

That information is in the e-mail. 그 정보는 이메일에 있어요.

It's on the meeting agenda. 회의 안건에 있어요.

John knows better than I do. 존이 저보다 더 잘 알아요.

Visit our Web site for details.
자세한 건 웹사이트를 방문해 주세요.

🎵 P2_28 정답 및 해설 p.64

대화를 듣고 적절한 응답을 고르세요. 다시 듣고 빈칸을 채우세요. (녹음은 두 번씩 들려줍니다.)

1. (A)   (B)   (C)

Are you _____ today?

(A) Sure, _____.

(B) A _____.

(C) It's _____.

| POSSIBLE ANSWERS |

Yes, _____ until 5 P.M.

_____ — I've _____

_____.

2. (A)   (B)   (C)

Isn't the catering company _____

at ten?

(A) _____.

(B) _____ was very nice.

(C) Yes, _____.

| POSSIBLE ANSWERS |

No, _____.

I _____.

3. (A)   (B)   (C)

Are there _____ in

the _____?

(A) Not _____.

(B) We _____.

(C) He _____ in a row.

| POSSIBLE ANSWERS |

Yes, _____.

_____.

4. (A)   (B)   (C)

Weren't the _____ last

night?

(A) It's _____.

(B) Yes, _____.

(C) _____.

| POSSIBLE ANSWERS |

Yes, I _____.

You'll _____.

5. (A)   (B)   (C)

Haven't the _____ yet?

(A) They're _____.

(B) No, _____.

(C) The _____ soon.

| POSSIBLE ANSWERS |

They _____.

_____.

6. (A)   (B)   (C)

Didn't you _____ online last

week?

(A) _____, please.

(B) This _____.

(C) The _____.

| POSSIBLE ANSWERS |

Yes, _____.

They are _____.

1. Mark your answer on your answer sheet. (A) (B) (C)

2. Mark your answer on your answer sheet. (A) (B) (C)

3. Mark your answer on your answer sheet. (A) (B) (C)

4. Mark your answer on your answer sheet. (A) (B) (C)

5. Mark your answer on your answer sheet. (A) (B) (C)

6. Mark your answer on your answer sheet. (A) (B) (C)

7. Mark your answer on your answer sheet. (A) (B) (C)

8. Mark your answer on your answer sheet. (A) (B) (C)

9. Mark your answer on your answer sheet. (A) (B) (C)

10. Mark your answer on your answer sheet. (A) (B) (C)

11. Mark your answer on your answer sheet. (A) (B) (C)

12. Mark your answer on your answer sheet. (A) (B) (C)

13. Mark your answer on your answer sheet. (A) (B) (C)

14. Mark your answer on your answer sheet.　　　　　(A)　(B)　(C)

15. Mark your answer on your answer sheet.　　　　　(A)　(B)　(C)

16. Mark your answer on your answer sheet.　　　　　(A)　(B)　(C)

17. Mark your answer on your answer sheet.　　　　　(A)　(B)　(C)

18. Mark your answer on your answer sheet.　　　　　(A)　(B)　(C)

19. Mark your answer on your answer sheet.　　　　　(A)　(B)　(C)

20. Mark your answer on your answer sheet.　　　　　(A)　(B)　(C)

21. Mark your answer on your answer sheet.　　　　　(A)　(B)　(C)

22. Mark your answer on your answer sheet.　　　　　(A)　(B)　(C)

23. Mark your answer on your answer sheet.　　　　　(A)　(B)　(C)

24. Mark your answer on your answer sheet.　　　　　(A)　(B)　(C)

25. Mark your answer on your answer sheet.　　　　　(A)　(B)　(C)

PART 2 | CHAPTER 02

⑨ 조동사 의문문

출제공식 1 Do 의문문은 사실/의견을, Have 의문문은 상태/경험을 확인하는 질문이 주로 출제된다. Yes/No로 시작하거나 이를 함축한 응답이 자주 나오며, 확인처를 제공하는 답변도 정답이 될 수 있다.

2 Can, Will 등으로 시작하는 의문문의 경우 가능성/사실 확인, 허락/조언 구하기, 제안하기 등 여러 가지 의도로 쓰이므로, 이에 따라 확인, 조언, 수락/거절 등 다양한 응답이 가능하다.

✏️ 빈출 질문 & 응답 패턴 🎧 P2_30

Do	**Q** Do you have the results from the customer survey? **A** Yes, I received them this morning.	고객 설문 조사 결과를 가지고 있나요? 네, 오늘 아침에 받았습니다.
Have	**Q** Have you finished the marketing report yet? **A** I've been in meetings all day.	마케팅 보고서 다 하셨나요? 저 하루 종일 회의에 참석했어요.
Can	**Q** Can we hire a catering service for the company picnic? **A** I heard it's expensive.	회사 야유회에 출장 음식 서비스를 불러도 될까요? 그게 비싸다고 들었어요.
May	**Q** May I ask a few questions about the hiring process? **A** Sure, go ahead.	채용 과정에 관해서 몇 가지 질문을 해도 될까요? 물론이죠, 하세요.
Will	**Q** Will the skills development workshop end before seven? **A** Here's the schedule.	기술 개발 워크숍이 7시 전에 끝날까요? 여기 일정표가 있어요.
Should	**Q** Should I take the bus to the convention center? **A** It's better to go by train.	컨벤션 센터에 버스를 타고 가야 할까요? 기차를 타고 가는 게 나아요.

만점 전략 Yes/No가 함축된 답변을 이해할 수 있어야 한다.

Q Has the new branch manager been named? 새 지점장이 임명 되었나요?

Yes 함축 It's Mr. Kim. 김 씨예요. (= 임명 완료)

No 함축 I hope it'll be Mr. Kim. 저는 김 씨가 되면 좋겠어요. (= 미정)

ETS CHECK-UP 🎧 P2_31 정답 및 해설 p.71

1.   (A)   (B)   (C)   **4.**   (A)   (B)   (C)

2.   (A)   (B)   (C)   **5.**   (A)   (B)   (C)

3.   (A)   (B)   (C)   **6.**   (A)   (B)   (C)

❿ 제안/요청문

출제공식

1 Would you like, Why don't we, How about, Let's 등으로 시작하는 제안문과 Can you, Would you, Please 등의 표현이 사용된 요청문이 주로 출제된다.

2 직접적으로 수락/동의, 거절/반대 의사를 나타내는 응답뿐만 아니라, 수락할 수 없는 이유를 말하는 등 우회적인 답변도 자주 나온다.

✏️ **빈출 질문 & 응답 패턴**　　　　　　　　　　　　　🎧 P2_32

제안	**Q** <u>Why don't we start</u> advertising on social media? **A** That's a great idea.	소셜 미디어 광고를 시작하는 게 어떨까요? 좋은 생각입니다.
	Q <u>Would you like to join</u> us for dinner tonight? **A** I have to work late.	오늘 밤에 우리랑 저녁 함께 할래요? 전 야근해야 해요.
	Q <u>Let's discuss</u> the business plan later this afternoon. **A** How about tomorrow morning instead?	이따 오후에 사업 계획에 대해 논의합시다. 오늘 오후 대신 내일 아침은 어때요?
요청	**Q** <u>Can/Could you send</u> me the link to that writer's blog? **A** My computer isn't working right now.	그 작가의 블로그 링크를 제게 보내줄 수 있나요? 지금 제 컴퓨터가 작동이 안 됩니다.
	Q <u>Will/Would you prepare</u> handouts for the workshop? **A** Sure, I'll do that after lunch.	워크숍 유인물을 준비해 줄래요? 물론이죠, 점심 시간 후에 하겠습니다.
	Q <u>Please make sure to bring</u> the form on your next visit. **A** I'll keep that in mind.	다음 번 방문 시 그 양식을 꼭 가져오세요. 명심하겠습니다.

만점 전략 우회적으로 수락/거절하는 응답 패턴에 익숙해지도록 한다.

Q <u>Would you mind updating</u> the employee directory? 직원 명부를 업데이트 해주시겠어요?

A1 Is it okay to do it tomorrow? 내일 해도 괜찮을까요? (= 조건부 수락)

A2 I need to finish this report by the end of the day. 퇴근 전까지 이 보고서를 끝내야 해요. (= 거절)

ETS CHECK-UP　　　　　　　　　　　　🎧 P2_33　정답 및 해설 p.72

1.	(A)	(B)	(C)
2.	(A)	(B)	(C)
3.	(A)	(B)	(C)

4.	(A)	(B)	(C)
5.	(A)	(B)	(C)
6.	(A)	(B)	(C)

ETS X-FILE | 수락 / 동의 및 거절 / 반대 응답 필수 표현

수락 / 동의

Suit yourself. 좋을 대로 하세요.

Yes, please. 네, 그렇게 해 주세요.

Yes, I would. 네, 그리고 싶어요.

Sure, no problem. 물론이죠. 문제 없어요.

Not at all. 전혀요.

No, I don't mind. 아니요, 상관 없습니다.

Certainly. / Absolutely. / Definitely. 물론이죠.

Be my guest. / Go ahead. / By all means. 그렇게 하세요.

I'd love to. / I'd be happy[glad, delighted] to.
그리고 싶어요.

It would be my pleasure. 기꺼이 하겠어요.

That sounds good[wonderful]. 좋은 것 같아요.

What an excellent idea! 그거 참 멋진 생각이네요.

That's a good idea[suggestion]. 좋은 생각[제안]이네요.

That should help our sales. 그럼 매출에 도움이 되겠네요.

Yes, I think we'd better. 네, 그게 낫겠어요.

Of course, here you go. 물론이죠. 여기 있어요.

I have some time right now. 제가 지금 시간이 돼요.

OK, I'll be sure to do that. 네, 꼭 그렇게 할게요.

Sure, I'll take care of that. 물론이죠. 제가 처리할게요.

OK, I'll work on that. 알았어요, 제가 할게요.

I'll do it right now. 제가 지금 바로 할게요.

Don't worry—I will. 걱정마세요. 그렇게 할게요.

Thanks, I'd like that. 고마워요, 그렇게 하고 싶어요.

I'd appreciate that. 그래 주시면 감사하겠습니다.

That would be nice. 그럼 좋겠네요.

That'll be very helpful. 그럼 아주 도움이 될 거예요.

Yes, that would be great. 네, 그럼 아주 좋겠네요.

If you don't mind. 괜찮으시다면요.

If you're not too busy. 당신이 많이 바쁘지 않다면요.

If it's not too much trouble.
그게 너무 수고스럽지 않다면요.

거절 / 반대

I'm sorry, (but) 미안하지만 ~

I'd rather not. 하지 않는 게 낫겠어요.

No, I don't think so. 아니요, 그렇게 생각하지 않아요.

I'm afraid I can't. / I'm afraid not.
그럴 수 없어서 유감이에요.

I wish I could, but I'm very busy.
그러고 싶지만 너무 바빠요.

I'm not sure I'm qualified.
적임자일지 잘 모르겠네요.

Actually, I already have. 실은 벌써 했습니다.

I'm already working overtime.
저는 이미 초과 근무를 하고 있어요.

I need to finish this report. 이 보고서를 끝내야 해요.

I have to return to the office right now.
저는 지금 바로 사무실로 돌아가야 해요.

I have a meeting early tomorrow morning.
내일 오전 일찍 회의가 있어요.

I'm on my break now. 지금은 제 휴게 시간 입니다.

Sorry, I'll be on vacation then.
미안하지만 제가 그때 휴가 중일 거예요.

Sorry, you'd better call Technical Support.
미안하지만 기술 지원부에 전화하시는 게 낫겠어요.

I have no technical expertise.
전 기술 관련 전문 지식이 없어요.

It's not in the budget. 그건 예산에 들어가지 않아요.

I heard they are expensive. 비싸다고 들었어요.

The copier is not working right now.
복사기가 지금 작동하지 않아요.

I can't connect to the Internet. 인터넷 연결이 안 되네요.

I'll consider it. 고려해 보죠.

Let me think about it. 생각해 보죠.

I'll try, but it's not going to be easy.
해보겠지만 쉽지 않을 거예요.

I have an appointment then. 그때 일정이 있어요.

Thanks, but I have other plans.
고맙지만, 다른 계획이 있어요.

No thanks, I'm already full.
고맙지만 됐어요, 전 이미 배불러요.

I'm almost done, thanks. 고맙지만, 거의 다 했어요.

I can manage on my own. 제가 혼자 할 수 있어요.

I can handle it, thanks. 제가 할 수 있어요, 고마워요.

That's OK—I'll do it later. 괜찮아요. 제가 나중에 할게요.

No, I'm just looking, thank you.
아니요, 저는 그냥 구경 중이에요. 고마워요.

대화를 듣고 적절한 응답을 고르세요. 다시 듣고 빈칸을 채우세요. (녹음은 두 번씩 들려줍니다.)

1. (A)   (B)   (C)

_____ for the construction

contract yet?

(A) _____ 50 years ago.

(B) Yes, and _____.

(C) _____.

| POSSIBLE ANSWERS |

Two so far, but _____.

_____.

2. (A)   (B)   (C)

Did you _____ for the

printer?

(A) _____.

(B) They're _____.

(C) _____ a minute.

| POSSIBLE ANSWERS |

Yes, _____.

I'm _____ them.

3. (A)   (B)   (C)

_____ yesterday's travel

expenses?

(A) _____.

(B) _____ one hundred fifty

dollars.

(C) _____ Tokyo.

| POSSIBLE ANSWERS |

Did you _____?

Sure, you will _____.

4. (A)   (B)   (C)

Could you _____ up to the

third floor?

(A) Around _____.

(B) She's _____.

(C) I'll _____.

| POSSIBLE ANSWERS |

Sorry, but _____ soon.

_____ over there?

5. (A)   (B)   (C)

_____ our fifteenth anniversary

gala?

(A) The _____.

(B) _____.

(C) _____.

| POSSIBLE ANSWERS |

_____?

Sure, _____.

6. (A)   (B)   (C)

Mr. Tan, _____ the results

of the survey?

(A) I'll _____.

(B) Is it alright _____?

(C) Across _____.

| POSSIBLE ANSWERS |

Sure, _____now.

_____ an urgent matter.

PART 2 | CHAPTER 02

ETS **TEST**

1. Mark your answer on your answer sheet. (A) (B) (C)

2. Mark your answer on your answer sheet. (A) (B) (C)

3. Mark your answer on your answer sheet. (A) (B) (C)

4. Mark your answer on your answer sheet. (A) (B) (C)

5. Mark your answer on your answer sheet. (A) (B) (C)

6. Mark your answer on your answer sheet. (A) (B) (C)

7. Mark your answer on your answer sheet. (A) (B) (C)

8. Mark your answer on your answer sheet. (A) (B) (C)

9. Mark your answer on your answer sheet. (A) (B) (C)

10. Mark your answer on your answer sheet. (A) (B) (C)

11. Mark your answer on your answer sheet. (A) (B) (C)

12. Mark your answer on your answer sheet. (A) (B) (C)

13. Mark your answer on your answer sheet. (A) (B) (C)

14. Mark your answer on your answer sheet.　　　　(A)　(B)　(C)

15. Mark your answer on your answer sheet.　　　　(A)　(B)　(C)

16. Mark your answer on your answer sheet.　　　　(A)　(B)　(C)

17. Mark your answer on your answer sheet.　　　　(A)　(B)　(C)

18. Mark your answer on your answer sheet.　　　　(A)　(B)　(C)

19. Mark your answer on your answer sheet.　　　　(A)　(B)　(C)

20. Mark your answer on your answer sheet.　　　　(A)　(B)　(C)

21. Mark your answer on your answer sheet.　　　　(A)　(B)　(C)

22. Mark your answer on your answer sheet.　　　　(A)　(B)　(C)

23. Mark your answer on your answer sheet.　　　　(A)　(B)　(C)

24. Mark your answer on your answer sheet.　　　　(A)　(B)　(C)

25. Mark your answer on your answer sheet.　　　　(A)　(B)　(C)

⑪ 평서문

출제공식 1 정보, 상황, 의견, 감정 등을 진술하는 문장으로, 매회 꾸준히 출제되며 비중이 높은 편에 속한다.

2 정보를 수용하는 응답, 문제 상황에 대해 조언하거나 해결책을 제시하는 응답, 동의 / 반대하는 응답 등 평서문의 의도와 내용에 따라 다양한 답변이 가능하다. 또한 관련 내용에 대해 질문하는 응답도 종종 나오므로, 문장의 키워드와 관련된 표현 및 상황을 떠올리며 보기를 들어야 한다.

✐ 빈출 질문 & 응답 패턴   🎧 P2_37

정보 전달	**Q** The city plans to build bike lanes along the river.	시에서 강을 따라 자전거 도로를 만들 계획이래요.	
	A That's good news.	좋은 소식이네요.	
상황 설명	**Q** The door to the conference room is broken.	회의실 문이 고장 났어요.	
	A I'll call the maintenance department.	제가 관리부서에 전화할게요.	
의사 표현	**Q** I need to stop at the grocery store on my way home.	집에 가는 길에 식료품점에 들렀다 가야 해요.	
	A What do you need to buy?	무엇을 사야 하는데요?	
제안 / 권유	**Q** I think we should hire more software engineers.	소프트웨어 기술자들을 더 고용해야 할 것 같아요.	
	A But the new project was canceled.	하지만 새 프로젝트가 취소되었잖아요.	
부탁 / 요청	**Q** I'd like you to help me with this logo design.	이 로고 디자인 작업을 도와줬으면 해요.	
	A I have some time in the afternoon.	제가 오후에 시간이 좀 있어요.	
감상 / 평가	**Q** Well, that was such a great movie!	와, 정말 좋은 영화였어요!	
	A I really enjoyed it, too.	저도 재미있게 봤어요.	

만점 전략 평서문에도 Yes / No로 응답할 수 있다. 이때 뒤따라오는 내용이 적절한 지 반드시 확인하자.

Q I can pick you up at the terminal later if you'd like. 원하시면 이따가 터미널에 모시러 갈 수 있어요. (= 도움 제안)

정답 No, you don't have to do that. 아니요, 그럴 필요 없어요. (= 거절)

오답 Yes, it's ready for pickup. 네, 수령해 가실 준비가 되었습니다. (다의어를 활용한 오답에 유의!)

ETS CHECK-UP   🎧 P2_38 정답 및 해설 p.80

1.　　(A)　(B)　(C)　　　　**4.**　　(A)　(B)　(C)

2.　　(A)　(B)　(C)　　　　**5.**　　(A)　(B)　(C)

3.　　(A)　(B)　(C)　　　　**6.**　　(A)　(B)　(C)

무료인강

⑫ 부가 의문문

출제공식
1 평서문 뒤에 붙는 〈be동사/조동사(n't) + 주어?〉 형태의 짧은 의문문으로, 사실 여부를 확인하거나 동의를 구하려는 목적으로 쓰인다. right, correct 등이 대신 출제되기도 한다.
2 〈Yes/No + 부연 설명〉 형태의 응답과 Yes/No를 우회적으로 표현한 응답이 자주 나온다. 확인해 보겠다고 하며 모른다는 것을 드러내는 답변도 정답이 될 수 있다.

✎ 빈출 질문 & 응답 패턴   ⌒◗ P2_39

Be	**Q** Our new Web site is well-designed, isn't it? **A** Yes, it's easy to navigate.	새 웹사이트가 잘 설계되었죠, 그렇지 않나요? 네, 둘러보기 편하더군요.
Do	**Q** Ms. Kim hired a new assistant recently, didn't she? **A** I haven't talked to her in a while.	김 씨가 최근 새 비서를 고용했죠, 그렇지 않나요? 그녀와 한동안 이야기하지 못했어요.
Have	**Q** You haven't checked the budget report, have you? **A** I looked it over twice.	예산 보고서 확인 못했죠, 그렇죠? 두 번 검토했습니다.
Will	**Q** Mr. Yoon will lead the training session, won't he? **A** I'll check with him.	윤 씨가 교육 시간을 진행할 거죠, 그렇지 않나요? 그에게 확인해 볼게요.
Can	**Q** We can reschedule the meeting for March seventh, can't we? **A** It's too late to change the date.	회의를 3월 7일로 바꿀 수 있죠, 그렇지 않나요? 날짜를 바꾸기엔 너무 늦었어요.
특수	**Q** Our supervisor booked the tickets for us, right? **A** No, she asked Mary to do it.	관리자가 우리 표를 예매했죠, 맞죠? 아니요, 메리에게 하라고 했어요.

만점 전략 부가 의문문 앞에 나온 내용에 초점을 맞추어 답을 선택해야 한다.

Q The last train to Amsterdam hasn't left yet, has it? 암스테르담으로 가는 마지막 기차가 아직 출발하지 않았죠, 그렇죠?

정답 No, you've got five minutes! 안 했어요, 5분 남았어요! (= No, it hasn't left yet.)

오답 Yes, we have some leftovers. 네, 남은 음식이 좀 있어요. (파생어를 활용한 오답에 유의!)

ETS **CHECK-UP**   ⌒◗ P2_40 정답 및 해설 p.81

1.	(A)	(B)	(C)		**4.**	(A)	(B)	(C)
2.	(A)	(B)	(C)		**5.**	(A)	(B)	(C)
3.	(A)	(B)	(C)		**6.**	(A)	(B)	(C)

🎧 P2_41

평서문

정보 수용

Q Our sales have doubled over the last month.
우리 매출이 지난 한 달간 두 배나 올랐어요.

A That's great news.
그거 좋은 소식이네요.

Q Construction on the new shopping mall is almost finished. 새 쇼핑몰 공사가 거의 끝났어요.

A Yes, I'm really excited about it!
네, 너무 기대돼요!

동의 / 수락

Q I think you should add more graphics to your slide show.
당신의 슬라이드 쇼에 그림을 더 넣어야 할 것 같아요.

A I was thinking that, too.
저도 그 생각을 하고 있었어요.

Q Hailey is the best designer that I've worked with.
헤일리는 제가 일해 본 디자이너 중에 최고예요.

A I agree. She's very talented.
동의해요. 그녀는 재능이 매우 뛰어나요.

반대 / 거절

Q We need to replace the air conditioner in the kitchen. 주방에 있는 에어컨을 교체해야 해요.

A I think it works fine.
전 잘 작동하는 거 같은데요.

Q I'll call the restaurant and make a reservation.
제가 그 식당에 전화해서 예약할게요.

A You don't have to—I'll do it now.
그러실 필요 없어요. 제가 지금 할 거예요.

문제 해결

Q I can't seem to open the link you e-mailed me.
당신이 이메일로 보내준 링크가 안 열려요.

A Let me send it to you again.
다시 보내드릴게요.

Q There's a leak in the ceiling of my office.
제 사무실 천장에 물이 새요.

A I'll come and have a look.
제가 가서 한 번 볼게요.

질문

Q I'm going to a jazz music festival this weekend.
이번 주말에 재즈 음악 축제에 가요.

A Oh, can I come with you?
오, 저도 같이 가도 돼요?

Q Mr. Stevens will leave the company next month.
스티븐스 씨가 다음 달에 퇴사하신대요.

A Where did you hear that?
어디서 들었나요?

기타 응답

Q Here's the new e-mail address of Mr. Yamada.
여기 야마다 씨의 새로운 이메일 주소예요.

A Fatima already called him.
파티마가 이미 전화했어요.

Q There are some customers waiting outside.
바깥에 기다리고 있는 손님들이 있어요.

A Sorry, I'll open the door right away.
죄송해요. 바로 문을 열게요.

부가 의문문

Yes / No + 부연 설명

Q The cafeteria will be closed for renovation soon, right? 구내 식당이 곧 보수 공사로 문을 닫죠, 그렇죠?

A Yes, it will reopen next month.
네, 다음 달에 다시 문을 열 거예요.

Q The instructions weren't very clear, were they? 설명서가 명확하지 않았죠, 그렇죠?

A No, they were very confusing.
명확하지 않았어요, 매우 헷갈렸죠.

Yes / No 생략 답변

Q There's no florist around here, is there?
이 근처에 꽃집이 없죠, 그렇죠?

A There's one across from the bank.
은행 건너편에 하나 있어요.

Q The play opens next week, doesn't it?
그 연극은 다음 주에 시작되죠, 그렇지 않나요?

A It starts on Thursday.
목요일에 시작해요.

LISTENING **PRACTICE**

P2_42 정답 및 해설 p.82

대화를 듣고 적절한 응답을 고르세요. 다시 듣고 빈칸을 채우세요. (녹음은 두 번씩 들려줍니다.)

1.　(A)　　(B)　　(C)

_____ on the top shelf.

(A) Maybe it's _____.

(B) No, I _____.

(C) There's _____.

| POSSIBLE ANSWERS |

Let me _____.

_____?

2.　(A)　　(B)　　(C)

_____ Ms. Jackson's order, correct?

(A) _____ Riverdale.

(B) _____ before.

(C) Yes, it _____.

| POSSIBLE ANSWERS |

No, _____.

_____ at the last minute.

3.　(A)　　(B)　　(C)

I suggest that the employee orientation _____.

(A) The _____.

(B) Let's see _____.

(C) I think _____.

| POSSIBLE ANSWERS |

_____.

But we've _____.

4.　(A)　　(B)　　(C)

_____ your e-mail recently, haven't you?

(A) I _____.

(B) _____.

(C) We _____.

| POSSIBLE ANSWERS |

Yes, I hope _____.

Do you _____, too?

5.　(A)　　(B)　　(C)

This is the _____ I've ever had.

(A) It's the _____.

(B) _____.

(C) Where did _____?

| POSSIBLE ANSWERS |

I'm sure _____ soon.

If you _____, just let me know.

6.　(A)　　(B)　　(C)

Dr. Chen is _____, isn't she?

(A) That's the _____.

(B) She's _____.

(C) No, _____.

| POSSIBLE ANSWERS |

She's _____ until May 20.

Let me _____.

ETS **TEST**

1. Mark your answer on your answer sheet. (A) (B) (C)

2. Mark your answer on your answer sheet. (A) (B) (C)

3. Mark your answer on your answer sheet. (A) (B) (C)

4. Mark your answer on your answer sheet. (A) (B) (C)

5. Mark your answer on your answer sheet. (A) (B) (C)

6. Mark your answer on your answer sheet. (A) (B) (C)

7. Mark your answer on your answer sheet. (A) (B) (C)

8. Mark your answer on your answer sheet. (A) (B) (C)

9. Mark your answer on your answer sheet. (A) (B) (C)

10. Mark your answer on your answer sheet. (A) (B) (C)

11. Mark your answer on your answer sheet. (A) (B) (C)

12. Mark your answer on your answer sheet. (A) (B) (C)

13. Mark your answer on your answer sheet. (A) (B) (C)

14. Mark your answer on your answer sheet. (A) (B) (C)

15. Mark your answer on your answer sheet. (A) (B) (C)

16. Mark your answer on your answer sheet. (A) (B) (C)

17. Mark your answer on your answer sheet. (A) (B) (C)

18. Mark your answer on your answer sheet. (A) (B) (C)

19. Mark your answer on your answer sheet. (A) (B) (C)

20. Mark your answer on your answer sheet. (A) (B) (C)

21. Mark your answer on your answer sheet. (A) (B) (C)

22. Mark your answer on your answer sheet. (A) (B) (C)

23. Mark your answer on your answer sheet. (A) (B) (C)

24. Mark your answer on your answer sheet. (A) (B) (C)

25. Mark your answer on your answer sheet. (A) (B) (C)

⑬ 선택 의문문

출제공식 1 〈A or B〉 구조의 선택 의문문은 둘 중 어느 것이 맞는지 확인하거나 상대방의 선호 사항을 묻는
질문이 주로 출제된다. 두 가지 선택지를 정확히 포착하는 것이 중요하다.

2 둘 중 하나를 직접적으로 선택하는 답변과 우회적으로 선택 사항을 드러내는 답변이 보편적이다.
둘 다 선택하거나 선택을 피하는 응답, 제3의 선택과 되묻는 응답도 나올 수 있다.

✏️ 빈출 질문 & 응답 패턴 🎧 P2_44

하나 선택	**Q** Would you like to have <u>lunch or dinner</u> with the client? **A** I'd prefer **lunch**. / **Dinner** would be better.	의뢰인과의 점심이 좋으세요, 저녁이 좋으세요? 저는 점심이 좋아요. / 저녁이 더 좋겠어요.
	Q Should we <u>walk or take a taxi</u> to the cinema? **A** **We need to hurry up.**	영화관에 걸어갈까요, 택시를 타고 갈까요? 우리 서둘러야 해요. (=우회적으로 택시 선택)
둘 다 선택	**Q** Does the hotel have <u>an indoor or outdoor pool?</u> **A** It has **both**.	그 호텔에 실내 수영장이나 실외 수영장이 있나요? 둘 다 있습니다.
제3의 선택	**Q** Is <u>Colin</u> going to give the presentation, or should <u>I</u>? **A** **Lisa** will do it.	그 발표를 콜린이 할 건가요, 아님 제가 할까요? 리사가 할 거예요.
선택 회피	**Q** Will you register for <u>Monday's workshop or Tuesday's?</u> **A** **I haven't decided yet.**	월요일, 화요일 워크숍 중 언제로 등록할 건가요? 아직 결정하지 않았어요.
되묻는 응답	**Q** <u>Can you fix the printer</u>, or <u>should I call the technician?</u> **A** **Why don't we get a new one?**	그 프린터를 고칠 수 있겠어요, 아니면 제가 기술자를 부를까요? 새 거 사는 게 어때요?

만점 전략 선택 의문문은 보통 Yes / No 응답이 불가능하지만, 문맥이나 구조에 따라 가능한 경우도 있다.

Q Are there <u>buses or trains</u> from here to the airport? 여기서 공항 가는 버스나 기차가 있나요?

Yes / No Yes, there are. / No, you should drive there. 네, 있습니다. / 아니요, 운전해서 가야 해요.

하나 선택 Well, there are buses but no trains. 음, 버스는 있는데 기차는 없어요.

ETS CHECK-UP 🎧 P2_45 정답 및 해설 p.89

1. (A) (B) (C)   4. (A) (B) (C)
2. (A) (B) (C)   5. (A) (B) (C)
3. (A) (B) (C)   6. (A) (B) (C)

⑭ 간접 의문문

출제공식
1 조동사 의문문이나 평서문 속에서 〈의문사 + (주어) + 동사〉, 〈의문사 + to부정사〉, 〈if / whether + 주어 + 동사〉 형태를 띠는 의문문으로, 출제 빈도가 낮은 편에 속한다.
2 〈Yes / No + 부연 설명〉 형태의 응답, 의문사에 해당하는 정보를 바로 말해주는 응답이 자주 나온다. 또한 모른다는 것을 드러내거나 되묻는 응답도 종종 등장한다.

✏ 빈출 질문 & 응답 패턴 🎧 P2_46

Yes / No + 부연 설명	**Q** Do you know where I can keep my belongings? **A** Yes, there's space in the cabinet.	제 소지품을 어디에 보관할 수 있는지 아세요? 네, 캐비닛에 공간이 있어요.
	Q Did you hear who will cover Andrew's shift tomorrow? **A** No, I didn't attend the staff meeting, either.	내일 누가 앤드류 대신 근무할 건지 들었어요? 아뇨, 저도 직원 회의에 참석하지 않았어요.
의문사 관련 답변	**Q** Can you tell me how to join the library book club? **A** Fill out this form.	도서관 독서 클럽에 가입하는 방법을 알려줄래요? 이 양식을 작성하세요.
	Q I wonder why there's so much traffic today. **A** Because there's a baseball game.	오늘 교통량이 왜 이렇게 많은지 궁금해요. 야구 경기가 있기 때문이에요.
'모른다' 응답	**Q** Do you know if the store offers free delivery service? **A** You'd better ask them.	그 가게가 무료 배송을 해주는지 알고 있나요? 그곳에 문의해 보는 게 나을 거예요.
되묻는 응답	**Q** I have no idea when I can get a parking permit. **A** When did you apply for it?	주차 허가증을 언제 받을 수 있을지 모르겠어요. 언제 신청했는데요?

만점 전략 '모른다', '궁금하다', '듣지 못했다' 등의 표현 뒤에는 간접 의문문이 올 확률이 높다.

Q I don't know which caterer to choose for the awards dinner.
시상식 저녁 식사를 위해 어떤 업체를 선택할지 모르겠어요.

A1 Let's hire the one we used last year. 지난해에 이용했던 곳으로 하죠.

A2 Diego might have some recommendations. 디에고가 몇 군데 추천할 수 있을지도 몰라요.

ETS **CHECK-UP** 🎧 P2_47 정답 및 해설 p. 90

1.	(A)	(B)	(C)		**4.**	(A)	(B)	(C)
2.	(A)	(B)	(C)		**5.**	(A)	(B)	(C)
3.	(A)	(B)	(C)		**6.**	(A)	(B)	(C)

🎧 P2_48

A, B 둘 중 하나 선택

One would[should] be fine. 하나만 해도 괜찮을 거예요.
I'd prefer to take a taxi. 택시를 타는 게 좋아요.
Monday works better. 월요일이 더 나아요.
Mornings are less busy. 아침이 덜 바쁘긴 하죠.
A slide show would be better. 슬라이드 쇼가 더 낫겠어요.
I'd like to eat here. 여기에서 먹고 싶어요.

I'd rather leave early. 저는 빨리 출발하는 게 좋겠어요.
Since it's raining, let's order in. 비가 오니 배달시켜 먹어요.
The soup sounds good. 수프가 좋을 것 같아요.
I'll take chocolate, please. 초콜렛 맛으로 할게요.
I'll go with the red one. 붉은 것으로 할게요.
I don't mind driving. 제가 운전해도 상관 없어요.

A, B 둘 중 어느 쪽도 괜찮은 경우

I don't care. 상관없어요.
Whichever you prefer[like]. 원하시는 대로요.
Whichever is convenient for you. 당신한테 편한 대로요.
We accept any of them. 둘 다 받습니다.
Either is fine. / Either one is fine with me.
아무거나 괜찮아요.

Any day except Monday. 월요일을 제외하고 언제라도요.
It doesn't matter (to me). 저는 상관없어요.
I'll leave it to you. / It's up to you. 당신이 결정해요.
I don't have a preference. 특별히 선호하는 게 없어요.
It doesn't make any difference.
별 차이 없을 거예요.

A, B 모두 선택/반대

I like both. / I like both of them. / I like all of them.
둘 다 좋아요.

I plan to do both. / I'm considering both.
둘 다 하려고요.

Neither, thanks. / Neither, actually.
고맙지만 둘 다 됐어요. / 사실 둘 다 아니에요.

I don't like either (of them).
모두 싫어요.

우회적 선택

Q Do you want to sit inside or out on the balcony?
실내에 앉고 싶어요, 아니면 발코니에 나가서 앉고 싶어요?

A It's quite hot today.
오늘 꽤 더운데요.

Q Would you like to drive or take a bus to the city hall? 시청까지 운전해서 갈래요, 아니면 버스 타고 갈래요?

A There's no parking nearby.
그 근처에 주차 공간이 없어요.

Q Will you give your presentation first, or should I?
먼저 발표하실래요, 아니면 제가 먼저 할까요?

A I need a few extra minutes to prepare.
전 준비할 시간이 몇 분 더 필요해요.

Q Should we have the meeting this week or next week? 회의를 이번 주에 할까요 다음 주에 할까요?

A We need to finalize the design as soon as possible. 가능한 한 빨리 디자인을 마무리해야 해요.

되묻는 응답

How about at 1:30?
1시 30분 어때요?

Why don't you try green instead?
대신에 초록색을 써보면 어때요?

Why don't we eat out?
외식하는 게 어때요?

Isn't it supposed to rain?
비 오기로 되어 있지 않아요?

Which is more urgent?
어떤 것이 더 급하죠?

Which is more convenient for you?
어느 쪽이 더 편하세요?

Which option is cheaper?
어떤 게 더 저렴하죠?

Is there a discount for buying two?
두 개를 사면 할인이 되나요?

LISTENING **PRACTICE**

대화를 듣고 적절한 응답을 고르세요. 다시 듣고 빈칸을 채우세요. (녹음은 두 번씩 들려줍니다.)

1. (A)   (B)   (C)

Should we go to the _____?
(A) Yes, _____.
(B) _____, please.
(C) I'd _____.

| POSSIBLE ANSWERS |

_____.
The _____ today.

2. (A)   (B)   (C)

_____ or do I have to pay cash?
(A) No, _____.
(B) Yes, _____.
(C) _____.

| POSSIBLE ANSWERS |

We _____.
_____ for you.

3. (A)   (B)   (C)

Do you want to _____ in London?
(A) _____ for five years.
(B) It _____.
(C) _____ yesterday.

| POSSIBLE ANSWERS |

_____.
_____ a direct flight?

4. (A)   (B)   (C)

Do you know _____ another travel agent?
(A) _____ next week.
(B) _____ a better rate.
(C) You'll need a _____.

| POSSIBLE ANSWERS |

The existing _____.
We need _____ business travel.

5. (A)   (B)   (C)

Would you like _____?
(A) _____ in the recipe.
(B) The _____?
(C) I _____.

| POSSIBLE ANSWERS |

I'll _____.
_____?

6. (A)   (B)   (C)

_____ the bus leaves for Madrid?
(A) _____.
(B) _____, please.
(C) No, _____.

| POSSIBLE ANSWERS |

_____.
The schedule is _____.

1. Mark your answer on your answer sheet.   (A)   (B)   (C)

2. Mark your answer on your answer sheet.   (A)   (B)   (C)

3. Mark your answer on your answer sheet.   (A)   (B)   (C)

4. Mark your answer on your answer sheet.   (A)   (B)   (C)

5. Mark your answer on your answer sheet.   (A)   (B)   (C)

6. Mark your answer on your answer sheet.   (A)   (B)   (C)

7. Mark your answer on your answer sheet.   (A)   (B)   (C)

8. Mark your answer on your answer sheet.   (A)   (B)   (C)

9. Mark your answer on your answer sheet.   (A)   (B)   (C)

10. Mark your answer on your answer sheet.   (A)   (B)   (C)

11. Mark your answer on your answer sheet.   (A)   (B)   (C)

12. Mark your answer on your answer sheet.   (A)   (B)   (C)

13. Mark your answer on your answer sheet.   (A)   (B)   (C)

14. Mark your answer on your answer sheet.   (A)   (B)   (C)

15. Mark your answer on your answer sheet.   (A)   (B)   (C)

16. Mark your answer on your answer sheet.   (A)   (B)   (C)

17. Mark your answer on your answer sheet.   (A)   (B)   (C)

18. Mark your answer on your answer sheet.   (A)   (B)   (C)

19. Mark your answer on your answer sheet.   (A)   (B)   (C)

20. Mark your answer on your answer sheet.   (A)   (B)   (C)

21. Mark your answer on your answer sheet.   (A)   (B)   (C)

22. Mark your answer on your answer sheet.   (A)   (B)   (C)

23. Mark your answer on your answer sheet.   (A)   (B)   (C)

24. Mark your answer on your answer sheet.   (A)   (B)   (C)

25. Mark your answer on your answer sheet.   (A)   (B)   (C)

PART 2

Directions: You will hear a question or statement and three responses spoken in English. They will not be printed in your test book and will be spoken only one time. Select the best response to the question or statement and mark the letter (A), (B), or (C) on your answer sheet.

7. Mark your answer on your answer sheet.

8. Mark your answer on your answer sheet.

9. Mark your answer on your answer sheet.

10. Mark your answer on your answer sheet.

11. Mark your answer on your answer sheet.

12. Mark your answer on your answer sheet.

13. Mark your answer on your answer sheet.

14. Mark your answer on your answer sheet.

15. Mark your answer on your answer sheet.

16. Mark your answer on your answer sheet.

17. Mark your answer on your answer sheet.

18. Mark your answer on your answer sheet.

19. Mark your answer on your answer sheet.

20. Mark your answer on your answer sheet.

21. Mark your answer on your answer sheet.

22. Mark your answer on your answer sheet.

23. Mark your answer on your answer sheet.

24. Mark your answer on your answer sheet.

25. Mark your answer on your answer sheet.

26. Mark your answer on your answer sheet.

27. Mark your answer on your answer sheet.

28. Mark your answer on your answer sheet.

29. Mark your answer on your answer sheet.

30. Mark your answer on your answer sheet.

31. Mark your answer on your answer sheet.

MEMO

PART

3

대화

LC

PART 3 기본 전략

PART 3

대화
CONVERSATIONS

두 사람, 혹은 세 사람의 대화를 듣고 이와 관련된 세 개의 문제를 푸는 유형으로, 총 13세트 39문항이 출제된다. 매회 3인 대화가 2세트씩 포함되며, 문제 유형은 다음과 같이 크게 두 가지로 나눌 수 있다.

전체 내용 관련 문제	주제/목적, 대화가 이루어지는 장소, 화자들의 직업/업종, 근무지
세부 내용 관련 문제	세부 사항, 문제점/걱정거리, 화자의 요청/제안/추천 사항, 화자의 의도 파악, 앞으로 할 일/다음에 일어날 일, 시각 정보 연계

기본 풀이 전략

🎧 P3_01

파트 3은 듣기와 읽기 모두 중요한 파트이다. 듣기와 읽기를 동시에 하는 것은 쉽지 않기 때문에, 반드시 대화를 듣기 전에 질문 및 보기를 읽어두어야 한다. 보통 문제 순서에 맞춰 대화 내 단서가 차례대로 주어지므로, 질문을 보고 대화의 흐름을 예상해 보는 것도 도움이 된다.

STEP 01 문제 파악하기
- 대화 듣기 전에 질문 및 보기 읽기
- 의문사, 주어, 동사를 중심으로 키워드 파악하기 (화자 성별 구분 필수)
- 키워드 표시하고 노력 듣기

STEP 02 대화 들으며 정답 체크하기
- 관련 내용 확인하는 즉시 답 체크하기
- 다음 문제로 넘어가서 노력 듣기
- 대화 종료 후 성우가 질문을 읽어주는 동안 다음 대화의 문제 파악하기

📑 문제지

32. What is the **man** asking about?
(A) The deadline for a project
(B) The status of a delivery
(C) The location of a meeting
(D) The amount of an invoice

33. Why is the **man** concerned?
(A) He cannot print some documents.
(B) Some files are missing.
(C) The wrong items were sent.
(D) A shipment was canceled.

34. What does the **woman** offer to send the man?
(A) A model number
(B) A cost estimate
(C) A tracking number
(D) A brochure

🔊 음원

M Hi, Christine. ㉜ Do you know if any office supplies were delivered today? We're out of color toner for the printers.

남자가 문의하는 내용: 사무용 비품 배송 완료 여부

W I didn't see anything arrive.

M Mmm. ㉝ I'm a bit worried because I can't print out my color handouts for this afternoon.

남자가 걱정하는 이유: 유인물을 인쇄할 수 없어서

W I have to go to a meeting in a few minutes, but ㉞ I have the tracking number for the order. How about I forward it to you so you can follow up?

여자가 보내주겠다고 하는 것: 배송 조회 번호

*이후 질문만 읽어주며, 그 사이에 공백이 주어진다.

104

1 문제 유형별 출제 비율

세부 사항 문제의 비율이 가장 높고, 주제/목적 및 장소/직업을 묻는 문제가 20퍼센트 내외로 꾸준히 출제된다. 매회 의도 파악 문제가 2문항, 시각 정보 연계 문제가 3문항씩 나온다.

2 대화 내용별 출제 비율

업무 관련 대화가 주를 이루며, 쇼핑, 교통, 부동산 등 다양한 일상 생활 관련 내용도 등장한다.

패러프레이징 PARAPHRASING

패러프레이징이란 '다른 말로 바꾸어 표현하는 것'을 뜻한다. 대화 내의 단서가 보기에 그대로 나오는 경우도 있지만, 패러프레이징되어 제시되는 경우가 많으므로 대표적인 유형을 미리 파악해 두면 실전에 도움이 된다.

1 동의어, 유의어, 사전적 의미 활용

W All you need to do to get the discount is show the coupon to the cashier. **여** 할인을 받으시려면 계산원에게 그 쿠폰을 보여주시기만 하면 됩니다.	**Q** How can the man receive a discount? **A** By presenting a voucher **질문** 남자는 어떻게 할인을 받을 수 있는가? **정답** 할인권을 제시함으로써

2 포괄적 개념을 지닌 상위어 활용

M I'm afraid I don't have enough boxes to pack all the books. **남** 모든 책을 포장할 만큼 박스가 충분하지 않은 것 같아요.	**Q** What problem does the man mention? **A** He does not have enough supplies. **질문** 남자가 언급한 문제점은? **정답** 비품을 충분히 가지고 있지 않다.

3 품사 변경

W I submitted my application for the editor position last week. **여** 제가 지난주에 편집자 직무에 지원서를 제출했어요.	**Q** What did the woman do last week? **A** She applied for a job. **질문** 여자가 지난주에 한 일은? **정답** 일자리에 지원했다.

4 내용 축약

M I got a bill from the credit card company today. It was higher than I expected. **남** 오늘 신용카드 회사에서 청구서를 받았는데, 제가 예상했던 것보다 더 많이 나왔어요.	**Q** What are the speakers discussing? **A** A credit card bill **질문** 화자들은 무엇에 관해 이야기하는가? **정답** 신용카드 청구서

문제 유형별 전략

❶ 주제/목적 문제

출제공식

1 대화 주제나 전화/방문 목적을 묻는 질문은 주로 첫 번째 문제로 출제되며, 간혹 두 번째로 나오는 경우도 있다.

2 단서는 보통 대화 초반에 등장한다. 하지만 초반에서 확인이 불가능하다면 중반까지 듣고 다른 문제와 함께 풀어나가야 한다.

문제유형

[주제] What are the speakers (mainly) discussing[talking about]?
화자들이 (주로) 이야기하는 것은?

What is the conversation (mainly) about? 대화는 (주로) 무엇에 관한 것인가?

What is the main topic of the conversation? 대화의 주제는 무엇인가?

[목적] Why is the man calling? 남자는 왜 전화를 하는가?

Why is the woman at[Why has the woman come to] ~? 여자는 왜 ~에 왔는가?

What is the purpose of the man's call / visit? 남자가 전화한 / 방문한 목적은 무엇인가?

✎ **핵심 전략 |** 초반부의 주제 / 목적을 나타내는 단서 표현에 귀를 기울인다. 🎧 P3_02

W Hi Abdul, I'm calling to make sure you saw the e-mail I sent earlier this morning about the quarterly sales report. We need to review the report by the end of the day.

목적을 나타내는 단서 표현: I'm calling to
전화 목적: 상대방의 이메일 수신 확인

M No, I didn't. I've been having trouble with my computer all morning and I haven't gotten any e-mails today.

W OK, I'm glad I called then. This report's a top priority, so let's meet in my office at three o'clock to discuss it.

Q. Why is the **woman** calling the man?
(A) To resolve a technical problem
(B) To follow up on an e-mail message
(C) To finalize an agenda
(D) To discuss a recent order

단서 to make sure you saw the e-mail
정답 (B) 이메일이 어떻게 되었나 확인하기 위해

여 안녕하세요 압둘, 제가 오늘 아까 아침에 보냈던 분기 영업 보고서 관련 이메일을 당신이 보았는지 확인하려고 전화해요. 오늘 퇴근 전까지 우리가 그 보고서를 검토해야 해요.

남 아니요, 보지 않았어요. 아침 내내 컴퓨터에 문제가 있어서 오늘 아무 이메일도 받지 못했답니다.

여 그렇군요. 제가 전화해서 다행이네요. 이 보고서가 최우선순위이니, 3시에 제 사무실에서 만나서 논의하도록 하죠.

여자는 왜 남자에게 전화하는가?
(A) 기술적인 문제를 해결하기 위해
(B) 이메일이 어떻게 되었나 확인하기 위해
(C) 안건을 마무리하기 위해
(D) 최근 주문건에 대해 논의하기 위해

✏️ 주제 / 목적을 나타내는 단서 표현

🎧 P3_03

바람 / 희망	**I'd like to ~ / I want to ~ / I hope to ~** **I'd like to** talk about the recent feedback we got from one of our biggest clients. 우리의 주요 고객사 중 한 군데에서 최근에 받은 피드백에 대해 이야기하고 싶습니다.
필요	**I need to ~ / We should[have to] ~** **We need to** review the marketing budget for our new line of moisturizing lotions. 우리의 신제품 수분 로션을 위한 마케팅 예산을 검토해야 해요.
전화 목적	**I'm calling about ~ / I'm calling to ~ / I'm calling because ~** **I'm calling to** find out about your room availability on April third. 4월 3일에 이용 가능한 방이 있는지 알아보려고 전화 드려요.
방문 목적	**I'm here to ~ / I'm here for ~ / I came to ~** **I'm here to** ask about a problem I'm having with my mobile phone. 제 핸드폰에 문제가 있어 이에 대해 문의하러 왔습니다.
기타	**상황 설명하기** I bought this shirt from your store yesterday, but then I found that one of the buttons is missing. 어제 귀하의 가게에서 이 셔츠를 샀는데, 단추 하나가 없는 걸 발견했어요. **질문하기** Did you hear that Joe Cooper will deliver a speech at the conference next week? 조 쿠퍼가 다음 주에 있을 회의에서 연설할 거라는 이야기 들었나요?

PART 3 | CHAPTER 01

ETS CHECK-UP

🎧 P3_04 정답 및 해설 p. 104

1. What is the conversation mainly about?

(A) Increasing a workforce
(B) Updating some software
(C) Changing a company policy
(D) Improving employee satisfaction

2. Why has the woman come to the library?

(A) To tour a facility
(B) To pay a late fee
(C) To attend a presentation
(D) To pick up a book

❷ 장소/직업 문제

출제공식 1 화자의 신분, 직업, 업종이나 근무지, 대화 장소 등을 묻는 질문도 첫 번째 문제로 자주 출제된다.

2 대화 초반에 장소 및 직업이 직접적으로 언급되거나, 특정 업계 관련 어휘가 대화 곳곳에 등장하기도 한다.

문제유형 [장소] Where do the speakers (most likely) work? 화자들은 어디에서 근무하는가?

Where is the conversation (most likely) taking place? 대화가 일어나는 장소는 어디인가?

What type of business does the man work for? 남자는 근무하는 어떤 업체에 근무하는가?

[직업] Who (most likely) is the woman? 여자는 누구인가?

What field / industry / department do the speakers (most likely) work in?
화자들은 어느 분야 / 업계 / 부서에서 일하는가?

What (most likely) is the man's job[profession]? 남자의 직업은 무엇인가?

✏️ **핵심 전략 |** 초반부의 장소/직업명이나 대화 내 특정 업계 관련 어휘를 포착한다. 🎧 P3_05

M Gia. I was looking at our list of guests for our radio show, and I noticed we aren't interviewing anyone on July fifteenth.

업계/근무지 관련 어휘 등장: 라디오 쇼 ●————

W Actually, I just had to remove Elke Woods from the schedule. She was supposed to come and read from her new book that day, but she can't make it.

M Oh no. I was looking forward to interviewing her about her historical novel. Well, at least she told us in advance so we can find another guest.

W That's true. We have a folder with profiles of people we want to interview. I think it's in one of the cabinet drawers. I'll go and look for it.

Q. Where do the speakers most likely work?
(A) At a publishing house
● (B) At a radio station
(C) At a bookstore
(D) At a television network

단서 our list of guests for our radio show

정답 (B) 라디오 방송국

남 지아. **우리 라디오 쇼에 나올 초대손님 명단을 찾아봤는데,** 7월 15일에는 우리가 아무도 인터뷰하지 않더군요.

여 실은, 그 일정표에서 엘크 우즈를 삭제해야만 했어요. 그날 그녀가 와서 자신의 신간을 읽기로 했는데 오지 못하거든요.

남 저런. 그녀의 역사 소설에 관해 인터뷰하기를 고대했는데. 그래도, 최소한 그녀가 우리에게 미리 알렸으니 다른 초대손님을 찾을 수 있겠군요.

여 맞아요. 우리가 인터뷰하고 싶은 사람들의 프로필을 모아둔 폴더가 있어요. 캐비닛 서랍 중 하나에 있을 거예요. 제가 가서 찾아볼게요.

화자들은 어디에서 일하겠는가?
(A) 출판사
(B) 라디오 방송국
(C) 서점
(D) 텔레비전 방송국

첫 인사	**Welcome to ~ / Good morning, ~ / You've reached ~** **Welcome to** the Bristol Museum of Art. How can I help you? 브리스톨 미술관에 오신 것을 환영합니다. 무엇을 도와드릴까요? → 미술관
본인 소개	**This is ~ / I'm calling from ~** **This is** Jenny Wilson, the receptionist at Morningside Medical Group. 저는 모닝사이드 메디컬 그룹 접수원인 제니 윌슨입니다. → 접수원
관련 어휘	**장소 / 직업을 추론할 수 있는 어휘 사용** Have you noticed how fast we've been selling out of our freshly baked **breads** recently? 우리가 최근에 갓 구운 빵을 얼마나 빨리 다 팔았는지 알고 있나요? → 제과점
기타	**상대방의 업무 / 부서 / 회사 언급** So on the phone you said you're looking for a new office space for **your company**. 전화상으로 귀사의 새로운 사무 공간을 찾고 있다고 말씀하셨죠. → 화자: 부동산 중개업자, 상대방: 사업주

PART 3 | CHAPTER 01

✎ 신분 / 직업 관련 어휘

caterer 출장 요리 공급자	receptionist 접수원	job applicant[candidate] 지원자
architect 건축가	accountant 회계사	supervisor 관리자
landscaper 조경사	pharmacist 약사	colleague 동료
mechanic / technician 정비공 / 기사	publisher 출판인, 출판사	representative / employee 직원
reporter / journalist 기자 / 언론인	real estate agent 부동산 중개인	sales associate 영업 사원
photographer 사진 작가	property manager 부동산 관리인	executive 임원, 경영자

ETS CHECK-UP 　　　　　  🎧 P3_07 　정답 및 해설 p. 105

1. Who most likely is the man?

(A) A marketing specialist
(B) An interior decorator
(C) A photographer
(D) A banker

2. Where is the conversation taking place?

(A) At a parking garage
(B) At a department store
(C) At a dental office
(D) At a community center

대화에 등장하는 단서가 알맞게 패러프레이징된 보기를 선택하세요.

W I've just called our warehouse, and it looks like **the brand of photo printer paper you wanted is not in stock.**

M When do you think it will become available? We really need it to get the best quality photos of our new product for a trade show next week.

1. What is the conversation mainly about?

(A) An out-of-stock item
(B) A misplaced form

M We got **a huge bill from the electric company** today. It's much higher than usual.

W Oh, I guess it's because of the heater we bought last month. The salesperson warned us that that could happen.

2. What are the speakers discussing?

(A) A broken appliance
(B) An electricity bill

W Hi, **I'm calling from Conference Room A. I've been trying to connect to the wireless Internet but it doesn't seem to work.**

M Yes, the network is down. Sorry about that. We are currently looking into the matter, so it should be fixed very soon.

3. Why is the woman calling?

(A) To cancel a meeting
(B) To report a problem

W I was impressed with your audition and **would like you to take the lead role in our upcoming play** in June.

M I'd love to. When will the rehearsals begin?

4. Who most likely is the man?

(A) An actor
(B) A musician

M Amanda, how's **the special order of chocolate muffins** for Beans Café coming along?

W **I'm putting them in the oven now.** We're supposed to deliver them by three this afternoon, right?

5. Where do the speakers most likely work?

(A) At a shipping company
(B) At a bakery

M I'm moving to Seoul next month, **and I'd like your help finding a one-bedroom apartment.**

W **We'd be happy to help you.** Can you tell me more about what you're looking for?

6. Who most likely is the woman?

(A) A real estate agent
(B) An interior designer

LISTENING **PRACTICE**

🎧 P3_09 정답 및 해설 p.107

대화를 들으면서 정답을 고르세요. 그리고 다시 들으면서 빈칸을 채우세요. (녹음은 두 번씩 들려줍니다.)

1. What is the main purpose of the call?

(A) To renew a contract
(B) To buy some furniture

2. What kind of business does the man most likely work for?

(A) A clothing manufacturer
(B) A laundry service

W This is Annette Murphy from the Winbridge Restaurant. I'm calling because _____ is almost up. We'd like to _____.

M Certainly, Ms. Murphy. I can send you _____—unless there are any changes you'd like to make?

W Actually, the restaurant is _____. So we'll be sending you more linens to be cleaned each week. Would it be possible to _____?

M Well, that would _____. I'll check with him this afternoon and let you know.

---

3. Where do the speakers work?

(A) At a pharmacy
(B) At a fitness center

4. Who is Min-Jung Won?

(A) A possible customer
(B) A job applicant

M Mitra, have you had time to _____ of the person _____?

W The one for Min-Jung Won? Yes, I did. She _____. I think she'd be great for our gym because she has a lot of _____.

M I agree. I'll give her a call now _____ later this week. I hope she's available.

---

5. What are the speakers mainly discussing?

(A) A job transfer
(B) A store opening

6. What most likely is the woman's job?

(A) Sales team leader
(B) Computer programmer

M Nancy, I heard that _____ in Hong Kong. What will you be doing there?

W Oh, it'll be the same thing I've been doing here. The company's ready to start _____ in Asia—and since my team's had _____ here, they've asked me to move to Hong Kong to _____.

M That sounds like a great opportunity. You know, my cousin works in Hong Kong _____. I'll give you her e-mail address _____. I'm sure she'd be happy to help you find an apartment there.

PART 3 | **CHAPTER 01**

1. Where does the woman work?
   (A) At a manufacturing plant
   (B) At a delivery service
   (C) At a machine repair shop
   (D) At an office supply store

2. Why is the woman calling?
   (A) To offer a product warranty
   (B) To ask for feedback on a prototype
   (C) To give updated information about an order
   (D) To request payment of an overdue invoice

3. Why is Mr. Yamaguchi out of the office?
   (A) He is away on holiday.
   (B) He is having lunch.
   (C) He is not feeling well.
   (D) He is working at another location.

4. What are the speakers discussing?
   (A) A product price
   (B) A business location
   (C) A doctor's prescription
   (D) An upcoming appointment

5. Why is the man behind schedule?
   (A) A staff member is out sick.
   (B) A doctor has not arrived yet.
   (C) A computer is not working.
   (D) A pharmacy has been busy.

6. What does the woman say she will do next?
   (A) Sign a receipt
   (B) Go to a nearby store
   (C) Make a phone call
   (D) Fill out a form

7. Who most likely is the man?
   (A) A construction worker
   (B) A magazine reporter
   (C) A financial investor
   (D) A software developer

8. What does the woman say will happen in June?
   (A) A magazine will be redesigned.
   (B) A facility will be inspected.
   (C) Some construction will begin.
   (D) Some new products will be tested.

9. According to the woman, how will Riverside residents benefit?
   (A) Their electricity bills will decrease.
   (B) Their electronics will be cheaper.
   (C) They will have quiet neighborhoods.
   (D) They will have more work opportunities.

10. What type of business does the woman work for?
    (A) A public utilities company
    (B) A graphic design firm
    (C) A delivery service
    (D) An electronics store

11. Why is the man calling?
    (A) To provide payment information
    (B) To inquire about a replacement part
    (C) To complain about a service
    (D) To request a user's manual

12. What does the man say he will provide?
    (A) A receipt
    (B) A credit card
    (C) A survey
    (D) A valid warranty

13. Where does this conversation most likely take place?
(A) In an office supply store
(B) In a restaurant
(C) In a library
(D) In a bank

14. What does the man inquire about?
(A) Product prices
(B) Business hours
(C) A credit card
(D) A lunch reservation

15. What does the man say he will do later?
(A) Visit a Web site
(B) Pick up a lost item
(C) Meet with the manager
(D) Stop by a showroom

16. What is the purpose of the woman's visit?
(A) To make travel arrangements
(B) To discuss a contract
(C) To pick up a package
(D) To promote a business

17. What does the man inquire about?
(A) A country's cuisine
(B) A company's location
(C) Payment options
(D) Business hours

18. What is the man planning to do?
(A) Read customer reviews
(B) Register for a cooking class
(C) Eat at a new restaurant
(D) Look for an online coupon

19. What type of organization do the speakers most likely work for?
(A) A city council
(B) A sports club
(C) A research institute
(D) A theater group

20. What are the speakers mainly discussing?
(A) Customer service policies
(B) Elections for a board of directors
(C) Corporate sponsorship
(D) Marketing costs

21. What does the woman say about a proposal?
(A) She cannot agree to it right away.
(B) She thinks it will be too expensive.
(C) She hopes it will be approved quickly.
(D) She is surprised by the sudden request.

22. What is the purpose of the man's call?
(A) To invite the woman to give a speech
(B) To arrange an interview
(C) To request a financial consultation
(D) To discuss a company retreat

23. What industry does the woman work in?
(A) Hospitality
(B) Publishing
(C) Marketing
(D) Health care

24. Why does the man suggest making travel arrangements soon?
(A) Hotel availability is limited.
(B) The reimbursement process takes time.
(C) Fares are expected to increase.
(D) A corporate discount will expire soon.

❸ 세부 사항 문제

출제공식 1 What, Why, How 등 다양한 의문사로 시작해 세부 정보를 묻는 문제는 가장 많이 출제되는 유형이다. 질문 및 보기의 키워드가 그대로, 혹은 패러프레이징되어 대화에 등장한다.

2 특정 대상에 대해 언급한 내용을 묻는 문제는 서술형 보기로 구성되어 있다. 따라서 대화가 나오기 전에 보기까지 다 읽어야 정답 찾기가 수월하다.

문제유형 [세부 정보] What(+ 명사) does / did the man ~? 남자가 무엇을(어떤 ~을) ~하는가 / 했는가?

Why does the woman ~? 여자는 왜 ~하는가?

When / Where / How did the man ~? 남자가 언제 / 어디서 / 어떻게 ~ 했는가?

According to the woman, what is ~? 여자에 따르면, ~는 무엇인가?

[언급한 내용] What does the man say[mention] about ~? 남자가 ~에 대해서 뭐라고 말하는가?

What is mentioned about ~? ~에 대해서 언급된 바는 무엇인가?

✏️ **핵심 전략 |** 문제의 키워드가 어떻게 패러프레이징될 지 예상하며 노려 듣는다.   🎧 P3_11

M I'd like to purchase a desk for my home office. I heard that your store has a thirty percent off sale on all furniture right now. 패러프레이징: want to buy → I'd like to purchase 남자가 사고 싶은 것: 자택 사무실용 책상 **W** I'm sorry—that sale actually ended last week. But we do have another excellent deal: if you buy any desk made by the Chester Furniture Company, it comes with a matching chair. **M** Thanks. That sounds like a good deal, but I already have an office chair. I wonder if, instead, you'd be able to give me a discount on the desk. **W** I'm not sure… Let me check with a store manager to see what we can do.	**Q.** What does the **man** want to buy? (A) A desk (B) An appliance (C) Construction materials (D) Printing supplies 단서 I'd like to purchase a desk 정답 (A) 책상

남 자택 사무실에 필요한 책상을 하나 구입하고 싶은데요. 귀하의 매장에서 현재 모든 가구를 30퍼센트 할인 판매한다고 들었습니다.

여 최송합니다. 그 세일은 지난주에 끝났어요. 하지만 정말 괜찮은 혜택이 있어요. 체스터 가구회사의 책상을 사시면 어울리는 의자를 드려요.

남 고마워요. 괜찮은 구매 혜택이지만 사무용 의자가 이미 있어요. 대신에 책상을 할인해 주실 수 있는지 궁금하네요.

여 글쎄요… 그럴 수 있는지 점장님께 확인해 볼게요.

남자가 사고 싶어 하는 것은?

(A) 책상

(B) 전자 제품

(C) 시공 재료

(D) 인쇄 용품

✎ 세부 사항 문제 단서 제시 방식　　　　　　　　🎧 P3_12

질문의 키워드가 그대로 나오는 경우

① 명사 키워드

질문 What does the man say about Dr. Chen ? 남자는 첸 박사에 대해 뭐라고 하는가?

단서 Dr. Chen is away on vacation and she won't be back until next Thursday.
첸 박사님은 휴가로 떠나 계시고, 다음 주 목요일 전에는 돌아오시지 않을 거예요.

정답 She is not available. 자리에 없다.

② 시점 키워드

질문 What did the company do last month ? 회사는 지난달에 무엇을 했는가?

단서 Since we replaced the old machinery last month , production has been up by twenty percent. 지난달에 낡은 기계를 교체한 뒤 생산량이 20퍼센트 가량 증가했어요.

정답 It upgraded some equipment. 장비를 개선했다.

질문의 키워드가 패러프레이징 되는 경우

① 질문의 명사

질문 What does the woman say about a new product ?
여자는 신제품에 대해 뭐라고 하는가?

단서 Our new air conditioner doesn't use much energy, so you can save money on electricity. 저희의 새로운 에어컨은 에너지를 많이 소모하지 않아서 전기세를 아끼실 수 있습니다.

정답 It is energy efficient. 에너지 효율이 좋다.

② 질문의 동사

질문 Why does the woman apologize ? 여자가 사과하는 이유는?

단서 I'm sorry—we've completely sold out of those sweaters in your size.
최송합니다. 귀하의 사이즈에 해당하는 스웨터는 품절입니다.

정답 Some items are out of stock. 물품 재고가 없다.

질문 What does the man give the woman? 남자가 여자에게 주는 것은?

단서 Here's her phone number. She'd be willing to answer your questions.
여기 그녀의 번호예요. 당신의 질문에 흔쾌히 답변해 줄 겁니다.

정답 Some contact information 연락처

ETS CHECK-UP　　　　　　　　🎧 P3_13　정답 및 해설 p.115

1. Why does the man apologize?

(A) He disagrees with an opinion.
(B) He did not hear what was said.
(C) He was late to an event.
(D) He made a technical error.

2. What does the woman say about Yamamoto's Restaurant?

(A) The business hours are convenient.
(B) The prices are reasonable.
(C) The staff is friendly.
(D) The food is delicious.

PART 3 | CHAPTER 01

❹ 문제점/걱정거리 문제

출제공식
1. 대화 초반부에서 문제점/걱정거리가 바로 언급되거나, 한 화자가 던지는 질문과 상대방의 대답에서 드러나는 경우가 많다.
2. 기기 고장, 문서 오류, 비효율적인 시스템, 비용/매출 문제, 일손 부족, 시간 제약, 예약 불가능, 교통편을 놓친 상황 등 다양한 소재가 등장한다.

문제유형
[문제점] What is the (woman's) problem? (여자의) 문제는 무엇인가?

What problem do the speakers have? 화자들은 어떤 문제를 겪고 있는가?

What problem does the man mention / report? 남자는 어떤 문제를 언급/보고하는가?

[걱정거리] What is the woman concerned about? 여자가 걱정하는 것은 무엇인가?

Why is the man concerned? 남자는 왜 걱정을 하고 있는가?

✏️ **핵심 전략** | 대조/반전의 표현, 부정적인 의미를 지닌 표현에 주목한다. 🎧 P3_14

W Arshad, did you place the order for the new work desks?
M Yes, I did. But I'm having trouble tracking the shipment on their Web site. The furniture store sent me a link to monitor the delivery of our order. I can't seem to open it, though, so I'm not sure when the desks will arrive.
문제점을 나타내는 단서 표현: But, trouble, can't, though ●
남자가 언급한 문제: 웹사이트 링크 오류 ●
W Hmm, could you call the store and check? Our office's grand-opening celebration is on Monday, so we need the desks to arrive by then.
M Oh you're right—we need the furniture here in time for that event. I'll give them a call right away.

Q. What problem does the **man** mention?
(A) He has misplaced some important files.
● (B) He cannot access a Web page.
(C) He has not hired enough part-time employees.
(D) He will not be available next week.

단서 I'm having trouble ~ on their Web site

I can't seem to open it (= a link)

정답 (B) 웹페이지에 접속할 수 없다.

여 아샤드, 새 업무용 책상들을 주문했나요?

남 네, 했어요. **그런데 업체 웹사이트에서 배송을 추적하는 데 문제가 있어요.** 가구점에서 제게 주문품 배송 상황을 추적할 수 있는 링크를 보내주었는데요. **하지만 링크가 열리지 않는 것 같아서** 책상이 언제 도착하는지 알 수가 없네요.

여 음, 매장에 전화해서 확인해 줄 수 있어요? 사무실 개장 축하 행사가 월요일에 있어서 그때까지는 책상이 도착해야 해요.

남 아, 그렇네요. 행사 시간에 맞춰 이곳에 가구가 필요하죠. 업체에 즉시 전화해 볼게요.

남자는 무슨 문제를 언급하는가?
(A) 중요한 파일을 제자리에 두지 않았다.
(B) 웹페이지에 접속할 수 없다.
(C) 시간제 직원을 충분히 채용하지 않았다.
(D) 다음 주에 시간 여유가 없을 것이다.

부정어	can't / wasn't / didn't / won't / haven't My bus is running late, so I **won't be able to** make it there until about 2 P.M. 제가 탄 버스가 지연되고 있어서 거기에 2시 정도까진 가지 못할 것 같아요.
대조 / 반전	but / however / though / unfortunately / actually **But unfortunately**, that model was recently discontinued. 하지만 유감스럽게도, 그 모델은 최근에 단종되었습니다.
문제	problem / trouble I'm having **trouble** connecting my laptop to the projector in the auditorium. 강당에 있는 프로젝터에 제 노트북을 연결하는 데 애를 먹고 있어요.
걱정	I'm worried[concerned] that ~ / The only thing that worries me is ~ / **My biggest concern is that ~** There's a lot of traffic on the road—**I'm worried that** I'll miss the flight. 도로에 교통량이 너무 많아요. 항공편을 놓칠까 걱정돼요.
부정적 의미의 어휘	wrong / incorrect / mistake / error I noticed that some of the interviewees' names were spelled **wrong**. 면접자 몇몇의 이름이 잘못 적혀 있는 걸 발견했습니다. go down / slow / delay / malfunction / break down Our car sales have **gone down** every month for the past two years. 우리 자동차 매출이 지난 2년간 매달 하락해 왔습니다.

PART 3 | **CHAPTER 01**

ETS CHECK-UP　　　　　　🎧 P3_16　정답 및 해설 p.116

1. What do the women express concern about?

　(A) A project schedule
　(B) A late delivery
　(C) A potential expense
　(D) A shortage of workers

2. What problem does the man mention?

　(A) Rain is predicted.
　(B) Some paperwork is missing.
　(C) Some garden tools are broken.
　(D) Workers are unavailable.

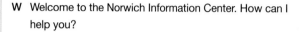

🎧 P3_17 정답 및 해설 p.116

대화에 등장하는 단서가 알맞게 패러프레이징된 보기를 선택하세요.

W Welcome to the Norwich Information Center. How can I help you?

M Hello. **I moved to this city last week after accepting a job here.** I'd like to get to know the area, and I was wondering if you could help me with that.

1. What did the man do recently?

(A) He opened a business.

(B) He relocated for a new job.

W I heard from one of my colleagues that conference attendees are eligible for a twenty-percent discount on hotel rooms. Is that correct?

M Yes—all you have to do is **show your ID badge at the front desk when you check in.**

2. How can the woman receive a discount?

(A) By presenting a form of identification

(B) By entering a special code online

W Our readers are very interested in learning about how your company has grown so quickly over the past year.

M Yes, it's amazing to think that I started it with only a few people but now there are over one hundred employees. **I'd like to attribute our success to them, because they're the best in the field.**

3. What does the man say about the employees?

(A) They need technical training.

(B) They are highly competent.

W I'm sorry I didn't make it to the staff meeting yesterday. I **had to finish an important report that was due today.**

M No problem. Here's a copy of the meeting minutes. Just let me know if you have any questions.

4. Why did the woman miss the meeting?

(A) She was busy with a report.

(B) She was on a business trip.

M Hello, I placed an order from your store a week ago. The package arrived this morning, but **one of the products I ordered was missing**—the label maker.

W Oh, I apologize for that. Let me check what happened. Could you tell me your name and order number?

5. What problem does the man mention?

(A) An item has not been delivered.

(B) Some equipment is out of order.

W I've been waiting for the number nine bus for the last thirty minutes, but it hasn't come. I have an interview in an hour, and **I'm worried I might be late.**

M I'm sorry, the driver just called and said his bus broke down on Roaster Avenue. But don't worry, the replacement bus is on its way.

6. Why is the woman concerned?

(A) She left her belongings on a bus.

(B) She might not arrive on time for an interview.

LISTENING **PRACTICE**

d b P3_18 정답 및 해설 p. 118

대화를 들으면서 정답을 고르세요. 그리고 다시 들으면서 빈칸을 채우세요. (녹음은 두 번씩 들려줍니다.)

1. What does the man remind the woman about?

(A) There will be traffic delays.
(B) The cost of parking is high.

2. What information will the man search for?

(A) A bus route
(B) A ticket price

W I'm glad several of our colleagues can join us for the baseball game tomorrow. But I wonder _____ _____. Should we drive?

M Well, _____ last time we went to the stadium for a concert?

W Oh yeah… I think it'll actually be _____. And it should drop us off right at the front gate.

M OK, let me _____.

---

3. What problem does the man mention?

(A) He does not have enough supplies.
(B) He has not been trained.

4. What does the man reassure the woman about?

(A) A form is easy to complete.
(B) A delivery will be made on time.

M Seema, I just finished _____ Toronto on the truck, but there's a problem.

W What's the matter?

M Well, I don't have _____ in the truck.

W Oh no, those sculptures are very fragile. Can you find _____?

M You know, I think John _____, so he might have some. And _____ _____. We won't get behind schedule.

---

5. How is the woman trying to improve efficiency?

(A) By training workers to operate more machines
(B) By rearranging some workstations

6. What does the woman say about some photos?

(A) They were taken on-site.
(B) They will be informative.

W Glad you're attending today's training, Felipe. I'm trying to _____ at our factory. Having staff _____ will help with that.

M I'm looking forward to learning how the rubber-injection molding machine works.

W We'll go step-by-step through the handbook I created. _____.

M Great. And after the training, if I don't understand something, should I ask you?

W Actually, Paul's been at the injection molding station for years. _____.

---

1. What is the conversation mostly about?
   (A) An office celebration
   (B) A cooking competition
   (C) A restaurant opening
   (D) A renovation project

2. Why does the man say he is worried?
   (A) Some materials will be expensive.
   (B) Some work will be noisy.
   (C) A parking area is too small.
   (D) A shipment has not arrived.

3. What does the woman inform the man about?
   (A) A special schedule has been arranged.
   (B) A partial payment has been made.
   (C) An employee has been promoted.
   (D) An event will be filmed.

4. What was the woman trying to do?
   (A) Check a bill
   (B) Watch a video
   (C) Download a song
   (D) Repair a device

5. According to the man, why was the woman having trouble?
   (A) A technical problem occurred.
   (B) A payment was not received.
   (C) An order was placed incorrectly.
   (D) A password was expired.

6. What will the man send the woman?
   (A) A letter of apology
   (B) A replacement part
   (C) An access code
   (D) A confirmation notice

7. Where does the conversation most likely take place?
   (A) At an architecture company
   (B) At a storage facility
   (C) At an accounting firm
   (D) At an advertising agency

8. What problem does the woman mention?
   (A) Her company's sales have decreased.
   (B) She does not have enough investors.
   (C) A factory has been closed.
   (D) A business location is inconvenient.

9. What does the woman give to the men?
   (A) Parking passes
   (B) Office keys
   (C) Budget information
   (D) Product designs

10. What topic does the woman bring up?
    (A) A recent vacation
    (B) A product launch
    (C) A health program
    (D) An employee luncheon

11. What does the man say about his work?
    (A) He has joined a new team.
    (B) He has been very busy.
    (C) His project needs more funds.
    (D) His business trip has been canceled.

12. What will the woman do next?
    (A) Check a policy
    (B) Visit a doctor
    (C) Provide a list of names
    (D) Give a demonstration

13. Who most likely are Ibrahim and Natalie?
(A) Apartment managers
(B) Maintenance workers
(C) Safety inspectors
(D) Potential home buyers

14. What are Ibrahim and Natalie concerned about?
(A) The placement of smoke detectors
(B) The size of a property
(C) The cost of major repairs
(D) The number of tenants

15. What is mentioned about the owner?
(A) She is starting a new job.
(B) She owns several properties.
(C) She can recommend qualified workers.
(D) She is available in the afternoon.

16. Who most likely is the man?
(A) A stage manager
(B) An assistant chef
(C) A talk show host
(D) A city official

17. What does the woman say about the Vaden Theater?
(A) It is where she began her acting career.
(B) It is her favorite theater to perform at.
(C) It has an excellent sound system.
(D) It has unique architecture.

18. What is the woman surprised to learn?
(A) A show has been nominated for an award.
(B) A building will be renovated.
(C) A close friend is retiring.
(D) A restaurant is still open.

19. What problem does the man mention?
(A) A document was not received on time.
(B) A report has incorrect data.
(C) A meeting has been canceled.
(D) An account has been closed.

20. What does the woman say she will do?
(A) Replace a file
(B) Download some software
(C) Check a schedule
(D) Order a desk

21. What will the man be doing tomorrow?
(A) Revising a budget
(B) Conducting an interview
(C) Delivering some special orders
(D) Meeting with clients

22. What does the speakers' company sell?
(A) Books
(B) Clothes
(C) Video games
(D) Kitchen appliances

23. What would the man like the Web site to do for customers?
(A) Show 3D images of products
(B) Indicate when a product is sold out
(C) Save purchasing histories
(D) Provide recommendations

24. Why is the woman unable to help?
(A) She is not going to be in the office.
(B) She does not have the necessary skill.
(C) Some equipment is not working.
(D) A supervisor has not given approval.

❺ 다음에 할 일/일어날 일 문제

출제공식 1 화자가 다음에 할 일은 묻는 질문은 주로 세 번째 문제로 출제되며, 마지막 대사에서 단서가 주어지는 경우가 많다.

2 일어날 일을 묻는 문제는 미래의 특정 시점을 나타내는 키워드가 단서로 등장한다.

문제유형 [할 일] **What will the man probably[most likely] do next?**
남자가 다음에 할 것 같은 일은 무엇인가?

What does the woman say she will do (next / later)?
여자는 (다음에 / 이따가) 무엇을 하겠다고 하는가?

[일어날 일] **What will happen[take place] ~?** ~에 무슨 일이 일어나는가?

✎ **핵심 전략 | 미래 계획이나 의지/결심을 나타내는 표현에 귀를 기울인다.** 🎧 P3_20

M Hi Kelly. This is Stan from the shipping department. I'm preparing the order of shirts for Clark Restaurant. According to the form, they want two hundred white shirts, but that number seems rather high.

W Yeah, it does. It's just a small family restaurant, so I doubt they have that many employees.

M I'm guessing that an extra zero was added by mistake. Could you check on that before I finish preparing the shipment?

W Definitely. I'll call the restaurant owner right now to confirm the number of shirts they want. Thanks for bringing this to my attention.

계획 및 의지를 나타내는 단서 표현: I'll ●
여자가 하겠다고 한 일: 식당 업주에게 전화 ●

Q. What does the **woman** say she will do?
(A) Inspect some merchandise
(B) Make an appointment
(C) Confirm a delivery date
● (D) Contact a business owner

단서 call the restaurant owner
정답 (D) 사업주에게 연락하기

남 안녕하세요, 켈리. 발송부의 스탠이에요. 클라크 식당에 보낼 셔츠 주문품을 준비하고 있어요. 양식에 따르면, 그들이 원하는 게 흰색 셔츠 200벌인데, 수량이 좀 많은 것 같아요.

여 네, 그러네요. 작은 패밀리 레스토랑인데 직원이 그렇게 많지는 않을 거예요.

남 제 추측으로는 실수로 0이 하나 더 붙은 것 같아요. 발송 준비를 끝내기 전에 확인해 줄 수 있어요?

여 그럼요. **지금 바로 식당 주인에게 전화해서 원하는 셔츠 수량을 확인할게요.** 알려줘서 고마워요.

여자는 무엇을 하겠다고 말하는가?
(A) 상품을 조사한다.
(B) 약속을 잡는다.
(C) 배송 날짜를 확인한다.
(D) 사업주에게 연락한다.

✏️ 다음에 할 일 / 일어날 일을 나타내는 단서 표현 🎧 P3_21

① 단순 미래 시제 will (계획 + 의지 / 의도)

I'll call the photographer and see if he's available the next day.

제가 사진작가에게 전화해서 그 다음 날 시간이 되는지 확인할게요.

② be going to / be planning to

Now I'm going to post the notice by the entrance to the conference room.

지금 회의실 출입구 옆에 그 공지를 게시하려고요.

계획

③ be -ing

We are interviewing applicants for the graphic designer position this week.

이번 주에 그래픽 디자이너직에 지원한 사람들을 면접할 예정입니다.

④ 단순 현재 시제

I just wanted to remind you that the winter internship program begins next Tuesday. 동계 인턴십 프로그램이 다음 주 화요일에 시작된다는 걸 상기시켜주고 싶었어요.

결심

I should ~

Maybe I should make an online reservation at the hotel right now.

지금 당장 그 호텔에 온라인 예약을 해야겠네요.

제안

Let me ~ / I can[could] ~

Let me ask the manager of the training division if we can change the date.

날짜를 변경할 수 있는지 직무교육과 담당자에게 물어볼게요.

기타

상대방의 제안 / 요청 / 안내

Let's get started by taking a tour of the facilities.

시설을 돌아보는 것으로 시작합시다.

Just fill out this form to sign up for our membership card.

멤버십 카드를 신청하시려면 이 양식을 작성하시기만 하면 됩니다.

ETS CHECK-UP 🎧 P3_22 정답 및 해설 p.126

1. What will the man do next?

(A) Meet with his boss
(B) Call potential advertisers
(C) Make an announcement
(D) Write an article

2. What does the woman say will happen next week?

(A) Qualified candidates will be interviewed.
(B) Computer systems will be upgraded.
(C) A new office branch will open.
(D) A hiring manager will lead an information session.

❻ 요청/제안 사항 문제

출제공식 1 화자의 요청이나 제안 사항을 묻는 문제 역시 주로 마지막에 출제된다.

2 요청/제안 사항 문제가 첫 번째나 두 번째 문제로 나올 경우, 앞으로 일어날 일이나 해야 할 일에 대해 묻는 질문이 함께 출제될 가능성이 높다.

문제유형 [요청] What does the woman ask the man to do? 여자는 남자에게 무엇을 해 달라고 요청하는가?

What is the man asked to do? 남자는 무엇을 하도록 요청받는가? (상대방의 대사에 단서 등장)

What does the woman request[ask for]? 여자는 무엇을 요청하는가?

[제안] What does the man suggest[recommend]? 남자는 무엇을 제안/추천하는가?

What does the woman encourage the man to do? 여자는 남자에게 무엇을 하라고 독려하는가?

What does the man offer to do? 남자는 무엇을 해 주겠다고 제안하는가?

✎ 핵심 전략 | 대화에 등장하는 요청/제안의 표현에 주목한다.　　🎧 P3_23

W So Carlo, it looks like Julia, the receptionist at the front desk, will be going on holiday next week. Since you're the receptionist in the marketing department, could you take over for her while she's gone? **M** Sure, but the front desk phones have a different system for transferring calls. Would Julia be free to give me a quick tutorial before she leaves? **W** Definitely, but why don't you take a look at the system manual before she goes over it with you? 제안의 표현: **why don't you** ● 여자가 제안하는 일: 시스템 설명서 읽기 ●	**Q.** What does the **woman** suggest? (A) Meeting with a manager (B) Creating a registration form ● (C) Reading a manual (D) Taking some measurements 단서 take a look at the system manual 정답 (C) 설명서 읽기

여 카를로, 안내 데스크의 접객 담당 줄리아가 다음 주에 휴가를 갈 것 같아요. 당신이 마케팅부의 접객 담당이니 그녀가 없는 동안 대신 업무를 봐줄 수 있나요?

남 물론이죠. 하지만 안내 데스크 전화기들은 전화 연결 방식이 달라요. 줄리아가 떠나기 전에 제게 잠깐 설명해 줄 시간이 있을까요?

여 그럼요. 하지만 그녀가 당신과 함께 그것을 살펴보기 전에 당신이 먼저 시스템 설명서를 보는 게 어때요?

여자는 무엇을 제안하는가?
(A) 관리자 만나기
(B) 등록 신청서 작성하기
(C) 설명서 읽기
(D) 치수 재기

Can[Could] you ~ / Please ~ / Would you ~? / I'd like you to ~ / I was wondering if ~

요청

Could you pick up some snacks and beverages for our department meeting?
부서 회의 때 먹을 간식과 음료 좀 사다 줄래요?

Would you be able to look over the proposal before I submit it?
제가 제안서를 제출하기 전에 검토해 주실 수 있나요?

I'd like you to write a feature article for next month's issue of our magazine.
우리 잡지의 다음 달 호에 실을 특집 기사를 써주셨으면 해요.

I was wondering if you could reserve seats for me and Mr. Thompson.
당신이 저와 톰슨 씨를 위해 자리를 맡아줄 수 있나 해서요.

제안

① 방법 제안: **Why don't you ~? / You might want to ~ / I suggest / we should ~**

You might want to come back next week, because we're having a big sale then.
다음 주에 오시는 게 좋을 지도 모르겠어요. 왜냐하면 그때 저희가 대대적인 할인행사를 하거든요.

I suggest buying your ticket at least two weeks ahead—that play is very popular.
적어도 2주 전에는 표를 구매하시길 권해드립니다. 그 연극이 굉장히 인기가 높거든요.

I think **we should** carry out a customer survey about our new application.
저는 우리의 새로운 애플리케이션에 대한 고객 설문조사를 실시해야 한다고 생각해요.

② 도움 제안: **I can[could] ~ / I'd be happy to ~ / I will ~ / Would you like me to ~**

If you'd like, **I could** help you sort through the applications.
원하시면 지원서 정리하는 것을 도와드릴 수 있어요.

I'd be happy to let you know when a vacancy comes up.
공석이 생기면 알려드리겠습니다.

I'll give you some samples so that you can try them before you make a purchase. 구매 전에 사용해 보실 수 있게 샘플을 드릴게요.

ETS CHECK-UP　　　　　　　🎧 P3_25　정답 및 해설 p. 127

1. What does the man offer to do for the woman?

(A) Add her name to a list
(B) Give her an estimate
(C) Waive a fee
(D) Send a bill in the mail

2. What does the man ask the woman to do?

(A) Provide some information
(B) Offer free samples
(C) Extend business hours
(D) Host an event

대화에 등장하는 단서가 알맞게 패러프레이징된 보기를 선택하세요.

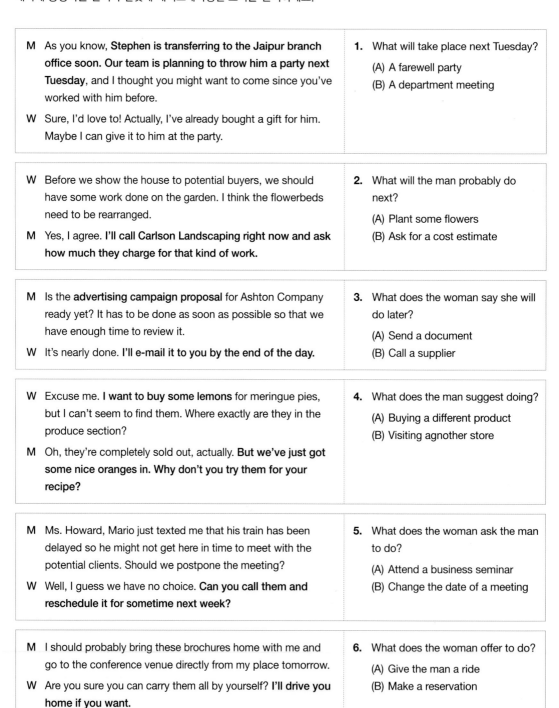

M As you know, **Stephen is transferring to the Jaipur branch office soon. Our team is planning to throw him a party next Tuesday**, and I thought you might want to come since you've worked with him before.

W Sure, I'd love to! Actually, I've already bought a gift for him. Maybe I can give it to him at the party.

1. What will take place next Tuesday?
(A) A farewell party
(B) A department meeting

W Before we show the house to potential buyers, we should have some work done on the garden. I think the flowerbeds need to be rearranged.

M Yes, I agree. **I'll call Carlson Landscaping right now and ask how much they charge for that kind of work.**

2. What will the man probably do next?
(A) Plant some flowers
(B) Ask for a cost estimate

M Is the **advertising campaign proposal** for Ashton Company ready yet? It has to be done as soon as possible so that we have enough time to review it.

W It's nearly done. **I'll e-mail it to you by the end of the day.**

3. What does the woman say she will do later?
(A) Send a document
(B) Call a supplier

W Excuse me. **I want to buy some lemons** for meringue pies, but I can't seem to find them. Where exactly are they in the produce section?

M Oh, they're completely sold out, actually. **But we've just got some nice oranges in. Why don't you try them for your recipe?**

4. What does the man suggest doing?
(A) Buying a different product
(B) Visiting agnother store

M Ms. Howard, Mario just texted me that his train has been delayed so he might not get here in time to meet with the potential clients. Should we postpone the meeting?

W Well, I guess we have no choice. **Can you call them and reschedule it for sometime next week?**

5. What does the woman ask the man to do?
(A) Attend a business seminar
(B) Change the date of a meeting

M I should probably bring these brochures home with me and go to the conference venue directly from my place tomorrow.

W Are you sure you can carry them all by yourself? **I'll drive you home if you want.**

6. What does the woman offer to do?
(A) Give the man a ride
(B) Make a reservation

LISTENING **PRACTICE**

🎧 P3_27 정답 및 해설 p. 129

대화를 들으면서 정답을 고르세요. 그리고 다시 들으면서 빈칸을 채우세요. (녹음은 두 번씩 들려줍니다.)

1. According to the man, what will happen in two weeks?

(A) A store will be renovated.
(B) A sale will begin.

2. What does the woman recommend?

(A) Distributing a survey
(B) Placing an advertisement in a newspaper

M Fatima, our storewide _____. We've got lots of merchandise left from last season, so it's important _____.

W I think we should _____. I know we've done that for sales in the past.

M That's a great idea. But before you submit anything, _____ both half-page and quarter-page advertisements. That way we can _____.

---

3. What does the man ask the woman for?

(A) Driving directions
(B) A deadline extension

4. What does the woman say she will do?

(A) Make some copies
(B) Speak with a supervisor

M This is Shinji calling from the marketing department. I know _____, but I was wondering if I _____.

W We don't usually allow that, unless _____.

M Well, to be honest, I'm not sure _____ and I need to find them before I fill out the request form.

W I'll have to _____. But in the meantime, fill out as much of the form as you can so we can at least get started _____.

---

5. Why is the woman at the bookstore?

(A) To return an item
(B) To attend a book reading

6. What does the man offer to do?

(A) Contact the woman when an item arrives
(B) Introduce an author

W Hello, I bought this novel at this bookstore a few days ago as a gift for a friend, but I just found out that she already has it. _____?

M Yes, of course, but we don't give cash refunds. You can _____, though.

W That's fine. I thought of _____. It's called *The Dog's Trail* by Kavi Mittal. Could you check and see if you carry it?

M Sure . . . It looks like the book is _____, but a new shipment is on the way. I'd be happy to _____.

1. Who is the man?
(A) A photographer
(B) A caterer
(C) A hotel manager
(D) A conference organizer

2. What does the man suggest the woman do?
(A) Arrange transportation
(B) Pay by credit card
(C) Hire his colleague
(D) Change a reservation

3. What does the woman ask the man for?
(A) A refund
(B) An upgrade
(C) An event program
(D) Some samples

4. What type of business is the man asking about?
(A) A catering company
(B) An advertising agency
(C) A law firm
(D) A printing business

5. What does the woman say about P.J.'s?
(A) Its orders are delivered quickly.
(B) It has positive online reviews.
(C) It has a large variety of options.
(D) It has reasonable prices.

6. What does the woman offer to do?
(A) Look up a telephone number
(B) Forward a Web site address
(C) Write a recommendation
(D) Find some paperwork

7. What does the woman request?
(A) An invoice
(B) A map
(C) A signature
(D) A replacement part

8. What does the man say he has to do?
(A) Find his security pass
(B) Talk with a supervisor
(C) Unlock a door
(D) Check inventory

9. What does the man ask the woman to do?
(A) Return later
(B) Lower a price
(C) Move a vehicle
(D) Remove some boxes

10. What do the women suggest doing?
(A) Participating in a local festival
(B) Hiring an advertising agency
(C) Expanding land used for farming
(D) Recruiting volunteers for an event

11. What does the man think their business should do?
(A) Arrive earlier than other participants
(B) Offer a coupon for fruit picking
(C) Provide free samples
(D) Review a budget

12. What will the man do next?
(A) Call a customer
(B) Register for an event
(C) Install a sign
(D) Schedule a construction project

13. What type of business does the man work for?
    (A) A construction company
    (B) A delivery service
    (C) A car repair shop
    (D) A sporting goods store

14. Why does the woman recommend TMK boots?
    (A) They will last a long time.
    (B) They are inexpensive.
    (C) They come in many colors.
    (D) They are available in many sizes.

15. What does the woman encourage the man to do?
    (A) Purchase a warranty
    (B) Sign up for a discount program
    (C) Increase the quantity of an order
    (D) Try on an item

16. What kind of product is the woman calling about?
    (A) A software program
    (B) A digital projector
    (C) An alarm system
    (D) An air conditioner

17. According to the man, what is special about the product?
    (A) It is portable.
    (B) It is inexpensive.
    (C) It has a long battery life.
    (D) It provides customized suggestions.

18. What will the man most likely do next?
    (A) Schedule a maintenance check
    (B) Share pricing information
    (C) E-mail a customer survey
    (D) Consult a user manual

19. Where do the speakers most likely work?
    (A) At a library
    (B) At a bank
    (C) At a movie theater
    (D) At a fitness center

20. What does the man suggest doing?
    (A) Reducing a loan period
    (B) Ordering more items
    (C) Posting a sign-up sheet
    (D) Charging higher fees

21. What event will take place next week?
    (A) A fund-raiser
    (B) A board meeting
    (C) A training session
    (D) An interview

22. What department does the man work in?
    (A) Graphic Design
    (B) Human Resources
    (C) Product Development
    (D) Information Technology

23. What does the woman mention about Waterson Pharmaceuticals?
    (A) It is a large company.
    (B) It has a good reputation.
    (C) It was on a news program.
    (D) It is located in a big city.

24. What will the woman most likely do next?
    (A) Provide photo identification
    (B) Attend a networking session
    (C) Complete a training module
    (D) Join a company staff meeting

PART 3 | CHAPTER 01

129

❼ 화자의 의도 파악 문제

출제공식
1 제시된 문장의 숨은 의도를 묻는 문제로 매회 2문항이 고정으로 출제된다.
2 단서는 제시문 앞뒤 문장이나 상대 화자의 대사에 있다.
3 같은 표현이라도 문맥에 따라 의미가 달라질 수 있으므로 맥락을 잘 이해하는 것이 중요하다.

문제유형
What does the man mean when he says, "~"?
남자가 "~"라고 말할 때 의미하는 바는 무엇인가?

What does the woman imply when she says, "~"?
여자가 "~"라고 말할 때 암시하는 바는 무엇인가?

Why does the man say, "~"?
남자가 "~"라고 말하는 이유는 무엇인가?

🖊 **핵심 전략 | 제시문의 의미와 보기를 파악한 후 대화의 흐름을 예상한다.**　　🎧 P3_29

M Angela, have you had a chance to look at the cost estimate for the repairs on the warehouse roof? There are several leaks, so the project will start as soon as the budget is approved.

　　남자의 질문: 견적서 확인했는지 문의 ●

W Uhm… **I've been in meetings all morning**…. Actually, since you met with the contractor, could you just stop by my office at two o'clock and tell me what he said about the roof?

　　여자의 답변: 오전 내내 회의 참석 = 미확인 ●

M Well, I'm leaving early this afternoon for an appointment at my bank. But Maria also spoke with the contractor. I'll tell her now that you'd like to talk with her at two.

W OK. Thank you.

Q. Why does the **woman** say, "I've been in meetings all morning"?
(A) She wants the man to change a deadline.
(B) She is unhappy about her schedule today.
(C) She has already been updated about a project.
(D) She did not have time to look at a document.

단서 Angela, have you had a chance to look at the cost estimate ~?

정답 (D) 문서를 볼 시간이 없었다.

남 안젤라, 창고 지붕 수리비 견적서를 볼 기회가 있었나요? 여러 군데가 새서 예산이 승인되는 대로 작업이 시작될 거예요.
여 음… **제가 오전 내내 회의를 했어요**… 사실, 당신이 하청업자를 만나 봤으니 **2시에 제 사무실에 들러 그가 지붕에 관해 무슨 얘기를 했는지 말해줄 수 있나요?**
남 이런, 저는 은행에 약속이 있어 이따가 오후에 일찍 나갈 거예요. 하지만 마리아도 그 하청업자와 이야기를 나눴어요. 당신이 2시에 그녀와 대화하고 싶어 한다고 지금 그녀에게 말할게요.
여 좋아요. 고마워요.

여자는 왜 "제가 오전 내내 회의를 했어요"라고 말하는가?
(A) 남자가 마감 시한을 변경해 주었으면 한다.
(B) 오늘 일정표가 마음에 들지 않는다.
(C) 프로젝트 현황에 대해 이미 들었다.
(D) 문서를 볼 시간이 없었다.

✏️ 맥락에 따른 화자의 의도 파악하기

의도 파악 문제는 문장의 표면적 의미가 아닌 문맥상 드러나는 화자의 의도를 묻기 때문에, 맥락 이해가 필수적이다. 같은 문장이 다른 맥락에서 어떤 의미를 갖는지 살펴보자.

대화문 1) P3_30

Q Why does the man say, "I can't believe it"? (A) He is disappointed with a situation. (B) He is happy about some news.	**Q** 남자는 왜 "믿을 수가 없어요"라고 말하는가? **(A) 상황에 실망스럽다.** (B) 소식을 듣고 기쁘다.

W I'm so glad we've come back to this restaurant. The chocolate cake we had for dessert last time was delicious. Let's order it again.

M Definitely. Wait… it's not listed in the dessert section anymore! **I can't believe it**. I'm going to ask the server about this.

→ 좋아하는 디저트가 메뉴에서 빠진 것에 대한 실망감 표현

여 이 레스토랑에 다시 와서 너무 기뻐요. 지난번에 왔을 때 먹었던 초콜렛 케이크 너무 맛있었잖아요. 우리 또 주문해요.

남 당연하죠. 잠깐만요… 더 이상 디저트 메뉴에 그게 안 보이는데요! 믿을 수가 없어요. 종업원한테 이것에 대해서 물어봐야겠어요.

대화문 2) P3_31

Q Why does the woman say, "I can't believe it"? (A) She is disappointed with a situation. (B) She is happy about some news.	**Q** 여자는 왜 "믿을 수가 없어요"라고 말하는가? (A) 상황에 실망스럽다. **(B) 소식을 듣고 기쁘다.**

M We're having a sixty-percent-off sale on shirts this week, so your purchase comes out to just twenty-three euros.

W For all of these shirts? **I can't believe it!** In that case, let me pick out a few more.

→ 셔츠가 할인 판매 중이라는 소식에 대한 기쁨 표현

남 이번 주에 셔츠를 60퍼센트 할인 판매 중이라서요. 귀하의 구매품은 단돈 23유로입니다.

여 이 셔츠들 전부가요? 믿을 수가 없어요! 그렇다면 몇 개 더 골라올게요.

ETS CHECK-UP 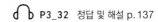 P3_32 정답 및 해설 p.137

1. Why does the man say, "Our new catalog is coming out next week"?

(A) To offer the woman reassurance
(B) To complain about a workload
(C) To suggest that the woman wait
(D) To express surprise

2. What does the woman imply when she says, "I volunteered last year"?

(A) She is able to help train other volunteers.
(B) She is proud of some volunteer work.
(C) She did not enjoy an event last year.
(D) She does not plan to attend an event.

PART 3 | CHAPTER 01

대화에 등장하는 단서를 보고 화자의 의도를 파악해 보세요.

W **Is there anything I can help you with?** I'm done with my sales report, so I have some time till tomorrow afternoon.

M Oh, really? I'm working on the Warren Footwear presentation. Here is the data for the graphics. **It needs to be turned into charts and tables.**

1. Why does the man say, "Here is the data for the graphics"?

(A) To fulfill a request

(B) To accept an offer

M Hi, Luisa. I was in a meeting with important clients, and so I missed the marketing workshop earlier. **Can I borrow your notes for a couple of hours?**

W Actually, the workshop was canceled. **I was told that it would be rescheduled next month.**

2. What does the woman mean when she says, "the workshop was canceled"?

(A) She is available to help the man.

(B) She cannot provide some materials.

W Oh, I forgot to bring the discount coupon that came with the advertisement for your store. **I'll go back to my office and get it. Could you hold my items until I come back?**

M Sure, but is your office nearby? We close at six. **But if you don't make it, I can extend the hold through tomorrow.**

3. What does the man imply when he says, "We close at six"?

(A) The woman's plan may not work.

(B) The woman is mistaken about a schedule.

M I don't know where to stay during my holiday in Barcelona. **There are so many hotels in the area and I just can't make a decision!**

W Well, Regis Inn was renovated and redecorated recently. **I'll send you the link to its Web site.**

4. Why does the woman say, "Regis Inn was renovated and redecorated recently"?

(A) To make a recommendation

(B) To correct a misunderstanding

W Hi, Paul. **Can you cover my shift this Saturday** from five to nine? There's a big jazz concert that night, and I really want to go.

M Uh… I'm planning a weekend getaway with friends. **Why don't you ask Jason?**

5. What does the man mean when he says, "I'm planning a weekend getaway with friends"?

(A) He wants the woman to join him.

(B) He cannot work on Saturday.

W Mathew, **I just heard we can't use this room now to practice our sales presentation.** Mr. Stevens will be holding interviews at 2 P.M.

M Really? **Should we find another room** or wait until he's finished?

6. What does the woman imply when she says, "Mr. Stevens will be holding interviews at 2 P.M."?

(A) A room will be occupied.

(B) A position has not been filled yet.

LISTENING **PRACTICE**

대화를 들으면서 정답을 고르세요. 그리고 다시 들으면서 빈칸을 채우세요. (녹음은 두 번씩 들려줍니다.)

1. What does the woman mean when she says, "Oh, don't thank me"?

(A) Someone else did the work.
(B) An assignment was not difficult.

2. What will the man most likely do next?

(A) Make an appointment
(B) Leave a message

M Hi, I'm with Spellman Technologies, and I'm calling to thank you and your company for the great job you did _____ last week.

W Oh, don't thank me. Your event was _____, Nadia. I'm sure she'll be happy to hear that you were pleased.

M If Nadia's in the office, I'd like to tell her myself.

W Actually, _____ today. But I can put you through to her voice mail so that you can _____.

---

3. Where most likely do the speakers work?

(A) At a supermarket
(B) At a restaurant

4. What does the man imply when he says, "I don't know"?

(A) He is not sure about the date of an event.
(B) He cannot fulfill the woman's request.

W Hi Carlo, I was just checking my schedule, and I see I'm working the lunch and dinner shifts all weekend. I worked both Saturday and Sunday last week, too, so I was hoping I could _____ _____ this weekend.

M Hmm… I don't know. We _____ right now. I've actually scheduled you this week to train two new employees who don't have much experience waiting tables…. But once they're fully trained, I'll be able to _____.

W Oh, I see. I'm glad we'll be getting more help.

---

5. Why is the woman calling the man?

(A) To order some gifts
(B) To find a new apartment

6. Why does the man say, "How's your afternoon"?

(A) To request help completing a project
(B) To suggest a meeting time

W Hi, Peter, this is Tanya Bryant. You helped me find an apartment last year. I was wondering if _____ _____ in the same neighborhood.

M Oh—hi, Tanya. I'd be happy to help. You're currently in the Mount Eldon area, aren't you?

W Yes, and I really like it. But I've _____, designing jewelry and selling it online, so I'd like to _____. I need to have another room to use as an office.

M I have _____. How's your afternoon?

---

1. What does the woman imply when she says, "My next meeting isn't until three"?
   (A) She wants to volunteer for a task.
   (B) She thinks a schedule should be revised.
   (C) She does not need to use a meeting room.
   (D) She is available to talk.

2. What problem are the speakers discussing?
   (A) A shipment has been delayed.
   (B) A product has not been selling well.
   (C) Some employees have not reported to work.
   (D) Some merchandise has been damaged.

3. What do the speakers agree to do?
   (A) Find a new supplier
   (B) Offer some discounts
   (C) Collect customer feedback
   (D) Talk to a marketing director

4. What task is the man doing?
   (A) Scanning some documents
   (B) Revising a spreadsheet
   (C) Filling out an invoice
   (D) Contacting some patients

5. What does the man thank the woman for?
   (A) Helping him carry some packages
   (B) Setting up some equipment
   (C) Locating an important file
   (D) Giving him a reference

6. Why does the man say, "There's a company in town that buys used office furniture"?
   (A) To express concern about a budget
   (B) To recommend redecorating a lobby
   (C) To emphasize that a location is convenient
   (D) To suggest selling some items

7. Where do the speakers most likely work?
   (A) At a bookstore
   (B) At an art museum
   (C) At a magazine publishing company
   (D) At a computer accessory shop

8. What does the man mean when he says, "there are a lot of details"?
   (A) He is impressed with an image.
   (B) He will explain a decision later.
   (C) A description should be written.
   (D) A design should be simplified.

9. What will the company celebrate in February?
   (A) A retirement
   (B) An anniversary
   (C) A branch opening
   (D) A successful merger

10. What event are the speakers discussing?
    (A) An annual reunion
    (B) A grand opening
    (C) A product launch
    (D) A company dinner

11. What does the man imply when he says, "The weather's been so nice lately, though"?
    (A) He is disappointed in a decision.
    (B) He is reluctant to plan an outdoor event.
    (C) He would like more vacation time.
    (D) He expects the weather will change tonight.

12. What does the woman suggest?
    (A) Rescheduling a dinner
    (B) Setting up video equipment outside
    (C) Serving some food in a different location
    (D) Offering a discount

13. What problem is discussed?
(A) A cost has increased.
(B) A schedule has changed.
(C) A property was damaged.
(D) A file was misplaced.

14. Why does the woman say, "the business next door did some landscaping recently"?
(A) To criticize a decision
(B) To refuse an offer
(C) To make a suggestion
(D) To apologize for a mistake

15. What does the man ask the woman to do?
(A) Reserve a table
(B) Buy some beverages
(C) Print presentation slides
(D) Make a phone call

16. Why is the woman calling the man?
(A) To report an equipment problem
(B) To confirm a schedule
(C) To request personnel information
(D) To ask about a lost item

17. What does the woman mean when she says, "I'm interviewing someone in here in five minutes"?
(A) She needs help urgently.
(B) She does not want to be disturbed.
(C) She is unhappy with an assignment.
(D) She will not attend another meeting.

18. What does the woman say is unusual about the interview?
(A) It will be recorded.
(B) It will be held on a weekend.
(C) It will be conducted face-to-face.
(D) It will last for more than an hour.

19. Where do the speakers most likely work?
(A) At a travel agency
(B) At a marketing firm
(C) At a hotel
(D) At a television station

20. What does the woman imply when she says, "but summer's almost over"?
(A) She does not want to take a vacation now.
(B) The man will complete a task soon.
(C) An advertisement will come out too late.
(D) A sales event must be rescheduled.

21. What will the man do next?
(A) Order more brochures
(B) Visit a branch office
(C) Create a survey
(D) Call some vendors

22. What are the speakers mainly discussing?
(A) An employee evaluation
(B) A sales report
(C) A new client
(D) A travel itinerary

23. Why does the man say, "there isn't a company policy about this"?
(A) To postpone an announcement
(B) To give the woman permission
(C) To offer an explanation
(D) To suggest a policy change

24. Why is the manager unavailable?
(A) She is speaking at a conference.
(B) She is training new employees.
(C) She is finishing a report.
(D) She is meeting some clients.

⑧ 시각 정보 연계 문제

출제공식
1 목록, 지도, 그래프 등 다양한 시각 정보와 대화 내용을 연계해서 풀어야 하는 문제로 매회 고정으로 3문항씩 출제된다.
2 질문의 키워드나 시각 정보 상에서 보기와 상응하는 부분이 대화 내에 단서로 등장할 가능성이 높다.

문제유형 Look at the graphic. What / Which / Where / Who / How ~?
시각 정보에 따르면, 무엇이 / 어떤 것이 / 어디에서 / 누가 / 어떻게 ~?

✏️ **핵심 전략 |** 질문의 키워드 및 보기에 상응하는 정보를 미리 확인한다. 🎧 P3_36

W Hello. I'm Yoon-Hee Min from Kent International Corporation. I'm one of the four people listed on your sign who are attending the trade show. You're going to drive us to our hotel right?

M Hi, Ms. Min. Yes, you're the first one to arrive. I just checked, and your colleagues' flight from Paris has been delayed for three hours.

W Oh, no. We'll miss the opening reception for the trade show if we wait for them.

M Don't worry. We'll only wait for your colleague coming from Glasgow. I'll drive the two of you to the hotel and then return for the others.

보기와 상응하는 정보인 출발 도시가 키워드로 등장
다음에 오는 사람: 글라스고에서 오는 동료

Names	Departure City
Monica Lavalle	Paris
Rosemarie Kunkel	Paris
Yoon-Hee Min	Seoul
Frank Martin	Glasgow

Q. Look at the graphic. Who will arrive next?
(A) Monica Lavalle
(B) Rosemarie Kunkel
(C) Yoon-Hee Min
(D) Frank Martin

단서 colleague coming from Glasgow
정답 (D) 프랭크 마틴

여 안녕하세요. 켄트 인터내셔널 사의 윤희 민입니다. 저는 댁의 팻말에 적혀 있는 대로 무역박람회에 참석하는 네 사람 중 한 명입니다. 저희를 호텔까지 태워 주시는 거죠?
남 안녕하세요, 민 씨. 맞습니다. 첫 번째로 도착하셨네요. 제가 방금 확인했는데, 동료 분들이 탄 파리발 항공기가 세 시간 지연되고 있습니다.
여 오, 이런. 우리가 그분들을 기다리다가는 무역박람회의 개막 축하연을 놓치고 말 거예요.
남 염려하지 마세요. **우리는 글래스고에서 오시는 동료 분만 기다릴 겁니다.** 제가 두 분부터 호텔로 모신 다음 다른 분들을 태우러 돌아올 겁니다.

시각 정보에 따르면, 다음에 누가 도착할 예정인가?
(A) 모니카 라발
(B) 로즈메리 쿤켈
(C) 윤희 민
(D) 프랭크 마틴

✏️ 시각 정보 유형별 전략

1. 목록(List)

가장 많이 출제되는 유형으로, 사람 / 제품 / 서비스 등의 목록, 일정표, 가격표, 주문서, 전화번호부 등이 나온다. 보기에 상응하는 정보를 키워드로 삼고 노려 들어야 한다.

Customer Service: 555-0146	
Services	**Extension #**
Registration	111
Facilities	121
Cleaning	131
Lost and Found	141

Look at the graphic. Which extension number will the man have to dial ?

(A) Ext. 111
(B) Ext. 121
(C) Ext. 131
(D) Ext. 141

남자가 전화할 내선 번호는?
각 번호에 상응하는 서비스(Registration, Facilities, Cleaning, Lost and Found) 노려 듣기

대화 내 단서

M Let me give our facilities department a call and see what they can do.
Facilities (시설과) → 121

2. 지도(Map)

마을, 도로 등의 지도, 회사 / 사업장의 평면도(floor plan), 대중교통 노선도, 공연장 등의 좌석 배치도(layout)가 출제된다. 위치나 방향 관련 빈출 표현들(next to, on the left, in front of, on the corner of 등)을 반드시 익혀 두어야 한다.

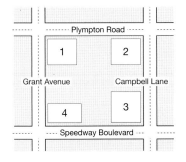

Look at the graphic. Where is the salon located?

(A) Building 1
(B) Building 2
(C) Building 3
(D Building 4

살롱이 위치한 곳은?
각 건물의 위치 확인 후 주변 도로명(Pylmpton, Campbell, Grant, Speedway) 노려 듣기

대화 내 단서

W We are right on the corner of Speedway Boulevard and Grant Avenue.
Speedway Boulevard와 Grant Avenue가 만나는 곳 → Building 4

3. 테이블(Table)

두 가지 이상의 대상을 서로 비교하는 차트나 테이블이 출제된다. 주어진 정보를 분석해야 하기 때문에 난이도가 약간 높을 수 있다. 두 대상이 나올 경우 차이점 / 변별점을 눈여겨보고, 여러 대상이 있을 경우 순위를 파악해 둔다.

Features	**Sabon Tacos**	**Julio's Tacos**
Free delivery	✓	✓
Loyalty program	✓	✓
Late-night service	✓	
Vegetarian menus		✓

Look at the graphic. Which feature does the woman suggest focusing on ?

(A) Free delivery
(B) Loyalty program
(C) Late-night service
(D) Vegetarian menus

여자가 중점을 두자고 제안하는 부문은?
두 업체간의 차이점 확인: Late-night service, Vegetarian menus 제공 여부

대화 내 단서

W Let's focus on promoting the feature that Julio's Tacos doesn't have.
Julio's Tacos에 없는 것 → Late-night service (심야 서비스)

4. 그래프(Graph) / 차트(Chart)

막대 그래프, 원 그래프, 선 그래프 등의 형태로 출제되며, 수익이나 매출, 시장 점유율, 선호도 등을 보여준다.
최고점이나 최저점, 순위, 또는 급락, 급등과 같이 특별히 눈에 띄는 변화 등을 미리 확인해 둔다.

Employee Preferences for New Cafeteria Food

- Cookies 17%
- Pudding 14%
- Carrot cake 41%
- Ice cream 28%

Look at the graphic. What item does the man recommend purchasing?
(A) Pudding
(B) Cookies
(C) Ice cream
(D) Carrot cake

남자가 구매하자고 추천하는 품목은?
퍼센트가 높은 순서대로 순위 파악하기

대화 내 단서

M In that case, we should order the second most popular item.

두 번째로 인기 있는 품목 = 28% → Ice cream

---

5. 쿠폰(Coupon) / 티켓(Ticket)

무료 쿠폰, 할인 쿠폰, 상품권 등이 출제되면 쿠폰의 종류, 혜택, 만료일 등 특이 사항을 파악한다.
시설 입장권, 대중교통 티켓, 주차권 등이 나오면 해당 시간, 좌석 종류, 혜택 대상 등을 살펴보아야 한다.

The Little Platter
COUPON
Half-priced appetizers
OR
Buy one main dish,
get another one free
OR
Free coffee with a dessert purchase

Look at the graphic. What special offer will the woman receive?
(A) A daily special
(B) A discounted appetizer
(C) A free main dish
(D) A free cup of coffee

여자가 받게 될 혜택은?
쿠폰에 나온 혜택 확인: 애피타이저 반값 할인,
메인 요리 1+1, 디저트 구매 시 커피 무료

대화 내 단서

W Yes, I'll take the chocolate cake. And I brought this coupon with me.

케이크(= dessert) 구매 시 커피 무료 → A free cup of coffee

---

6. 기타

교통상황 정보 안내판, 고장/수리 관련 안내문, 상품 정보 및 취급 가이드, 그림이 있는 광고/웹페이지 등 점점 더
다양한 시각 정보가 출제되고 있다. 문제의 보기로 제시되는 숫자, 요일, 이름 등과 연계되는 정보에 주목한다.

Modern Office Building
1230 Oak Blvd., Clarkston, PA 19075

$1,140,000
1,050 Square Meters
Built in 2008
Six-Story Office Building

Look at the graphic. Which number does the woman say is incorrect?
(A) 1230
(B) 19075
(C) 1,140,000
(D) 1,050

여자가 틀렸다고 하는 숫자는?
숫자 관련 정보(주소, 우편번호, 금액, 면적) 노려 듣기

대화 내 단서

W I was going to tell you that there's a typo in the listing I sent you. It's
actually nearly double the size.

매물 정보에 있는 오타: 크기(= 면적, Square Meters) → 1,050

LISTENING **PRACTICE**

🎧 P3_37 정답 및 해설 p. 147

대화를 들으면서 정답을 고르세요. 그리고 다시 들으면서 빈칸을 채우세요. (녹음은 두 번씩 들려줍니다.)

ITEM	PRICE
Phone case	$30
Monthly service plan	$50
Extended warranty	$100
Mobile phone	$200
TOTAL	**$380**

1. Look at the graphic. Which amount will be removed from the bill?

(A) $30 (B) $50
(C) $100 (D) $200

W Will that be all for today? Just the new phone and service upgrade?

M I just have one more question before I buy the phone. _____? I travel a lot for work, so I'm not always home when the bill comes.

W Yes, you can! You can _____ on our Web site. I also recommend _____ so you can view the status of your account at any time.

M OK, great... But... I think I _____. I don't think I really need it. Could you _____ _____?

W Of course.

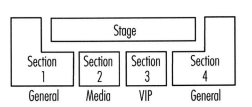

2. Look at the graphic. Where will the speakers sit?

(A) Section 1 (B) Section 2
(C) Section 3 (D) Section 4

W Hello, Kang-Min?

M Yaping? I just parked. I'm _____ now. Are you inside?

W Kang-Min, listen. Right before I left work, I told our editor we were seeing this show and she _____ it for the magazine. So our seats have been moved from the general area to a section _____, right _____.

M Really? Wow. Neither one of us usually _____.

W I know, but it'll be an interesting show to review.

Jerry's Department Store

Discount Coupon

$15 off clothing purchase of $50 or more

Expires May 8

100123456782010

3. Look at the graphic. Why is the coupon rejected?

(A) It has expired.
(B) It is for a different department.
(C) It must be approved by a manager.
(D) It is for purchases of at least $50.

W OK, sir. Your _____.

M Oh, wait—I have a discount coupon I want to use _____... I think I've got it here somewhere... Oh, here it is.

W OK—thanks... Hmm, it looks like the computer _____. Let me take a look ...

M Ah—I see the problem. Is it OK if I go back and _____ that I need?

W Certainly. I can keep these shirts here at the register for you if you'd like.

PART 3 | CHAPTER 01

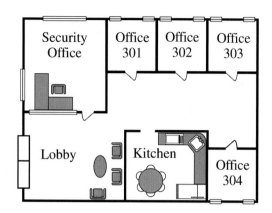

Minami Medical Group
Hours by Location

Creekside	6 A.M.–8 P.M.
Hillside	7 A.M.–5 P.M.
Linden	12 P.M.–6 P.M.
Storytown	1 P.M.–9 P.M.

1. Where do the speakers work?
(A) At a printing company
(B) At a hotel
(C) At a law firm
(D) At a bank

2. What must the woman do at eleven o'clock?
(A) Meet with her manager
(B) Have her picture taken
(C) Attend a team meeting
(D) Conduct a training session

3. Look at the graphic. What is the man's office number?
(A) 301
(B) 302
(C) 303
(D) 304

4. Why does the man say he needs an appointment?
(A) He recently moved.
(B) He started a new job.
(C) He is going on a trip.
(D) He is training for a sporting event.

5. Look at the graphic. Where will the man's appointment be?
(A) At Creekside
(B) At Hillside
(C) At Linden
(D) At Storytown

6. What does the woman tell the man to do before his appointment?
(A) Send his health records
(B) Fill out some documents
(C) Make a payment
(D) Confirm an appointment time

Item #	Date Checked Out	Date Due
232	October 5	October 7
117	October 6	October 7
105	October 8	October 9

7. What does the woman ask the man to do?
(A) Record a performance
(B) Save some seats
(C) Check the time of a meeting
(D) Arrange for transportation

8. Look at the graphic. When does the man plan to arrive at the concert hall?
(A) At 5:30 P.M.
(B) At 6:00 P.M.
(C) At 6:30 P.M.
(D) At 7:00 P.M.

9. What will the woman do next?
(A) Print a confirmation
(B) Send an e-mail
(C) Approve a purchase
(D) Request contact information

10. What did the business recently purchase?
(A) Some software
(B) Some trucks
(C) Office furniture
(D) Protective eyewear

11. What type of business do the speakers most likely work for?
(A) A laundry service
(B) A computer store
(C) A cleaning company
(D) A delivery service

12. Look at the graphic. When is the conversation taking place?
(A) On October 5
(B) On October 7
(C) On October 8
(D) On October 9

PART 3 | CHAPTER 01

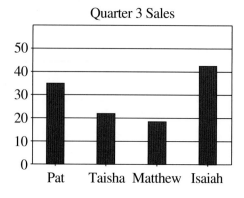

Quarter 3 Sales

13. What needs to be printed?
(A) Some promotional flyers
(B) Some area maps
(C) Some business cards
(D) Some garden layouts

14. Why is the man unable to pick up the order?
(A) He does not have a car.
(B) He has the day off.
(C) He does not feel well.
(D) He has a client meeting.

15. Look at the graphic. Which street name needs to be updated in the application?
(A) Wescott Avenue
(B) Holly Street
(C) Thompson Boulevard
(D) Meadow Lane

16. What is the conversation about?
(A) A job opening
(B) A product launch
(C) A salary increase
(D) A budget proposal

17. Look at the graphic. Which employee is the man most likely talking about?
(A) Pat
(B) Taisha
(C) Matthew
(D) Isaiah

18. What does the woman say she will do?
(A) File some applications
(B) Update a Web page
(C) Call a colleague
(D) Schedule a sales meeting

Departures	Gate	Time	Status
Atlanta	B1	16:30	Delayed
Chicago	A13	16:30	On time
Dallas	A9	16:45	Canceled
Philadelphia	C24	17:00	On time

Category	Number of Questions
Printing	5
Adding text	8
Changing size	2
Ruler	4

19. What type of event are the speakers traveling to?
- (A) An arts festival
- (B) A sports competition
- (C) A business conference
- (D) An awards ceremony

20. Why is the man staying just a short time?
- (A) He must return for a meeting.
- (B) He is about to go on holiday.
- (C) He has a limited budget.
- (D) He could not find a later flight.

21. Look at the graphic. What city are the speakers flying to?
- (A) Atlanta
- (B) Chicago
- (C) Dallas
- (D) Philadelphia

22. What happened last week?
- (A) A company moved to a different location.
- (B) The woman received a promotion.
- (C) A senior director retired.
- (D) The man designed a poster.

23. Look at the graphic. How many questions will the man respond to?
- (A) 5
- (B) 8
- (C) 2
- (D) 4

24. Why will the woman post a notice?
- (A) To tell users that a Web site will be down
- (B) To invite colleagues to a party
- (C) To advertise a vacant position
- (D) To explain a new company policy

대화 내용별 전략

❾ 일반 업무 및 인사

출제공식
1 일반적인 업무 논의, 작업 일정/진행 상황 점검, 업무 협조 요청 등의 내용이 주로 출제된다.
2 직원 채용, 면접, 승진, 전근, 퇴직 등의 인사 관련 내용도 자주 출제된다.

✏️ 대화 흐름 파악하기 | 업무 언급 → 도움 요청 → 수락 후 피드백   🎧 P3_39

M Fatima, ① I'm ready to add the changes to the employee directory on our company Web site. Would you mind checking it over before I upload them?	① 주제: 회사 웹사이트의 직원 명부 수정
W Hmm, it looks good so far. But—uh—wait, ② there's a problem here. You've misspelled the name of the vice president. Actually, her name should only have one "L" at the end.	② 문제점: 여자가 검수 도중 철자 오류 발견
M Oh, ③ I can't believe I didn't see that earlier! Thanks for catching it.	③ 여자의 의도: 남자가 자책한 후 감사를 표하자 여자가 격려
W It's easy to miss. The important thing is that we have the correct information for visitors to our Web site.	

주제	1. What are the speakers mainly talking about ? 화자들이 주로 이야기하는 것은?	Updating a company's Web site 회사 웹사이트 업데이트
문제점	2. What problem does the **woman** notice? 여자가 알아차린 문제점은?	A name is spelled incorrectly. 이름이 부정확하게 표기되었다.
의도 파악	3. Why does the **woman** say, "It's easy to miss" ? 여자가 "놓치기 쉬운 거잖아요"라고 말하는 이유는?	To express her understanding 이해하는 마음을 표현하려고

남   파티마, **회사 웹사이트의 직원 명부에 변동사항을 추가할 준비가 됐어요.** 업로드하기 전에 살펴봐 주겠어요?
여   음, 현재까지는 괜찮아 보여요. 그런데, 어, 잠깐만요. **여기에 문제가 있네요. 부사장님 성함을 잘못 표기했어요.** 실은 이름 끝부분에 L자가 하나만 있어야 해요.
남   이런, **내가 그걸 일찌감치 알아채지 못했군요! 실수를 잡아줘서 고마워요.**
여   **놓치기 쉬운 거잖아요.** 중요한 건 우리 웹사이트를 방문하는 사람들에게 정확한 정보를 제공하는 일이죠.

일반 업무 및 인사 빈출 상황 　　　　　　　　　　　　　　　　　　　🎧 P3_40

진행 상황 점검	How are the preparations going[coming along] for the two-day leadership workshop? 이틀간 열리는 리더십 워크숍 준비는 어떻게 되어가고 있나요?
업무 협조 요청	Do you have time to take a look at the draft of the new agreement? 신규 계약서 초안을 봐주실 시간이 있으실까요?
업무 지시	I'd like you to make a short presentation on our corporate culture at the orientation. 오리엔테이션에서 우리 기업 문화에 관해 간략한 발표를 해주었으면 해요.
일정 변경	Let's move up the application deadline so that we have enough time to hold interviews. 지원 마감일을 앞당겨서 면접 볼 시간이 충분히 있게끔 합시다.
면접	We reviewed your application, and you seem to be well qualified for the photo editor position. 귀하의 지원서를 검토했는데, 사진 편집 직책에 적합한 것으로 보입니다.
승진 제안	We've been impressed with your work, so we'd like to offer you the project manager position. 당신의 업무 능력에 깊은 인상을 받아서, 프로젝트 매니저 자리를 제안하고 싶습니다.
인력 충원	Since our business is growing so fast, it might be a good idea to hire more workers. 우리 회사가 아주 빠르게 성장하고 있으니 추가 인력을 고용하는 것이 좋겠습니다.
전근/은퇴 소식	Noah's transferring to Paris at the end of the month—we have to find someone to replace him. 노아가 이번 달 말에 파리로 전근을 갑니다. 그를 대체할 사람을 찾아야 해요.

PART 3 | CHAPTER 02

ETS CHECK-UP 　　　　　　　　　　　　　　　　　🎧 P3_41 정답 및 해설 p.155

1. What is the purpose of the conversation?
(A) To discuss an employment opportunity
(B) To propose a department relocation
(C) To revise an itinerary
(D) To introduce a new colleague

2. What does the man ask about?
(A) The location of a company headquarters
(B) The process for reimbursement
(C) The requirement to move overseas
(D) The start date of a position

3. What does the man say he needs to do?
(A) Talk to his manager
(B) Renew a passport
(C) Open a bank account
(D) Purchase an airplane ticket

회의 / 일정 / 회계

prepare for the meeting 회의 준비를 하다
attend a conference (대)회의에 참석하다
set up a conference call 전화 회의를 열다
host a videoconference 화상회의를 열다
add A to the agenda 의제에 A를 추가하다
come up with ideas 아이디어를 내놓다
cancel[call off] a meeting 회의를 취소하다
available / unavailable 시간이 되는 / 되지 않는
have a scheduling conflict 일정이 겹치다
reschedule the appointment 예약 일정을 조정하다
arrange a time to**부정사** ~할 일정을 잡다
postpone[put off] a project 프로젝트를 연기하다
ahead of / behind schedule 일정보다 앞서다 / 뒤처지다

meet a deadline 마감일을 맞추다
move up the deadline 마감일을 당기다
ask for a deadline extension 마감일 연장을 요청하다
audit a business 사업체 회계를 감사하다
review[look over] some sales figures 매출액을 검토하다
request a price estimate[quote] 가격 견적서를 요청하다
submit a proposal 제안서를 제출하다
revise the budget report 예산 보고서를 수정하다
within the budget 예산 범위 내의
have a limited budget 예산이 한정되다
exceed the quarterly budget 분기 예산을 초과하다
restrict one's spending 지출을 제한하다
cut[reduce] expenses 비용을 삭감하다

생산 / 마케팅 / 계약

raw materials 원료, 원자재
workforce 노동자, 노동력
assembly line 조립 라인
shut down production 생산을 중단하다
product release date 제품 출시일
be in high demand 수요가 높다
meet[satisfy] demand 수요를 맞추다
increase[improve] productivity 생산성을 제고하다
check on the progress of ~의 진행 상황을 점검하다
market a product 제품을 시장에 내놓다, 광고하다
promote sales 판촉하다
selling point 판매에 유리한 장점
put an advertisement 광고를 내다

plan a publicity campaign 홍보 캠페인을 기획하다
edit a commercial 광고를 수정하다
feedback from clients 고객의 피드백
customer satisfaction 고객 만족도
conduct market research 시장 조사를 하다
compile the answers to a survey 설문 답변을 집계하다
find a new supplier[vendor] 새로운 납품업체를 구하다
terms and conditions of the contract 계약 조건
win / renew a contract 계약을 따내다 / 갱신하다
reach an agreement 합의에 이르다
negotiate a deal 계약을 협상하다
valid 유효한 (= good)
M&A 합병 및 인수 (= mergers and acquisitions)

고용 및 인사 / 업무 평가

hire 고용하다 (= employ, recruit)
job opening 일자리 공석 (= job vacancy)
job description 직무기술서
entail 수반하다 (= involve, include)
responsibilities 업무, 임무 (= duties)
employee benefits 직원 혜택, 복리후생
flexible working hours 탄력근무제
apply for a position 일자리에 지원하다
qualified applicants[candidates] 자격을 갖춘 지원자들
meet the requirements 자격 요건을 충족시키다
lack experience 경험이 부족하다
fill out an application form 지원서를 작성하다
résumé and cover letter 이력서와 자기소개서

qualifications 자격(증)
expertise 전문성, 전문지식
reference 추천서 (= recommendation letter), 추천인
have a lot of connections 인맥이 넓다
train new employees 신입직원을 교육시키다
performance evaluation[appraisal, review]
업무 평가, 인사 고과
transfer 전근 보내다 (= reassign), 전근가다
get[receive] a promotion 승진하다
be promoted to + **직책** ~로 승진하다
raise 급여 인상
retire 퇴직하다, 은퇴하다
career move 전직, 직업 전환

LISTENING **PRACTICE**

P3_43 정답 및 해설 p. 156

대화를 들으면서 정답을 고르세요. 그리고 다시 들으면서 빈칸을 채우세요. (녹음은 두 번씩 들려줍니다.)

1. Why is the company looking for a new employee?

(A) They are opening another office.
(B) An employee is retiring.

2. What would the man like Mary to do?

(A) Advertise a job opening
(B) Train a new staff member

M	You know, Mary's _____, so we're going to have to hire a new office assistant fairly quickly. _____ yet?
W	Yes. In fact, I've already received a lot of résumés, and _____.
M	That's great. If we can get someone before Mary leaves, _____.

3. What does the woman imply when she says, "These are important clients"?

(A) She is glad to be assigned a project.
(B) The man should attend a meeting.

4. What does the woman say the company will do?

(A) Reschedule a meeting
(B) Pay for an expense

W	Ramon, I'll see you _____, right?
M	Well, I was hoping to return my rental car today, so _____.
W	These are important clients. Don't worry about returning the car today. The company will _____—you were using it for company business, after all.
M	OK, great. I'd better _____.

5. Where do the speakers most likely work?

(A) At a newspaper office
(B) At a local school

6. When does the man have to complete an assignment?

(A) On Thursday
(B) On Friday

W	Scott, _____of our newspaper have been excellent. Even though you're relatively new here, I'd like you to _____ on Thursday.
M	That's the one about _____, right? I heard the mayor's going to make an important announcement. When's the deadline for the article?
W	In order to make the Sunday edition, you'll have to _____. Oh, and I'm going to send one of our staff photographers to take some pictures to go with your piece.

PART 3 | CHAPTER 02

1. What is the woman preparing to do?
   (A) Visit a client
   (B) Give a presentation
   (C) Hire a new department head
   (D) Revise a pricing policy

2. Why is the woman's work taking extra time to finish?
   (A) Some résumés have not been received.
   (B) A computer is not working.
   (C) A colleague is on vacation.
   (D) Some data are incorrect.

3. What does the man say he will do?
   (A) Reschedule a meeting
   (B) Contact department managers
   (C) Add another person to a project
   (D) Prepare a job description

4. What did the man do recently?
   (A) He hired an assistant.
   (B) He won a contract.
   (C) He completed a certification.
   (D) He conducted some research.

5. What does the woman encourage the man to consider?
   (A) Attending a conference
   (B) Organizing a training
   (C) Applying for a job
   (D) Reviewing a policy

6. What will the woman do next week?
   (A) Start a new project
   (B) Move to another office
   (C) Go on vacation
   (D) Appear on television

7. What is the conversation mainly about?
   (A) Training new staff
   (B) Filming an advertisement
   (C) Publishing an article
   (D) Attending a play

8. Why does the woman suggest July 25 ?
   (A) Some employees will be available.
   (B) A national holiday will be celebrated.
   (C) A facility will stay open late.
   (D) A famous author will be visiting.

9. What does the man say he wants to do on July 25 ?
   (A) Go on a tour
   (B) Visit some local shops
   (C) Order some refreshments
   (D) Conduct some interviews

10. What problem does the woman mention?
    (A) A research error was made.
    (B) Some project deadlines have passed.
    (C) A department lacks funding.
    (D) Some staff members are inexperienced.

11. What does the woman mean when she says, "Now that's an idea"?
    (A) She would like some more advice.
    (B) The man has made a useful suggestion.
    (C) The current plan is too complex.
    (D) A change is happening at the right time.

12. What will the speakers most likely do next?
    (A) Discuss a proposal
    (B) Offer a promotion
    (C) Conduct an interview
    (D) Read a report

13. What industry do the speakers most likely work in?
(A) Tourism
(B) Fashion
(C) Advertising
(D) Publishing

14. What does the woman say about a new product?
(A) It is durable.
(B) It is inexpensive.
(C) It is selling well.
(D) It is being redesigned.

15. What does the man suggest?
(A) Initiating product testing
(B) Creating a brochure
(C) Arranging a press conference
(D) Promoting a special feature

16. Where do the interviewers most likely work?
(A) At an electronics store
(B) At an employment agency
(C) At a television station
(D) At a movie theater

17. What job requirement do the speakers discuss?
(A) Being professionally certified
(B) Owning the proper equipment
(C) Having management experience
(D) Having a flexible schedule

18. What does the man agree to do next?
(A) Show a video
(B) Provide references
(C) Tour a facility
(D) Meet a supervisor

How Clients Found Us

19. Why is the woman calling the man?
(A) To thank him for doing some work
(B) To point out a mistake in a document
(C) To suggest a new marketing strategy
(D) To ask for details about some feedback

20. Look at the graphic. Which category does the woman mention?
(A) Offline Advertisement
(B) Referral from previous customer
(C) Online advertisement
(D) Other

21. What does the man say he will do?
(A) Double-check some data
(B) Contact more clients
(C) Revise part of a questionnaire
(D) Share a report with other coworkers

PART 3 | CHAPTER 02

1 대규모 회의, 회사의 교육 및 기념 행사 등의 준비나 참석 관련 내용이 자주 출제된다.
2 각종 비품·기기의 주문 / 배송, 기기 및 시스템 설치 / 수리, 시설 보수 관련 내용이 주로 출제된다.

✎ 대화 흐름 파악하기 | 행사를 위한 주문 지시 → 제안 및 논의 → 추가 요청 🎧 P3_45

W ① Jason, I need you to place a catering order for Insook's retirement party. I'd like to offer our staff some fresh and healthy food options.	① 준비하는 것: 동료의 은퇴 기념 파티
M Certainly. The Crestwood Café would be a great choice. ② They offer items made from local farm ingredients, so we'd be supporting farmers in our area. Should I order from there?	② 출장요리 업체(Crestwood Café) 추천: 지역 농장 식재료 사용
W Yes, that sounds promising. We'll need a variety of snacks and beverages for 30 people. ③ Please e-mail me your choices from their menu this afternoon so I can approve them.	③ 요청 사항: 메뉴 선택 후 이메일로 발송

세부 정보	**1.** What are the speakers preparing for? 화자들이 준비하고 있는 것은?	A retirement party 은퇴 기념 파티
세부 언급	**2.** What does the **man** say about the Crestwood Café? 남자가 크레스트우드 카페에 관해 한 말은?	It uses ingredients from local farms. 지역 농장에서 나는 식재료를 쓴다.
요청 사항	**3.** What does the **woman** ask the man to send? 여자가 남자에게 보내달라고 요청한 것은?	Some menu selections 선택한 메뉴

여 제이슨, 인숙의 **퇴직 기념 파티에 출장 요리를 주문해 주었으면** 해요. 직원들이 신선하고 건강에 좋은 음식을 골라 먹을 수 있게 하고 싶거든요.
남 알았습니다. 크레스트우드 카페가 훌륭한 선택일 거예요. **지역 농장에서 난 식재료로 만든 음식을 제공하니까 우리가 지역 농부들을 지원하게 되는 셈이죠.** 그곳에서 주문할까요?
여 네, 그것 괜찮겠네요. 다양한 간식과 음료 30인분이 필요할 거예요. **메뉴에서 당신이 고른 음식들을 승인할 수 있게 오늘 오후에 제게 이메일로 보내주세요.**

✏️ 회사 내·외부 행사 및 사무기기·시설 빈출 상황　🎧 P3_46

행사 준비	Is everything ready for tomorrow's training seminar for new employees? 내일 진행될 신입 사원 교육 세미나 준비가 다 되었나요?
행사 참여	We are new to this construction trade show. Where's the technical support desk? 저희는 이 건축 박람회에 처음인데요. 기술 지원 데스크가 어디에 있나요?
행사 등록	Hello, I'm calling about the annual engineering conference. Is it possible to register by phone? 안녕하세요, 연례 공학 학회 관련해서 전화드려요. 전화로 등록하는 게 가능한가요?
정보 요청	I was wondering if you could give me more details about the technology expo. 기술 박람회에 대해 더 자세한 정보를 주실 수 있을지 궁금합니다.
시스템 변경	Did you hear that we'll be switching to new scheduling software next month? 다음 달부터 새로운 일정 관리 소프트웨어로 교체하게 될 거라는 소식 들었어요?
시스템 오류	I've been having trouble accessing our client database all morning. 아침 내내 우리 고객 데이터 베이스에 접속하는 데 문제를 겪고 있어요.
기기 고장	I've just noticed that one of the conveyor belts is not working properly. 컨베이어 벨트 중 하나가 제대로 작동하지 않는다는 걸 조금 전에 발견했습니다.
기기·시설 수리	I'll have a repair person come by your office and check it out this afternoon. 오늘 오후에 당신의 사무실에 수리 기사를 보내 그것을 확인해 보라고 할게요.

PART 3 | CHAPTER 02

ETS CHECK-UP　🎧 P3_47 정답 및 해설 p. 163

1. What are the speakers discussing?

(A) A piece of equipment
(B) A work schedule
(C) A customer complaint
(D) A power failure

2. What has the woman noticed?

(A) An item was misplaced.
(B) An order was incomplete.
(C) A colleague is late.
(D) A warning light is on.

3. What does the woman ask the man to do?

(A) Contact a manufacturer
(B) Provide an updated recipe
(C) Turn off a machine
(D) Fill a customer's order

🎧 P3_48

회사 내·외부 행사

company retreat 회사 야유회	**accommodate** 수용하다
shareholders' meeting 주주총회	**catering order** 출장요리 주문
opening ceremony 개회식	**provide refreshments** 다과를 제공하다
corporate event 기업 행사	**participant** 참석자 (= attendee)
conference/convention 대회의	**turnout** 참석자 수
fundraiser 자금 모금 행사	**confirm participation[attendance]** 참석을 확인하다
career[job] fair 취업 박람회	**register for** ~에 등록하다 (= enroll in, sign up for)
trade show 무역박람회	**online registration** 온라인 등록
retirement party 은퇴 기념 파티	**photo identification** 사진이 부착된 신분증
reception 축하[환영] 연회	**complete a form** 양식을 작성하다
training session 교육 시간	**submit the form electronically** 양식을 온라인으로 제출하다
training materials 교육 자료	**keynote speaker** 기조 연사
refresher course 재교육 과정	**make[give, deliver] a presentation** 발표하다
upcoming[future] events 향후 행사	**distribute handouts** 유인물을 나누어 주다
celebrate 기념하다, 축하하다 (= mark)	**rearrange chairs** 의자를 재배치하다
organize an event 행사를 준비[조직]하다	**limited seating** 한정된 좌석
conference organizer[planner] 회의 기획자	**stop by a booth** 부스에 들르다
post[put up] a notice 공지를 게시하다	**booth assignment** 부스 자리 지정
book the venue 행사장을 예약하다	**exhibit area** 전시 구역
reserve a banquet hall 연회장을 예약하다	**watch a product demonstration** 제품 시연을 보다

사무기기·시설

place an order 주문하다	**inefficient system** 비효율적인 시스템
rush the order 주문을 빨리 처리하다	**give an error message** 오류 메시지가 뜨다
purchase office supplies 사무용품을 구매하다	**keep crashing** 계속 오류가 나다
run out of supplies 비품이 다 떨어지다	**warning light** 경고등
stockroom 비품 저장실	**control panel** 제어판
take inventory 재고 조사를 하다	**technical support** 기술지원(부)
computer components 컴퓨터 부품	**figure out** 알아내다, 처리하다
replacement parts 교체 부품	**pinpoint the problem** 문제를 정확히 짚어내다
arrive assembled 조립된 채 오다	**repair** 수리하다 (= fix)
set up[install] the equipment 장비를 설치하다	**inspect a facility** 시설을 점검하다
instruction manual[booklet] 사용설명서	**restart a machine** 기계를 다시 시작하게 하다
express delivery 빠른 우편, 속달	**maintenance department** 수리 부서
delayed shipment 지연된 배송품	**work crew** 작업반
shipping cost 배송비	**mechanic/technician** 수리공/기술자
in good condition 좋은 상태로	**building renovation** 건물 개조
damaged items 손상된 물품	**soundproofed** 방음장치가 되어 있는
out of order 고장 난 (= broken, malfunctioning)	**leak** (물 등이) 새다; 새는 부분
out-of-date 구식의, 낡은	**crack** 금이 간 곳
defective equipment 결함 있는 장비	**billing problem** 대금 청구 문제
warranty period 보증 기간	**overcharge** 과다 청구하다, 바가지를 씌우다

LISTENING **PRACTICE**

P3_49 정답 및 해설 p.164

대화를 들으면서 정답을 고르세요. 그리고 다시 들으면서 빈칸을 채우세요. (녹음은 두 번씩 들려줍니다.)

1. What is the problem with the order?

(A) The paper is the wrong size.

(B) A telephone number is incorrect.

2. According to the woman, what will take place this weekend?

(A) A cooking demonstration

(B) An opening celebration

W Hi, this is Meridith Lansky calling about _____. They arrived in the mail today, and, unfortunately, _____.

M I'm sorry to hear that, Ms. Lansky. We'll print _____, free of charge. They should be ready for you by the beginning of next week.

W Actually, we're having _____. Could you please rush the order so I get them by Friday?

---

3. What are the speakers discussing?

(A) An employee manual

(B) Work space arrangements

4. What does the woman suggest?

(A) Recruiting additional applicants

(B) Using a conference room

W Have you seen the e-mail saying that we'll have twenty new summer interns starting next week? Will we have _____?

M Hmmm... the computers are already here, but the desks and chairs—I'm not sure when they'll arrive. We'll have to find a _____.

W Well, the interns will be in training for most of the first week. _____ until their furniture comes in.

---

5. What is the man having trouble doing?

(A) Locating a schedule

(B) Changing a password

6. What does the man ask the woman to do?

(A) Install a software program

(B) Contact technical support

M Martina, _____ — the calendar software keeps on giving me an error message. I think I'm meeting Ms. Lee at one o'clock, right?

W Actually, she just called a while ago and asked if you could come at one thirty instead.

M Good – pushing it back to one thirty gives me more time to get ready. While _____, would you mind _____? I'd like to make sure my calendar works again soon!

PART 3 | CHAPTER 02

1. What department does the man probably work in?
   (A) Human Resources
   (B) Accounting
   (C) Technical Support
   (D) Public Relations

2. What does the man ask the woman to do?
   (A) Attend a meeting
   (B) Write a report
   (C) Check a manual
   (D) Restart a computer

3. What does the man say he can do?
   (A) Provide a reference
   (B) Visit the woman's office
   (C) Approve a request
   (D) Select a project team

4. What are the speakers going to celebrate?
   (A) A sales milestone
   (B) A business merger
   (C) A company anniversary
   (D) A product launch

5. What does the man mean when he says, "It's a big cake"?
   (A) The price of the cake is reasonable.
   (B) There will be enough cake for partygoers.
   (C) The cake would not fit in an office appliance.
   (D) Transporting the cake will require special arrangements.

6. What does the man offer to do next?
   (A) Make an announcement
   (B) Put up decorations
   (C) Change an order
   (D) Visit a bakery

7. What problem are the speakers discussing?
   (A) A power failure
   (B) A damaged wall
   (C) A broken appliance
   (D) A delayed delivery

8. What does the woman want to avoid?
   (A) Adjusting her store's hours
   (B) Relocating her business
   (C) Purchasing some equipment
   (D) Ruining some items

9. What does the woman agree to do?
   (A) Call back later
   (B) Give away some merchandise
   (C) Pay more for a service
   (D) Provide customer feedback

10. What type of event is being held?
    (A) A press release
    (B) A training session
    (C) A job interview
    (D) A client dinner

11. Why is Jack Krugman concerned?
    (A) He forgot his photo identification.
    (B) He has a scheduling conflict.
    (C) He did not register in advance.
    (D) He did not request a laptop.

12. What does the woman say is at the back of the room?
    (A) A variety of refreshments
    (B) Some audio visual equipment
    (C) Some training manuals
    (D) A program for the event

13. What type of software are the speakers discussing?
(A) Project management
(B) Accounting
(C) Desktop publishing
(D) Data protection

14. Why is the man dissatisfied with the software?
(A) It requires a lot of training.
(B) It lacks security features.
(C) It is unreliable.
(D) It is expensive.

15. What will happen on Thursday?
(A) Some demonstrations will be offered.
(B) Some sales figures will be available.
(C) A technician will make a visit.
(D) An office will close early.

16. What problem are the speakers mainly discussing?
(A) A flight has been canceled.
(B) Tickets are sold out.
(C) A credit card has expired.
(D) Hotel rooms are unavailable.

17. What solution does the man suggest?
(A) Reserving rooms in another area
(B) Postponing a business trip
(C) Calling a travel agent
(D) Taking public transportation

18. What is the woman worried about?
(A) Arriving late for a conference
(B) Exceeding a budget
(C) Missing a connecting flight
(D) Losing some documents

Table of Contents

19. Where does the conversation most likely take place?
(A) In a cafeteria
(B) In a computer lab
(C) In a copy room
(D) In a conference room

20. Look at the graphic. Which page does the woman turn to?
(A) Page 1
(B) Page 16
(C) Page 25
(D) Page 32

21. What does the man say he will do next?
(A) Go to the store
(B) Rearrange some chairs
(C) Find a coworker
(D) Take some measurements

PART 3 | CHAPTER 02

⑪ 쇼핑/교통/여행

출제공식
1 다양한 상품 및 서비스 구매, 문의, 교환/환불, 결제, 할인, 구매 혜택 등의 내용이 출제된다.
2 대중교통 이용, 교통 체증, 도로 공사, 길이나 주차 안내 등의 내용이 출제된다.
3 여행 계획 및 준비, 휴가 후 업무 복귀, 출장, 숙소/관광 문의 등의 내용이 출제된다.

✎ 대화 흐름 파악하기 | 구매하고 싶은 상품 문의 → 특징·장점이나 구매 혜택 설명　🎧 P3_51

W Excuse me, ① I like the twelve-piece cookware set on display in the store window. Where can I find it?	① 여자가 찾고 있는 것: 조리 기구 세트
M It's this way, let me show you. You know, we're having a promotion this week. ② If you spend more than one hundred dollars at one time, we'll give you a fifteen percent discount.	② 할인 받는 방법: 100달러 이상 구매
W Oh, that sounds great! I'd like to buy the entire set of pots and pans, but I came here by bus today so I won't be able to carry them home.	
M That's not a problem. ③ We can ship it to your house free of charge.	③ 이용 가능한 서비스: 집까지 무료 배송

세부 정보	**1.** What is the **woman** looking for ? 여자가 찾고 있는 것은?	Appliances 가전제품
세부 정보	**2.** What must the **woman** do to receive a discount ? 여자가 할인을 받으려면 해야 하는 일은?	Spend a certain amount 일정 금액 소비하기
세부 정보	**3.** According to the **man**, what service is available ? 남자에 따르면, 이용 가능한 서비스는?	Home delivery 가정 배달

여 실례합니다. **가게 쇼윈도에 진열된 12종 조리 기구 세트가 마음에 드는데요.** 어디서 찾을 수 있죠?
남 이쪽입니다. 안내해 드릴게요. 참고로, 이번 주에 판촉행사가 진행 중입니다. **한번에 100달러 이상 쓰시면 15퍼센트 할인을 해드려요.**
여 와, 잘 됐네요! 냄비랑 팬 전체 세트를 사고 싶거든요. 그런데 오늘 제가 여기에 버스로 와서 집까지 들고 갈 수가 없을 것 같아요.
남 그건 문제가 안됩니다. **저희가 무료로 댁까지 배송해 드릴 수 있어요.**

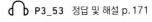

✎ 쇼핑 / 교통 / 여행 빈출 상황   🎧 P3_52

구입 의사	I'm looking for some high-quality filing cabinets for my new office. 제 새로운 사무실을 위한 고품질 서류 보관함을 찾고 있는데요.
교환 / 반품	I purchased these gloves here yesterday, but I'd like to exchange them for a different pair. 어제 여기서 이 장갑을 샀는데요, 다른 것으로 교환하고 싶습니다.
구매 혜택	We're having a promotional event this week. If you buy any of our cakes, you'll get a free drink. 이번 주에 특별 판촉 행사를 진행 중이에요. 저희 케이크 중 아무거나 사시면, 무료 음료 한 잔을 받게 되십니다.
길 안내 요청	Could you tell me how to get to Wolfburg Square from this hotel? 이 호텔에서 울프버그 광장까지 가는 길을 설명해 주시겠어요?
교통편 연착	My flight from London arrived late, so I missed my connection to Seoul. 영국에서 출발한 항공편이 늦게 도착해서, 서울로 가는 연결편을 놓쳤어요.
교통 체증	They're doing some repairs to the main road, so traffic is really slow. 간선 도로에 보수 작업을 하고 있어서 통행이 굉장히 더디네요.
호텔 이용	Hello, I'm staying in room 429, and I'd like to extend my stay for another night. 안녕하세요, 429호실에 머물고 있는데요. 숙박을 하룻밤 연장하고 싶습니다.
관광 문의	Do you have any suggestions about what to do and where to go in the city? 도시에서 무얼 하고 어디에 가는 게 좋을 지 추천해 주실만한 곳이 있나요?

PART 3 | CHAPTER 02

ETS CHECK-UP   🎧 P3_53   정답 및 해설 p.171

1. Where does the conversation most likely take place?

(A) At an airport
(B) At a travel agency
(C) At an office building
(D) At a hotel

2. What does the woman say she will do this afternoon?

(A) Visit an art gallery
(B) Meet a friend
(C) Change a reservation
(D) Purchase a gift

3. What does the woman want to keep?

(A) A map
(B) A catalog
(C) A ticket
(D) A calendar

쇼핑

retailer 소매상 ↔ **wholesaler** 도매상
business hours 영업 시간
look for ~를 찾다
carry 판매하다, 취급하다
in stock 재고가 있는 ↔ **out of stock** 품절된
clearance (sale) 재고 정리 (세일)
have a promotion 판촉 행사를 하다
receive a discount 할인을 받다
be under warranty 보증 기간 내에 있는
valid 유효한 ↔ **expired** 만료된
come with (제품에) ~가 함께 오다, 딸려오다
come in a variety of colors 다양한 색깔로 나오다
measurement 치수 (= dimension)

on display 진열되어 있는
environmentally[eco] friendly material 친환경 자재
locally made[produced] 현지에서 생산된
make a purchase 구매하다
make a payment 대금을 지불하다
affordable (가격이) 알맞은, 저렴한
free of charge 무료로 (= for free, at no extra charge)
original receipt 원본 영수증
return policy 반품 정책
issue a refund 환불해 주다
exchange A for B A를 B로 교환하다
inquire about a product 제품에 대해 문의하다
tracking number 배송 추적 번호

교통

public transportation 대중교통
express train 급행 기차
one-way[round] trip 편도[왕복] 여행
direct flight 직행 항공편
airfare 항공 요금
aisle[window] seat 통로[창가] 좌석
connection 연결 교통편
completely booked 예약이 꽉 찬 (= booked solid)
arrive on time 제시간에 도착하다
delay 지연, 지체; 지체 시키다
miss one's flight 비행기를 놓치다
behind schedule 예정보다 늦게
be running late 늦어지고 있다

departure 출발 ↔ **arrival** 도착
display board (전광) 게시판
timetable 시간표
provide directions 길 안내를 제공하다
give somebody a ride[lift] ~를 태워 주다
pick somebody up ~를 태우러 가다
at the last minute 막바지에, 최후의 순간에
roadwork 도로 공사
heavy traffic 교통 체증 (= traffic congestion)
have a flat tire 타이어에 바람이 빠지다
parking permit 주차 허가증
waive the parking fee 주차비를 면제하다
jet lag 시차증(장거리 비행 후 시차로 인한 피로감)

여행

leave 휴가; 떠나다
time off 휴가
take a day off 하루 쉬다
take a trip 여행 가다
go on holiday 휴가 가다
take a guided tour 가이드가 딸린 견학[여행]을 하다
travel agency[agent] 여행사 / 여행사 직원
processing fee 처리 수수료
itinerary 일정표
sightseeing 관광
destination 목적지
accommodations 숙박시설
apply for a visa 비자를 신청하다

book[reserve] a hotel room 호텔 방을 예약하다
booking confirmation 예약 확인
during one's stay / journey 머무는 동안 / 이동하는 동안
recommendation 추천사항
popular spot 인기있는 장소
tourist attraction 관광 명소
major landmarks 주요 지형지물
guidebook 안내 책자
souvenir shop 기념품 가게
get around (여기 저기) 돌아다니다
inclement[bad] weather 궂은 날씨, 악천후
travel expenses 여행 경비
travel reimbursement 출장 경비 환급

LISTENING **PRACTICE**

ᵈ ᵇ P3_55 정답 및 해설 p.171

대화를 들으면서 정답을 고르세요. 그리고 다시 들으면서 빈칸을 채우세요. (녹음은 두 번씩 들려줍니다.)

1. What does the man say will happen in five minutes?

(A) A press conference will start.
(B) A tour will begin.

2. What problem does the woman mention?

(A) She has limited time.
(B) She does not have cash.

W Excuse me. You work here at the national park, right? _____ and I'd like to learn more about the plants and animals here.

M Well, the best way to learn about our park is _____. There's one that starts in five minutes. It runs for about an hour and a half—_____?

W Thanks, but _____. I only have an hour before I have to catch the bus back into town. Are there _____?

M Yes, we have some excellent guidebooks in our gift shop. It's right downstairs.

3. Where are the speakers?

(A) In a coffee shop
(B) In an appliance store

4. Why does the woman say, "let me take a look around a bit first"?

(A) She would like to buy more merchandise.
(B) She is uncertain about a purchase.

W Hi, I'm wondering if you _____—you know, the one that makes the small single-serving cups of coffee.

M We sure do. It's just one hundred and nine dollars, and it comes with a free starter pack of coffee—enough for sixteen cups. We're _____ that offers this. _____ _____.

W Well, let me take a look around a bit first. Thanks.

5. What does the woman say she has done?

(A) Checked a schedule
(B) Prepared a presentation

6. Why is the man pleased?

(A) Tickets are still available.
(B) He expects to arrive on time.

M Excuse me, are you waiting for the 9:15 train to Linton? I'm a bit late, but I really hope I didn't miss it.

W No, you haven't missed it. When it didn't come on time, _____. But the ticket agent said all the trains on this line are _____ this morning.

M Oh, good. _____, then. I have to teach a class at the university. My students are giving presentations today, and I don't want to keep them waiting.

1. What did the man do on his holiday?
   (A) He shopped.
   (B) He swam.
   (C) He hiked.
   (D) He cycled.

2. What does the man say about the place he visited?
   (A) It was crowded.
   (B) It was expensive.
   (C) It was boring.
   (D) It was far away.

3. According to the woman, what did the company do recently?
   (A) They changed their business hours.
   (B) They completed a project.
   (C) They got a new client.
   (D) They opened a branch office.

4. What is the man interested in purchasing?
   (A) Computer software
   (B) Office furniture
   (C) Dental equipment
   (D) Advertising space

5. Why does the woman direct the man to a Web site?
   (A) To write a customer review
   (B) To apply for a store credit card
   (C) To try a new viewing feature
   (D) To register a serial number

6. What additional information does the man ask for?
   (A) Available colors
   (B) A delivery date
   (C) Warranty terms
   (D) Product measurements

7. What is the woman's problem?
   (A) She has missed her connecting flight.
   (B) She cannot print her boarding pass.
   (C) Her flight has been canceled.
   (D) Her luggage is missing.

8. What does the man say about Flight 5 ?
   (A) It is now boarding.
   (B) It is already full.
   (C) It is delayed for fueling.
   (D) It offers free refreshments.

9. What does the man tell the woman to do at Gate E9 ?
   (A) Present her ticket
   (B) Show her passport
   (C) Ask for a voucher
   (D) Fill out a form

10. What does the man say he will do soon?
    (A) Write an article
    (B) Attend an event
    (C) Meet an entertainer
    (D) Travel by train

11. Why does the man say, "I've never read any of his books before"?
    (A) To provide the reason for a selection
    (B) To express doubt about a recommendation
    (C) To explain why he cannot answer a question
    (D) To request assistance with a project

12. What does the woman say about a book?
    (A) It is exciting.
    (B) It is nonfiction.
    (C) It is a bestseller.
    (D) It is part of a series.

13. What will the man do in London next month?
(A) Attend a conference
(B) Visit corporate headquarters
(C) Meet with some clients
(D) Recruit new employees

14. What does the woman ask the man about?
(A) The length of his stay
(B) The topic of his presentation
(C) The cost of his tickets
(D) The names of his clients

15. What does the woman recommend?
(A) Making a hotel reservation
(B) Bringing additional cash
(C) Visiting a museum
(D) Taking a bus tour

---

16. Why is the man calling the hotel?
(A) To reserve a room
(B) To ask about transportation
(C) To leave a message for a guest
(D) To request a bill

17. What problem does the woman explain to the man?
(A) A credit card has expired.
(B) No rooms are currently available.
(C) A vehicle is being repaired.
(D) Some luggage has been misplaced.

18. According to the woman, what will be open until ten o'clock?
(A) An outdoor pool
(B) A business center
(C) A dining facility
(D) A gift shop

Tea Type	Time in Hot Water
White	2 minutes
Green	3 minutes
Black	4 minutes
Herbal	5 minutes

19. Why does the man want to try a new tea?
(A) It is popular with his coworkers.
(B) It is only sold at this shop.
(C) It has a mild flavor.
(D) It has health benefits.

20. What will the man receive with his purchase?
(A) An extra tea sample
(B) A membership card
(C) A free teapot
(D) A gift certificate

21. Look at the graphic. How long should the man leave the tea in hot water?
(A) 2 minutes
(B) 3 minutes
(C) 4 minutes
(D) 5 minutes

출제공식
1 식당, 부동산, 병원을 비롯해 도서관, 은행, 우체국, 방송국 등에서 일어나는 대화도 출제된다.
2 매물 문의, 각종 시설 및 서비스 이용, 해당 장소에 근무하는 직원 간의 대화 내용이 자주 등장한다.

✎ 대화 흐름 파악하기 | 식당 재료 수급 문제 → 해결 방안 제시   🎧 P3_57

M I just found out that ① the farm that supplies the tomatoes for our restaurant had a bad crop this season and can only give us half of what we usually order.	① 근무지: 식당, 재료 수급 문제 논의
W Oh, no. ② There's no way we can cook all of our dishes with only half. We'll have to find another supplier for the time being.	② 걱정하는 이유: 요리에 필요한 재료 부족
M Well, ③ the farm that we get our corn from, Johnson Farms, also plants tomatoes. I'll call them now to see if they have enough tomatoes to meet our needs.	③ 남자가 다음에 할 일: 다른 공급업체에 전화

근무지	1. Where do the speakers most likely work ?	At a restaurant
	화자들이 근무하는 곳은?	식당
걱정 거리	2. Why are the speakers concerned ?	An order cannot be filled.
	화자들이 걱정하는 이유는?	주문을 맞출 수 없다.
할 일	3. What will the **man** probably do next ?	Call a supplier
	남자가 다음에 할 일은?	공급업체에 전화하기

남 방금 알았는데 우리 식당에 토마토를 대주는 농장이 이번 계절에 작황이 안 좋아 우리가 평소 주문하던 양의 절반만 줄 수 있대요.
여 이런. 절반만 갖고는 우리 요리를 다 만들 방법이 없어요. 당분간 다른 공급업자를 찾아야겠어요.
남 저, 우리가 옥수수를 들이는 존슨 농장에서도 토마토를 재배해요. 지금 전화해서 우리가 필요한 만큼 토마토가 있는지 알아볼게요.

✏️ 기타 장소 빈출 상황

🎧 P3_58

식당 예약	Hello, I'm calling to make a reservation for dinner tonight. I'd like a table for two. 안녕하세요, 오늘 밤 저녁 식사 예약을 하려고 전화했습니다. 2인석 테이블로 부탁드려요.
재료 부족	We're almost out of the ingredients for the desserts. Can you go get some right away? 디저트 재료가 거의 떨어져가요. 지금 당장 가서 조금 사올래요?
부동산 임대	I'm moving to Tulsa next month and am looking to rent an apartment in the downtown area. 제가 다음 달에 털사로 이사를 갈 예정인데, 시내에 아파트를 임대하고 싶어요.
병원 예약 조정	Could you reschedule my appointment for sometime next week? 제 검진 예약을 다음 주 중으로 조정해주실 수 있을까요?
도서 대출	If you want, you can request that book through our inter-library loan service. 원하시면 도서관 상호 대출 서비스를 통해 그 책을 신청하실 수 있습니다.
은행 업무	I'm applying for a loan with your bank, and I have a question about the application documents. 은행에 대출 신청하려고 하는데, 지원 서류에 관해 질문이 하나 있습니다.
우편물 보관	Could you put a hold on my mail while I'm away for two weeks? 제가 2주간 떠나있을 동안 제 우편물을 맡아주실 수 있을까요?
방송 인터뷰	Joining me today is John Brown, one of the best-selling authors of all time. Welcome, John. 오늘 저와 함께하실 분은 존 브라운 씨입니다. 역대 최고의 베스트셀러 작가 중 한 분이죠. 어서 오세요, 존.

PART 3 | CHAPTER 02

ETS CHECK-UP

🎧 P3_59 정답 및 해설 p.178

1. What are the speakers mainly discussing?

(A) Job training
(B) Company policies
(C) Office space
(D) Market trends

2. What does the man suggest doing?

(A) Changing a date
(B) Going on a tour
(C) Talking to a consultant
(D) Reviewing a manual

3. What does the woman ask for?

(A) A floor plan
(B) A business card
(C) A cost estimate
(D) A project timeline

ETS X-FILE | 기타 장소 관련 빈출 표현

P3_60

식당

cuisine 요리	seasoning 양념, 조미료
culinary 요리의, 음식의	platter 모둠 요리, 큰 접시
vegetarian meal 채식주의 식사	diner 식사하는 사람, (소규모) 식당
entrée 주요리	server 서빙하는 사람
today's special 오늘의 요리	gourmet 미식가; (음식이) 고급인
assorted 여러 가지의, 갖은	supplier 공급[납품]업체
recipe 조리법	a table for four 4인용 테이블
flavor 맛, 풍미	private dining area 별도[전용] 식사 공간
ingredient 요리 재료, 성분	put somebody on the waitlist ~를 대기자 명단에 올리다

부동산

real estate agency/agent 부동산 중개소/중개인	residential/commercial area 주거/상업 지역
property 부동산, 건물	neighborhood 동네, 인근
rent 임대료; 임대하다	suburb 교외
lease 임대차 (계약); 임대하다	downtown 시내의, 중심가에
deposit 보증금	conveniently located 위치가 좋은
tenant 세입자	spacious (공간이) 넓은
utility bill 공과금(전기·가스·수도 요금)	have a nice view 전망이 좋다
landscaping 조경	fully furnished 가구를 모두 구비한
renovation 개조, 수리 (= remodeling / improvement)	relocate to ~로 이사하다

병원/약국

medical history 병력	remedy 치료법
medical check-up 건강 검진	prescription 처방전
fill in[out] a new patient form 초진용 서류를 작성하다	take medicine[medication] 약을 복용하다
examine a patient 환자를 검진하다	have a high fever 열이 높다
diagnose 진단하다	get a shot[an injection] 주사 맞다
treatment 치료, 처치	get some vaccinations 예방 접종하다

은행

deposit 예금하다 ↔ withdraw 인출하다	bank statement 은행 입출금 내역서
deposit[withdrawal] slip 입금[출금] 전표	balance 잔고, 잔액
transfer 송금하다	exchange rate 환율
open[set up] an account 계좌를 개설하다	apply for a loan 대출을 신청하다
savings/checking account 저축용/입출금용 계좌	endorse (수표에) 이서하다
account number 계좌 번호	transaction 거래, 처리

우체국 및 기타

regular delivery 일반 배송	exhibition 전시회
express mail service 속달 우편 서비스	admission fee 입장료
overnight delivery 익일 배송	have one's hair trimmed 머리를 다듬다
by courier 택배로	inter-library loan[borrowing] 도서관 상호 대출
pick up a package 소포를 찾아가다	check out (책을) 대출하다, (호텔) 퇴실하다

🎧 P3_61 정답 및 해설 p.179

대화를 들으면서 정답을 고르세요. 그리고 다시 들으면서 빈칸을 채우세요. (녹음은 두 번씩 들려줍니다.)

1. What does the woman tell the customer about?

(A) A discount on meals
(B) An addition to the menu

2. What will the woman do next?

(A) Consult the chef
(B) Find more menu

> **W** Good evening. I'm Kira, and I'll be your server. Tonight _____. It's roast chicken, and it's served with mashed potatoes and sautéed wild mushrooms.
>
> **M** That sounds delicious. But is it possible _____?
>
> **W** Oh, I'm not sure if we can serve it that way. But _____, and I'll let you know.

3. Who most likely is the man?

(A) An author
(B) A librarian

4. What does the man offer to do?

(A) Sign a form
(B) Obtain a book

> **W** Good morning. I wonder if the _____. It's called *Financial Matters*. The author is Gary Bork.
>
> **M** Um... I know we have the book, but _____ right now. The Hastings library has one, and we have an _____ with them. If you like, I can _____ _____ for you to borrow.
>
> **W** Oh, great. Is there a charge for this service?
>
> **M** Yes, there is. It's a dollar. And it will take two to three days for the book to get here.

5. What document does the woman ask to see?

(A) A bank statement
(B) Photo identification

6. When will the man most likely return?

(A) In the afternoon
(B) In a few days

> **M** Good morning. I'd like to _____.
>
> **W** Of course. We can open the account today, if you'd like. You'll just have to fill out this form, and then _____.
>
> **M** I'm afraid I don't have my driver's license with me. Why don't I _____, fill it out there, and _____ with my I.D.?

1. Where are the speakers?
   (A) At a doctor's office
   (B) At a travel agency
   (C) At a restaurant
   (D) At a pharmacy

2. Why does the woman apologize?
   (A) The man's account has been closed.
   (B) The man's bill is incorrect.
   (C) The man has to wait.
   (D) The man must resubmit a form.

3. What will the man most likely do next?
   (A) Forward an e-mail
   (B) Go to the airport
   (C) Make a telephone call
   (D) Provide credit card information

4. Where does the conversation take place?
   (A) In a library
   (B) In a utility company office
   (C) In a community center
   (D) At a real estate agency

5. What is the man asked to provide?
   (A) Photo identification
   (B) A credit card number
   (C) Proof of residence
   (D) A receipt

6. What does the woman suggest doing today?
   (A) Going to another location
   (B) Completing a form
   (C) Reviewing a policy
   (D) Making some copies

7. What is being delivered to the restaurant?
   (A) New plates
   (B) Cleaning supplies
   (C) Vegetables
   (D) Bread

8. Why does the man say, "Yuko's the restaurant manager"?
   (A) To explain why he cannot sign a document
   (B) To express surprise at Yuko's recent promotion
   (C) To suggest calling at a later time
   (D) To clarify why a delivery was delayed

9. What will Yuko ask an employee to do?
   (A) Taste some samples
   (B) Help unload boxes
   (C) Write down some directions
   (D) Clean a refrigerator

10. Who most likely is the man?
    (A) A real estate agent
    (B) A property owner
    (C) A building contractor
    (D) A government inspector

11. What does the woman mean when she says, "that was five years ago"?
    (A) She does not remember the steps of a process.
    (B) Her family needs more space than before.
    (C) An area has been used extensively.
    (D) Some records may be difficult to find.

12. What does the man ask about?
    (A) The terms of an agreement
    (B) The shape of a room
    (C) A budget for a project
    (D) A date for a site visit

13. Who most likely is the woman?
(A) A dentist
(B) A bank teller
(C) A pharmacist
(D) An insurance agent

14. What did the man do last week?
(A) He won a contest.
(B) He moved to a new place.
(C) He lost an identification card.
(D) He bought some glasses

15. What problem does the woman point out?
(A) Some paperwork is outdated.
(B) A signature is missing.
(C) A credit card machine is broken.
(D) Some prices are incorrect.

16. Why does the woman call the man?
(A) To check an e-mail address
(B) To cancel an appointment
(C) To respond to a message
(D) To give directions to a location

17. What problem does the man mention?
(A) He lost his keys.
(B) He forgot his password.
(C) He will not be on time for an appointment.
(D) He did not receive some instructions.

18. What does the man say he will do tomorrow?
(A) Go to the bank
(B) Call a client
(C) Work from home
(D) Have lunch with a colleague

Salazar's Southern Diner

Special discounts

Salads	10% off
Soups	15% off
Meat platters	20% off
Pasta platters	30% off

---

19. What does the woman say about the diner?
(A) It does not accept reservations.
(B) It has an outdoor eating area.
(C) It was recommended by a friend.
(D) It is located in the city center.

20. Look at the graphic. What discount will the woman receive?
(A) 10%
(B) 15%
(C) 20%
(D) 30%

21. What does the man suggest the woman do?
(A) Choose a beverage
(B) Place another order
(C) Ask for a refund
(D) Print out a coupon

PART 3 | CHAPTER 02

PART 3
기출

PARAPHRASING
LIST

PARAPHRASING LIST

1. **a copy of my report/ a résumé**
   내 보고서 한 부/ 이력서
   ▶ **a document**
   서류

2. **around 4/ later this afternoon**
   4시쯤에/ 이따 오후에
   ▶ **in the afternoon**
   오후에

3. **due**
   마감 기한인
   ▶ **deadline**
   마감일

4. **review**
   검토하다
   ▶ **go over**
   검토하다

5. **the new computers**
   새 컴퓨터
   ▶ **the new equipment**
   새 장비

6. **truck**
   트럭
   ▶ **vehicle**
   차량

7. **expensive electronics**
   값비싼 전자제품
   ▶ **valuables**
   귀중품

8. **come by**
   들르다
   ▶ **visit**
   방문하다

9. **the eatery**
   식당
   ▶ **a restaurant**
   식당

10. **finish**
    끝내다
    ▶ **complete**
    완료하다

11. **road work**
    도로 공사
    ▶ **a construction project**
    공사

12. **parking permit**
    주차권
    ▶ **parking pass**
    주차권

13. **the new assistant**
    새 보조
    ▶ **a new staff member**
    신입 직원

14. **the head of marketing**
    마케팅 부장
    ▶ **a department manager**
    부서장

15. **desk**
    책상
    ▶ **office furniture**
    사무용 가구

16. **take a look**
    확인하다
    ▶ **review**
    확인하다

17. **the music festival**
    음악 축제
    ▶ **an event**
    행사

18. **high ratings**
    높은 평가
    ▶ **a good reputation**
    좋은 평판

19. **a small tear**
    약간 터짐(찢어짐)
    ▶ **damaged**
    손상된

20. **highlight**
    강조하다
    ▶ **emphasize**
    강조하다

21.	rent 임대료	▶	rental charge 임대료
22.	reorganize 새로 진열하다	▶	rearrange 다시 진열하다
23.	book 예약하다	▶	reserve 예약하다
24.	pass out 나눠주다	▶	distribute 배포하다
25.	department managers 부서장들	▶	company managers 회사 부장들
26.	the accounting training 회계 교육	▶	a training session 교육
27.	sign up 등록하다	▶	register 등록하다
28.	membership 회원 자격	▶	account 회원 계정
29.	coffee, tea, and snacks 커피, 차, 간식	▶	a variety of refreshments 다양한 다과
30.	a picture and description of the chairs 의자 사진과 설명	▶	some information 정보
31.	a credit card number 신용카드 번호	▶	some payment information 지불 정보
32.	career move 이직	▶	career change 이직
33.	designed 디자인한	▶	created 만든
34.	look 모습	▶	appearance 외형
35.	amounts 금액	▶	cost of purchase 구매 비용
36.	fascinating 흥미진진한	▶	interesting 흥미로운
37.	remodeling 보수공사	▶	make some improvements 보수 공사하다
38.	show 보여주다	▶	demonstrate 보여주다
39.	wash 씻어 내다	▶	clean 청소하다
40.	join 가입하다	▶	become a member 회원이 되다

41.	some of us in the department 우리 부서 사람 몇 명	▷	a group 단체
42.	a rough version of the text 대략적인 문구	▷	a draft of a document 문서 초안
43.	less than that 그것보다 적은	▷	not high enough 충분히 높지 않은
44.	by a coworker 동료에 의해	▷	from a coworker 동료로부터
45.	e-mail addresses and phone numbers 이메일 주소와 전화번호	▷	contact information 연락처
46.	a lab coat and some safety glasses 실험복과 보안경	▷	protective gear 보호 장비
47.	express shipping 빠른 배송	▷	faster shipping method 더 빠른 배송 방법
48.	telecommuting 재택근무	▷	working from home 재택근무
49.	revise 수정하다	▷	make a correction 수정하다
50.	complicated 복잡한	▷	not easy to figure out 이해하기 쉽지 않은
51.	quarterly 분기마다	▷	every three months 3개월마다
52.	detour 우회도로	▷	alternate route 우회로
53.	at no charge/cost 무료로	▷	for free 무료로
54.	relocate to ~로 이전하다	▷	move to ~로 옮기다, 이사하다
55.	the price I quoted you 말씀드린 견적 가격	▷	a cost estimate 비용 견적서
56.	excellent selection of tasty dishes 훌륭하게 엄선된 맛있는 메뉴	▷	the quality of its food 음식의 질
57.	passwords and network addresses 암호와 네트워크 주소	▷	security details 보안 세부사항
58.	the company that supplies that equipment 장비를 공급하는 회사	▷	a supplier 납품업체
59.	the quality of our mobile phones 휴대폰의 품질	▷	product performance 제품 성능
60.	a tour of the assembly line 조립라인 견학	▷	a tour of the facilities 시설 견학

PARAPHRASING LIST

61. ideas for pieces to write this summer
올 여름에 쓸 글에 대한 아이디어
▶ **ideas for future articles**
향후 기사에 대한 아이디어

62. previous customers to write reviews
이전 고객들의 후기를 적은
▶ **customer feedback**
고객 의견

63. the printouts of what food was ordered
어떤 음식을 주문했는지 나타낸 출력 서류
▶ **order forms**
주문서

64. a special that's not listed on the menu
메뉴에 실리지 않은 특별 요리
▶ **an addition to the menu**
메뉴에 추가된 요리

65. looking for another job
다른 일자리를 알아보는
▶ **finding a new job**
새로운 일자리를 찾는

66. find somebody who can help us out
도와줄 수 있는 사람을 찾다
▶ **asking for assistance**
도움 요청

67. upgrading our office
사무 공간을 개선하는 것
▶ **an office renovation project**
사무실 보수 공사

68. going bicycle riding
자전거 여행
▶ **biking**
자전거 타기

69. adding a library wing
부속 도서관을 추가하는 것
▶ **a library addition**
도서관 증축

70. different way to promote our products
우리 상품을 홍보할 다른 방법
▶ **different promotional approach**
다른 홍보 방법

71. transferring to our office in Hong Kong
홍콩 지사로 옮기다
▶ **a job transfer**
일자리 이동

72. get together
모이다
▶ **meet**
만나다

73. speak about
이야기하다
▶ **describe**
설명하다

74. take a few days off
며칠을 쉬다
▶ **take some time off**
얼마간 휴가를 내다

75. take two weeks off
2주간 휴가를 내다
▶ **vacation**
휴가

76. make a list of job duties
직무 목록을 만들다
▶ **listing a job's duties**
직무 목록 작성하기

77. fax an order
팩스로 주문을 넣다
▶ **place an order**
주문을 하다

78. deal with
다루다
▶ **handle**
다루다

79. take place
열리다
▶ **be held**
개최되다

80. enroll in
등록하다
▶ **sign up/register for**
등록하다

81. ask the chef
주방장에게 묻다

▶ consult the chef
주방장과 상의하다

82. write up a report
보고서를 작성하다

▶ work on a report
보고서를 작성하다

83. isn't big enough
별로 크지 않다

▶ small
작은

84. a week earlier than scheduled
예정보다 일주일 앞당겨서

▶ rescheduled
일정이 바뀐

85. which aisle spaghetti is in
스파게티가 어느 통로에 있는지

▶ the location of a product
제품의 위치

86. focus on one area
한 분야에 집중하다

▶ specialize in one area
한 분야를 전문으로 하다

87. will be transferring
전근 갈 것이다

▶ will be away
멀리 떠날 것이다

88. perform the safety inspection
안전 점검을 하다

▶ conduct an inspection
안전 검사를 실시하다

89. come over to the security office
경비실에 오다

▶ visit an office
사무실을 방문하다

90. waive your delivery charge
고객의 배송비를 면제하다

▶ provide free shipping
무료 배송을 제공하다

91. promoting our store
가게를 홍보하는 것

▶ advertising a store
가게를 광고하는 것

92. describing the products
제품을 설명하는

▶ product details
제품 상세설명

93. will not be valid
유효하지 않을 것이다

▶ will expire
만료될 것이다

94. keep these shirts
이 셔츠들을 보관하다

▶ hold some items
몇 가지 물건들을 맡아두다

95. drive slowly
천천히 운전하다

▶ drive carefully
조심해서 운전하다

96. get off work
퇴근하다

▶ leave for the day
퇴근하다

97. offer a deal
저렴하게 제공하다

▶ reduce a price
할인하다

98. make a list
명단을 만들다

▶ complete a list
명단을 작성하다

99. mention this to our manager
부장님께 이 문제를 말씀드리다

▶ speak to a supervisor
상사에게 이야기하다

100. talk to the hotel receptionist
호텔 접수 직원과 이야기하다

▶ contact a hotel
호텔에 연락하다

PARAPHRASING LIST

101. give you a ride in my car
내 차로 태워주다

▶ drive her
그녀를 태워 주다

102. come back in about forty-five minutes
약 45분 뒤에 돌아오다

▶ return later
이따가 다시 오다

103. check online
온라인으로 알아보다

▶ find information on the Internet
인터넷에서 정보를 찾아보다

104. find out if the rates have gone up
요금이 올랐는지 알아보다

▶ ask about electricity rates
전기 요금에 대해 문의하다

105. leave the office
퇴근하다

▶ leave work
퇴근하다

106. work overtime
초과 근무하다

▶ work extended hours
연장 근무하다

107. put on this visitor's badge
방문자 배지를 착용하다

▶ wear a badge
배지를 착용하다

108. let the supervisor know
관리자에게 알리다

▶ notify a manager
매니저에게 통지하다

109. own a restaurant in Madrid
마드리드에서 레스토랑을 운영하다

▶ has a restaurant there
거기에 레스토랑을 소유하고 있다

110. show them around the hotel
호텔을 구경시켜 주다

▶ give a tour of a facility
시설을 견학시키다

111. reschedule the delivery for tomorrow
배송을 내일로 조정하다

▶ postpone a delivery
배송을 연기하다

112. having dinner at my parents' house
부모님의 집에서 저녁 식사를 하다

▶ visit her parents' home
부모님의 집을 방문하다

113. Let me know what they tell you.
뭐라고 하는지 내게 알려 주세요.

▶ tell her what he finds out
그가 알아낸 것을 그녀에게 말해주다

114. have a contract ready
계약서를 준비하다

▶ prepare a document
문서를 준비하다

115. take turns entering the data
교대로 데이터를 입력하다

▶ share job responsibility
업무를 나눠 하다

116. doesn't have the extra resources
여분의 재원이 없다

▶ has a limited budget
예산이 제한돼 있다

117. check the supplies in the storeroom
창고에서 물품을 확인하다

▶ check the inventory
재고를 확인하다

118. find out about pricing information
가격 정보를 알아보다

▶ research some prices
가격 조사를 하다

119. put the apartment up for sale
아파트를 팔려고 내놓다

▶ sell a property
부동산을 팔다

120. get a fitness center membership
헬스클럽 회원자격을 얻다

▶ join a fitness center
헬스클럽에 가입하다

121. Let me know when he is free.
그가 언제 시간이 있는지 알려 주세요.
▶ the man's availability
남자의 시간적 여유

122. give you the address of a Web site with information
정보가 있는 웹사이트 주소를 알려주다
▶ Direct the woman to a Web site
여자에게 웹사이트를 알려주다

123. temporarily stop my mail delivery
우편물 배달을 잠시 중단하다
▶ reschedule mail delivery
우편물 배달 일정을 조정하다

124. ask if it can be delivered before Jane's first day of work 제인의 첫 출근 전에 배달될 수 있는지 묻다
▶ check on the delivery date
배달 날짜를 확인하다

125. have more time to answer all the questions
모든 질문에 대답할 수 있도록 더 많은 시간을 가지다
▶ allowing more time for questions
질문에 더 많은 시간을 할애하다

126. The schedule's pretty full.
일정이 가득 찼다.
▶ a busy schedule
바쁜 일정

127. Our payment processing team was just moved.
결제처리팀이 옮겨왔다.
▶ relocated some of its staff
일부 직원들을 재배치했다

128. Our budget's been cut.
우리의 예산이 삭감되었다
▶ Some funding has been reduced.
일부 자금이 축소되었다.

129. You did a great job.
일을 훌륭하게 해냈다.
▶ It was done well.
잘 처리했다.

130. We had classes together.
우리는 수업을 같이 들었다.
▶ They went to the same university.
그들은 같은 대학에 다녔다.

131. Someone's already booked meeting room A.
누군가가 A 회의실을 벌써 예약했다.
▶ It's not available.
그것을 이용할 수 없다.

132. The machine is currently out of order.
현재 기계가 고장이다.
▶ A machine is not working.
기계가 작동되지 않는다.

133. That's the color of my house.
그것이 우리 집의 색깔이다.
▶ It is the same color as her house.
그녀의 집과 같은 색깔이다.

134. Some renovations are being done.
보수 공사를 하는 중이다.
▶ It is currently being renovated.
현재 보수 공사 중이다.

135. I'm missing the drawings with the measurements.
치수를 표시한 도면을 잃어버렸다.
▶ A document is missing.
문서가 없다.

136. have some phones for sale at half price
반값 세일 중인 전화기가 몇 가지 있다
▶ Some phones are available at a discount.
몇몇 전화기는 할인가로 구입 가능하다.

137. see the assembly line in full operation
조립라인 전체가 가동되는 것을 보다
▶ a complete process can be observed
전체 과정이 관찰될 수 있다

138. We tried last year and didn't have much success.
작년에 시도했지만 많은 성과는 얻지 못했다.
▶ It was not successful in the past.
과거에 성공적이지 않았다.

139. The weather's getting nicer.
날씨가 좋아지고 있다.
▶ The weather has improved.
날씨가 좋아졌다.

140. We just can't find enough people to hire who have the skills we need.
우리가 필요한 기술을 갖추고 있는 사람들을 충분히 구할 수 없다.
▶ There is a shortage of skilled workers.
숙련된 근로자들이 부족하다.

PART 3

Directions: You will hear some conversations between two or more people. You will be asked to answer three questions about what the speakers say in each conversation. Select the best response to each question and mark the letter (A), (B), (C), or (D) on your answer sheet. The conversations will not be printed in your test book and will be spoken only one time.

32. What did the woman e-mail the man about?
(A) An inspection
(B) A client order
(C) A company picnic
(D) A workshop

33. Where will the man go on Thursday?
(A) To a government office
(B) To a car dealership
(C) To a doctor's office
(D) To a construction site

34. What does the man agree to do?
(A) Fix a machine
(B) Join a committee
(C) Lead a tour
(D) Create a survey

35. What is the purpose of the call?
(A) To schedule repairs
(B) To arrange shipping
(C) To place a catering order
(D) To reserve a flight

36. Who most likely is the woman?
(A) A travel agent
(B) A truck driver
(C) A farmer
(D) A factory worker

37. What information will the woman provide next?
(A) An address
(B) A password
(C) A form of payment
(D) A meeting time

38. What type of event are the speakers most likely attending?
(A) A museum exhibition
(B) A store's grand opening
(C) A music concert
(D) A sports game

39. What does the woman not like about an item?
(A) The size
(B) The color
(C) The style
(D) The cost

40. What does the man suggest doing?
(A) Returning later
(B) Inviting a friend
(C) Paying with cash
(D) Getting some food

41. Where does the conversation most likely take place?
(A) At a mobile phone store
(B) At a bookshop
(C) At a convention center
(D) At a train station

42. What problem does the man mention?
(A) His phone battery is low.
(B) He lost his phone.
(C) He cannot access a ticket.
(D) He is running late.

43. What does Paloma ask the man to do?
(A) Provide a credit card
(B) Show a confirmation e-mail
(C) Call a help line
(D) Complete a form

44. What kind of company does the woman work for?
(A) A car manufacturer
(B) An employment agency
(C) An advertising firm
(D) A television network

45. Why does the man say, "I live in Berlin"?
(A) To invite the woman to visit
(B) To express uncertainty about an offer
(C) To explain a shipping delay
(D) To request an address change

46. What does the woman say she will do?
(A) Review some job applications
(B) Send some supplies
(C) Approve a proposal
(D) Contact Human Resources

47. What are the speakers mainly discussing?
(A) An employee health initiative
(B) A new product idea
(C) A marketing campaign
(D) A production schedule

48. What does the woman say she has tracked information about?
(A) Online searches
(B) Customer ratings
(C) Employee efficiency
(D) Monthly sales

49. Who will the speakers most likely meet with next week?
(A) A medical professional
(B) An accountant
(C) A director of sales
(D) A chief executive officer

50. Who most likely is the woman?
(A) A civil engineer
(B) A real estate agent
(C) A financial consultant
(D) A construction supervisor

51. What happened at the men's company last month?
(A) An important contract was signed.
(B) An international branch was added.
(C) Some technology upgrades were made.
(D) Some staff members received promotions.

52. What problem does the woman mention?
(A) A business trip went over budget.
(B) A moving truck is not available.
(C) Some equipment has been damaged.
(D) Some renovations are behind schedule.

53. Why did the man choose to attend a particular panel discussion?
(A) It received the most publicity.
(B) It required audience participation.
(C) It was the most relevant to his job.
(D) It was led by a speaker he likes.

54. What does the woman dislike about a conference?
(A) Having no opportunities to network
(B) Having too few seats in meeting rooms
(C) Having unsatisfactory meal options
(D) Having to miss some interesting sessions

55. What do the speakers plan to do?
(A) Send e-mails to their managers
(B) Share their notes with each other
(C) Complain to the conference organizers
(D) Meet in the lobby at the end of the day

Go on to the next page

56. What does the woman mean when she says, "This work isn't urgent"?
(A) She plans to leave work early.
(B) She is available to talk.
(C) She thinks a task is boring.
(D) She does not need any help.

57. What is the man organizing?
(A) A city tour
(B) An international trip
(C) A client visit
(D) A weekend outing

58. What does the woman suggest doing?
(A) Checking the weather
(B) Reading a menu
(C) Reserving transportation
(D) Moving a machine

59. Where do the speakers most likely work?
(A) At a clothing company
(B) At an automobile factory
(C) At a fashion magazine
(D) At an electronics company

60. According to the man, what does management want to do?
(A) Relocate a production facility
(B) Reduce some costs
(C) Move a release date
(D) Increase the price of a product

61. What approach has the man already tried?
(A) Hiring a consultant
(B) Changing a delivery schedule
(C) Negotiating a contract
(D) Meeting with employees

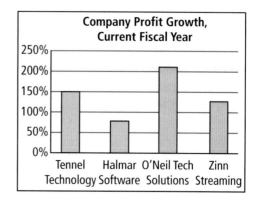

62. What is the man working on?
(A) A news article
(B) A technology survey
(C) An advertising campaign
(D) A recruitment strategy

63. What does the man request?
(A) Additional funding
(B) A day off from work
(C) A different assignment
(D) A deadline extension

64. Look at the graphic. Which company is the man referring to?
(A) Tennel Technology
(B) Halmar Software
(C) O'Neil Tech Solutions
(D) Zinn Streaming

Catering Menu	
Dessert platter	$50
Vegetable platter	$75
Fruit and cheese platter	$80
Shrimp cocktail platter	$95

65. Where is the conversation most likely taking place?
(A) At a restaurant
(B) At an office building
(C) At a supermarket
(D) At a storage warehouse

66. Why is the man unsure about ordering from Jupiter Restaurant?
(A) It might not have time to fill an order.
(B) It might not serve enough food.
(C) It does not have affordable prices.
(D) It does not have flavorful food.

67. Look at the graphic. How much will a catering order cost?
(A) $50
(B) $75
(C) $80
(D) $95

Schedule Wednesday, June 12	
9 A.M.–10 A.M.	
10 A M –11 A M	
11 A.M.–12 P.M.	Conference Call
12 P.M.–1 P.M.	
1 P.M.–2 P.M.	Haircut at Salon
2 P.M.–3 P.M.	
3 P.M.–4 P.M.	Sales Team Meeting
4 P.M.–5 P.M.	

68. Why is the man calling?
(A) To order a prescription
(B) To register for a workshop
(C) To ask a billing question
(D) To inquire about a research study

69. Look at the graphic. When does the man plan to go to Blustin Incorporated?
(A) Between 9 A.M. and 10 A.M.
(B) Between 10 A.M. and 11 A.M.
(C) Between 12 P.M. and 1 P.M.
(D) Between 2 P.M. and 3 P.M.

70. What does the woman say she will do?
(A) Consult a manager
(B) Send a questionnaire
(C) Print some documents
(D) Provide a receipt

PART
4

담화

PART 4 기본 전략

CHAPTER 01　문제 유형별 전략

CHAPTER 02　담화 유형별 전략

ETS ACTUAL TEST

한 사람의 담화를 듣고 이와 관련된 세 개의 문제를 푸는 유형으로, 총 10세트 30문항이 출제된다.

전체 내용 관련 문제	주제/목적, 담화가 이루어지는 장소, 화자/청자의 직업/업종, 근무지
세부 내용 관련 문제	세부 사항, 문제점/걱정거리, 화자가 청자에게 하는 요청/제안/추천 사항, 화자의 의도 파악, 앞으로 할 일/다음에 일어날 일, 시각 정보 연계

기본 풀이 전략

P4_01

파트 4에서도 반드시 담화를 듣기 전에 질문 및 보기를 읽어두어야 한다. 파트 3 문제에서 화자의 성별을 구분해야 했다면, 파트 4 문제에서는 화자/청자를 구분해야 한다.

STEP 01 문제 파악하기
- 담화 듣기 전에 질문 및 보기 읽기
- 의문사, 주어, 동사를 중심으로 키워드 파악하기
  (화자/청자 구분 필수)
- 키워드 표시하고 노려 듣기

STEP 02 담화 들으며 정답 체크하기
- 관련 내용 확인하는 즉시 답 체크하기
- 다음 문제로 넘어가서 노려 듣기
- 담화 종료 후 성우가 질문을 읽어주는 동안 다음 담화의 문제 파악하기

📄 문제지

🔊 음원

71. Where does the **speaker** work?
(A) At a university
(B) At a bookstore
(C) At a radio station
(D) At a bank

72. What will Dr. Mamat be discussing?
(A) Career choices
(B) Publishing opportunities
(C) Communication strategies
(D) Personal finances

73. What does the speaker encourage **listeners** to do?
(A) Call in with questions
(B) Register for a seminar
(C) Open an account
(D) Refer a friend

W ㉛ Welcome back to Money Talk on KQSF Radio.

화자의 근무지: 라디오 방송국

Our studio guest today is Dr. Anwar Mamat, professor of microeconomics at Benham University, and author of the recent bestseller *How to Make the Most of Your Money*.
㉒ Today, Dr. Mamat will be sharing tips on the best way to manage your personal finances.

마마트 박사가 이야기할 것: 개인 재정

Throughout the show, I will be taking questions from listeners over the phone.
㉓ So, if you have a question for Dr. Mamat, feel free to call us here at the station at 555-0194.

청자들에게 권유하는 일: 전화로 질문하기

*이후 질문만 읽어주며, 그 사이에 공백이 주어진다.

① 문제 유형별 출제 비율

세부 사항 문제의 비율이 가장 높고, 주제/목적 및 화자나 청자의 직업을 묻는 문제가 20퍼센트 내외로 꾸준히 출제된다. 매회 의도 파악 문제가 3문항, 시각 정보 연계 문제가 2문항씩 나온다.

② 담화 유형별 출제 비율

회의 및 업무 관련 공지, 전화 메시지가 가장 많이 출제되며, 방송/광고, 발표/소개, 관광/견학 담화도 나온다. 대화보다 내용 전개 패턴이 비교적 명확한 편이므로, 담화 유형별 흐름은 알아두는 것이 좋다.

패러프레이징 PARAPHRASING

파트 4에서는 한 사람이 담화를 이어가기 때문에 긴 문장이 등장하기도 하며, 단서가 정답으로 패러프레이징되는 방식도 복잡한 양상을 띠는 경우가 있다. 이러한 패턴을 미리 알아두고 실전에서 당황하지 않도록 한다.

① 두 개가 한 문장에 들어가는 경우

As you all know, the renovations to expand our lobby were completed yesterday. 여러분 모두 아시다시피, 로비를 확장하는 공사가 어제 완료되었습니다.	**Q** According to the speaker, what happened yesterday? **A** Some construction work was finished. **질문** 화자에 따르면 어제 일어난 일은? **정답** 공사 작업이 끝났다.

② 두 문장에 있는 단서를 조합해야 하는 경우

I wanted to make sure that everybody reviews the proposal before the client meeting. Here, I've prepared copies for everyone. 고객과의 회의 전에 모두들 꼭 제안서를 검토했으면 합니다. 여기요, 제가 모두를 위해 사본을 준비했어요.	**Q** What will the speaker most likely do next? **A** Hand out some documents **질문** 화자가 다음에 할 것 같은 일은? **정답** 문서 나눠 주기

③ 문제의 키워드와 단서가 떨어져 있는 경우

The management finally approved our request to install solar panels on the roof. The installation won't be cheap, but we will become able to generate our own electricity and thus reduce our expenses over the long term. 경영진에서 지붕에 태양 전지판을 설치하자는 요청을 마침내 승인했어요. 설치비가 저렴하진 않겠지만, 전기를 자체적으로 생산하게 되어 장기적으로 비용을 절감할 수 있을 거예요.	**Q** Why was the request approved? **A** To save money **질문** 요청이 승인된 이유는? **정답** 비용을 절약하기 위해

문제 유형별 전략

❶ 주제/목적 문제

출제공식
1 전화/회의/방송 등의 주제나 목적, 광고 대상 등을 묻는 유형으로, 주로 첫 번째 혹은 두 번째 문제로 출제된다.

2 화자의 인사말 바로 다음에 단서가 등장할 확률이 높다.

문제유형
[주제] **What is the speaker mainly discussing[talking about]?**
화자는 주로 무엇에 관해 이야기하는가?

What is the topic[focus] of the talk / broadcast / workshop?
담화 / 방송 / 워크숍의 주제는 무엇인가?

What is the news report / announcement mainly about?
뉴스 / 공지는 주로 무엇에 관한 것인가?

What (type of business) is being advertised? 무엇이(어떤 업체가) 광고되고 있는가?

[목적] **What is the purpose of talk / meeting / message?** 담화 / 회의 / 메시지의 목적은 무엇인가?

Why is the speaker calling? 화자는 왜 전화를 하는가?

Why did the speaker call a meeting? 화자는 왜 회의를 소집했는가?

✏ **핵심 전략 |** 화자의 인사말 바로 다음에 나오는 부분에 귀를 기울인다.　　🎧 P4_02

Hello, this is Min-Jee Choi, from the city transportation committee, calling about our proposed highway expansion project.

주제를 나타내는 단서 표현: **calling about** ●
전화 메시지 주제: 고속도로 확장 프로젝트 ●

I just read the environmental assessment for the project, and the impact of the construction was found to be acceptable. This means that we'll be able to proceed and get started while the weather is good. Can you arrange a meeting with the entire committee soon, so we can plan the next steps? Keep in mind, the rainy season starts in six months.

Q. What is the message mainly about?
(A) A roadwork project
(B) A job opening
(C) A pollution problem
(D) A local election

단서　our proposed highway expansion project

정답　(A) 도로 공사 프로젝트

안녕하세요. 시 교통위원회의 최민지입니다. **우리가 제안한 고속도로 확장 프로젝트에 관해 전화 드립니다.** 프로젝트의 환경 영향 평가서를 막 읽었는데요. 공사에 따른 영향이 용인될 수준인 것으로 보여집니다. 이대로 진행해서 날씨가 좋을 때 착수할 수 있다는 뜻이죠. 빠른 시일 내에 위원회 전체와의 회의를 소집해서 다음 단계를 계획할 수 있도록 해 주시겠어요? 6개월 후에 우기가 시작된다는 점 염두에 두세요.

메시지는 주로 무엇에 관한 것인가?
(A) 도로 공사 프로젝트
(B) 공석
(C) 공해 문제
(D) 지역 선거

✎ 주제 / 목적을 나타내는 단서 표현 ∩ P4_03

전화 메시지	**I'm calling about ~ / I'm calling to ~ / I'm calling because ~** **I'm calling about** tonight's awards dinner at the convention hall. 오늘 밤 컨벤션 홀에서 열릴 시상식 저녁 만찬 관련해서 전화 드려요.
회의	**I called this meeting to ~ / I want to discuss ~ / Next on the agenda is ~** **I called this meeting to** share with you the results of our latest market research. 최근 시장 조사 결과를 여러분에게 공유하고자 이 회의를 소집했습니다.
발표 / 설명	**I'm happy[pleased] to announce that ~ / Today's talk will focus on ~** **I'm happy to announce that** next month we'll be opening up a new branch office in Munich. 다음 달 뮌헨에서 신규 지점을 열게 된다는 것을 알리게 되어 기쁩니다.
공지	**I want to inform[remind] you that ~ / Let me tell you that ~** **I want to inform you that** we'll be repairing our factory's parking facility over the next two weeks. 향후 2주간 우리 공장의 주차 시설을 수리한다는 점을 알려 드리고 싶습니다.
광고	**Are you looking for ~ ? / Do[Did] you ~ ? / Have you ever ~ ?** **Are you looking for** the best legal services in town? 이 지역 최고의 법률 서비스 회사를 찾고 계신가요?
방송	**In local news, ~ / Today, we will be -ing ~** **In local news,** Hillside mayor Richard Suarez announced his retirement today. 지역 소식입니다. 힐사이드의 시장을 역임했던 리처드 수아레즈 씨가 오늘 은퇴를 발표했습니다.

PART 4 | CHAPTER 01

ETS CHECK-UP ∩ P4_04 정답 및 해설 p.195

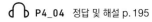

1. What is the topic of the workshop?

(A) Creating a résumé
(B) Using recording software
(C) Improving public speaking skills
(D) Networking with colleagues

2. What is the main purpose of the meeting?

(A) To distribute work assignments
(B) To explain a company policy
(C) To discuss sales strategies
(D) To plan a customer appreciation event

❷ 장소/직업 문제

출제공식
1 담화 장소, 화자나 청자의 직업/업계/근무지 등을 묻는 문제로, 단서는 주로 초반부에 언급된다.

2 화자가 직접 본인 또는 청자의 신분을 밝히거나, 주제/목적을 언급할 때 관련 어휘를 사용함으로써 간접적으로 드러내는 경우가 많다.

문제유형

[근무지 / 장소] Where does the speaker most likely work? 화자는 어디서 근무하겠는가?

Where does the speaker most likely work? 화자는 어디서 근무하겠는가?

What type of business does the speaker work for? 화자가 근무하는 업체는?

Where is the announcement being made? 안내가 나오는 장소는 어디인가?

[직업 / 업계] Who (most likely) are the listeners? 청자들은 누구인가?

What industry / department / field does the speaker work in?
화자가 일하는 업계 / 부서 / 분야는?

Who is the speaker calling / addressing? 화자는 누구에게 전화를 / 말을 하고 있는가?

Who is the (intended) audience for the announcement / talk?
공지 / 담화의 청중은 누구인가?

✎ **핵심 전략** | 화자와 청자를 구분하고, 장소/직업 관련 어휘에 집중한다. 🎧 P4_05

I'd like to thank the entire design team for your hard work on the user interface for the H100 smartphone. You did a great job designing the product,

청자들의 직업 앞에 나온 단서 표현: **I'd like to thank** •
청자들의 직업: 제품 디자인 팀원들 •

and we're ready for the next step in the project— we're going to show the interface to people who haven't seen it before and see what they think. We'll need someone to get in touch with people from other departments and ask them if they'd like to participate in the product testing sessions. Would someone volunteer to do that?

Q. Who most likely are the **listeners**?
(A) Computer technicians
(B) Human resources workers
(C) Product designers
(D) Sales representatives

단서 I'd like to thank the entire design team for your hard work, designing the product

정답 (C) 제품 디자이너들

H100 스마트폰의 사용자 인터페이스를 작업한 디자인팀 여러분 전체의 노고에 감사를 표합니다. 제품을 디자인하느라 수고 많으셨습니다. 이제 우리는 프로젝트 다음 단계를 위한 준비가 되었는데요. 인터페이스를 본 적이 없는 사람들에게 이걸 보여주면서 어떻게 생각하는지 알아볼 예정입니다. 다른 부서 사람들에게 연락을 취해서 제품 테스트 세션에 참가하고 싶은지 물어볼 사람이 필요합니다. 누군가 그 일을 자원해서 해주겠어요?

청자들은 누구겠는가?
(A) 컴퓨터 기술자들
(B) 인사부 직원들
(C) 제품 디자이너들
(D) 영업 사원들

전화 메시지	This is ~ (calling from) ~ / This message is for ~ / You've reached ~ / Thanks for calling ~ **This is** Anita Han calling from <u>the sales department at Howard Electronics</u>. 저는 하워드 전자 영업부 소속 아니타 한입니다. → 전자제품 회사, 영업부 직원
회의	Thanks for coming to this ~ meeting. / I called this meeting for ~ / I'd like to thank ~ **Thanks for coming to this** emergency <u>Web development team</u> **meeting**. 웹 개발팀 긴급 회의에 와주셔서 감사합니다. → 기술 분야, 웹 개발자
안내 방송	Attention ~ / Can I have the attention of ~ ? **Attention,** Wellington <u>Train Station passengers</u>. 웰링턴 기차역 승객 여러분께 안내 말씀 드립니다. → 기차역
발표 / 설명	Thank you (all) for attending[coming to] ~ / Welcome to ~ / On behalf of ~ **Thank you all for attending** <u>the grand opening of my new restaurant</u>. 저의 새 레스토랑 개업식에 참석해 주신 모든 분들께 감사 드립니다. → 식당, 식당 소유주
방송	On today's show ~ / And now for your local news. / This is ~, reporting live from ~ **On today's show,** I'll be talking with Frank Randell, the author of the best-selling book, *1986*. 오늘 방송에서는 베스트셀러 〈1986〉의 저자인 프랭크 랜덜 씨와 이야기를 나눌 것입니다. → 쇼 호스트(진행자)
관광 / 견학	Welcome to ~ / I'll be leading ~ / I'll show you ~ / Today, we'll ~ **Welcome to** <u>Manor Farm</u>! Today, **we'll** <u>look around the fields and see different farm animals</u>. 매너 농장에 오신 것을 환영합니다! 오늘 우리는 농장을 둘러보고 다양한 가축을 볼 겁니다. → 농장, 가이드

PART 4 | CHAPTER 01

ETS CHECK-UP　🎧 P4_07　정답 및 해설 p. 196

1. Where does the listener work?

(A) At a hotel

(B) At an airport

(C) At a museum

(D) At a print shop

2. What field does the speaker most likely work in?

(A) Tourism

(B) Education

(C) Radio broadcasting

(D) Information technology

담화에 등장하는 단서가 알맞게 패러프레이징된 보기를 선택하세요.

M Hello. This is Pierre Jean from Zenex Pharmaceuticals. **We reserved the Royal Hall for a press conference on March 25 at 10 A.M. However, now we would like a bigger hall that can accommodate up to 100 people**, as more journalists have decided to attend.

1. What is the main purpose of the message?
   (A) To confirm attendance at a meeting
   (B) To make changes to a reservation

W **Are you looking for a reliable company to keep your building safe? If so, GS Secure Solutions can help.** We have been providing security services to a variety of businesses in this area for the past ten years.

2. What is being advertised?
   (A) A security company
   (B) A fitness center

M **Welcome aboard, everyone! Thanks for joining this tour of Bayside Harbor.** My name is Harvey Jones, and I'll be your guide today. On this trip, you'll learn about the history of the harbor as well as enjoy some quality time out on the bay.

3. Where most likely are the listeners?
   (A) At a museum
   (B) On a boat

W Hello, Marco. **This is Stacey from Lafayette Travel. Unfortunately, there are no more seats on direct flights to Toronto for the date and time that you mentioned.** But if you leave one day earlier, there are several options available.

4. Who most likely is the speaker?
   (A) A travel agent
   (B) A hotel employee

M Good morning, everyone, and thank you for the warm welcome. It's my honor to **present Erikson Incorporated's latest product at the Digital Innovation Expo today. What I have here in my hand is our new mobile phone, the Aura 11.**

5. What industry does the speaker most likely work in?
   (A) Technology
   (B) Event planning

W **Before you enter the factory floor today**, let me give you a quick reminder. I know you're under pressure to work quickly as we're expanding our popular line of glass display cases, but please be extra careful **when using the cutting machine.**

6. Who is the audience for the talk?
   (A) Delivery drivers
   (B) Factory workers

LISTENING **PRACTICE**

⏺ P4_09 정답 및 해설 p.198

담화를 들으면서 정답을 고르세요. 그리고 다시 들으면서 빈칸을 채우세요. (녹음은 두 번씩 들려줍니다.)

1. Who is the message most likely intended for?

(A) A restaurant manager
(B) A bank teller

2. What is the speaker calling about?

(A) A lost item
(B) A new account

Hello, this is Natasha Klein. I _____ last night, and I think _____

_____. I was sitting in a booth at the back of the dining room, and my purse was on

the seat. The phone must have fallen out when I took out my credit card to pay for dinner. Could you

please _____? If so, I could stop by this afternoon to pick it up.

You can reach me at my work number—555-0196. Thank you.

---

3. What is the main purpose of the broadcast?

(A) To describe a recent trip
(B) To interview a local business owner

4. What type of business is Maxi's?

(A) A coffee shop
(B) A restaurant supplier

Good morning and thanks for listening to KS Radio's Entrepreneur Hour. _____

Mei Zhou, the owner of Maxi's, _____. Using money from a

small business start-up grant, Ms. Zhou converted an old warehouse into _____

_____ imported from all over the world. After a commercial break, we'll talk to Ms. Zhou about

the steps she took to _____.

---

5. Where most likely is the announcement being made?

(A) In a department store
(B) In a library

6. Who is Midori Nagai?

(A) A newspaper reporter
(B) An interior designer

Attention, _____. Stop by the home decorating department to

meet _____, Midori Nagai. At noon she'll be _____

_____ on her top ten home decorating tips. She will explain ways to decorate on a

budget by using items you probably already have around the house. She has included many of these

suggestions in her new book, *In Your Home*. And after her presentation, Ms. Nagai will be _____

_____. Don't miss today's special event, and thank you for shopping at

Tuckman's!

PART 4 | CHAPTER 01

1. What type of business is the speaker calling?
   (A) A law firm
   (B) A real estate office
   (C) An office supply store
   (D) An advertising agency

2. Why is the speaker calling?
   (A) To provide a change of address
   (B) To request a refund
   (C) To confirm a shipment
   (D) To make an appointment

3. What does the speaker say will happen in November?
   (A) A product will be advertised.
   (B) A contract will expire.
   (C) An office will open.
   (D) A Web site will be launched.

4. What is the purpose of the talk?
   (A) To introduce a speaker
   (B) To promote a product
   (C) To announce an award
   (D) To describe a trip

5. What field does Joan McLane most likely work in?
   (A) Economics
   (B) Transportation
   (C) Publishing
   (D) Medicine

6. What has Joan McLane recently done?
   (A) Edited a book
   (B) Advised a company
   (C) Conducted an experiment
   (D) Started an organization

7. Who most likely is the speaker?
   (A) A sales manager
   (B) A corporate trainer
   (C) A company president
   (D) A human resources representative

8. What is the speaker mainly discussing?
   (A) Sales results
   (B) Employee satisfaction
   (C) Customer feedback
   (D) Certification programs

9. What does the speaker ask the listeners to do?
   (A) Register for a seminar
   (B) Research a competitor
   (C) Create a list
   (D) Have small-group discussions

10. What type of business is being advertised?
    (A) A food company
    (B) A photography studio
    (C) A sporting goods store
    (D) A fitness center

11. Who is Mike Clark?
    (A) A television journalist
    (B) A famous film actor
    (C) A professional athlete
    (D) A city official

12. What does the speaker encourage listeners to do?
    (A) Try a free service
    (B) Arrive early to an event
    (C) Compare prices online
    (D) Enter a contest

13. Where most likely is the talk being given?
(A) At a career fair
(B) At a sales presentation
(C) At a training session
(D) At an employee luncheon

14. What does the speaker say is broken?
(A) A computer
(B) A projector
(C) A telephone
(D) A camera

15. What will the listeners do next?
(A) Return to their offices
(B) Introduce themselves
(C) Input some data
(D) Obtain identification badges

16. What is the focus of the broadcast?
(A) A health fair
(B) A laptop computer
(C) A training workshop
(D) A mobile application

17. According to the speaker, what can the listeners find on a Web site?
(A) Contest rules
(B) A review
(C) Driving directions
(D) A survey

18. What will the listeners hear next?
(A) A sports report
(B) A weather forecast
(C) A traffic report
(D) An interview

19. Where does the speaker work?
(A) At a recycling center
(B) At a pharmacy
(C) At a custom sign shop
(D) At a computer repair shop

20. What should customers be asked?
(A) Whether they need a plastic bag
(B) Whether they have a membership card
(C) How they prefer to pay for a purchase
(D) Where they would like a product delivered

21. Why will the speaker put up a sign?
(A) To provide a password for customers
(B) To remind employees of a policy
(C) To illustrate a new product
(D) To advertise an upcoming a sale

22. Who are the listeners?
(A) Bank tellers
(B) Factory workers
(C) Restaurant servers
(D) Hotel housekeeping staff

23. What is the purpose of the meeting?
(A) To prepare for an inspection
(B) To introduce an executive
(C) To train new employees
(D) To revise work schedules

24. What must listeners do on Friday?
(A) Return some equipment
(B) Attend a conference
(C) Update a password
(D) Sign a form

❸ 세부 사항 문제

출제공식

1 What, Why, How, Who 등 다양한 의문사로 시작해 세부 정보를 묻는 문제는 가장 많이 출제되는 유형이다. 질문 및 보기의 키워드가 그대로, 혹은 패러프레이징되어 대화에 등장한다.

2 특정 대상에 대해 언급한 내용을 묻는 문제는 서술형 보기로 구성되어 있다. 따라서 담화가 나오기 전에 보기까지 다 읽고 단서가 어떻게 패러프레이징될 지 예상하며 듣는 것이 좋다.

문제유형

[세부 정보]   **What(+ 명사) does / did / will the speaker ~?**
화자가 무엇을(어떤 ~을) ~하는가 / 했는가 / 할 것인가?

What / Where can the listeners ~?   청자들은 무엇을 / 어디서 ~할 수 있는가?

[방법]   **How can the listeners ~?**   청자들은 어떻게 ~ 할 수 있는가?

[이유]   **Why is / are / will / should + 주어 ~?**   ~는 왜 ~인가 / 할 것인가 / 해야 하는가?

[언급한 내용]   **What does the speaker say / emphasize about ~?**
화자는 ~에 대해 뭐라고 말하는가 / 강조하는가?

According to the speaker, what is special[unique] about ~?
화자에 따르면, ~의 특별한 점은?

What is mentioned about ~?   ~에 대해서 언급된 바는 무엇인가?

✏️ **핵심 전략 | 문제의 키워드와 패러프레이징될 단서를 노려 듣는다.**   🎧 P4_11

Thanks for joining us at this year's summer baking contest. The judges have tasted all the homemade cakes that were entered in the competition, and now it's time to reveal the results. But before I do that, I'd like to thank our competition sponsor, Rossman's Market. Its support is what makes this event possible.

문제의 키워드: Rossman's Market
화자가 로스만즈 마켓에 대해 말한 것: 제빵 대회 후원 업체

The cakes were judged on flavor and appearance. We had a lot of impressive entries. In fact, the judges met for a full hour. Without further delay, here are the results.

Q. What does the speaker say about Rossman's Market?
(A) It is family owned.
(B) It is sponsoring an event.
(C) It has been operating for 50 years.
(D) It is having a promotional sales event.

단서   our competition sponsor, Its support is what makes this event possible.

정답   (B) 행사를 후원한다.

이번 여름 제빵 대회에 함께해 주셔서 감사합니다. 심사위원들이 대회에 참가한 수제 케이크를 모두 맛보았고, 이제 결과를 발표할 시간입니다. 하지만 이에 앞서, **대회 후원업체인 로스만즈 마켓에 감사를 드리고 싶습니다. 지원해 주셔서 본 행사가 가능했습니다.** 케이크는 맛과 모양으로 판정했는데요. 인상적인 출품작이 많았습니다. 실제로 심사위원들이 한 시간 내내 회의를 했습니다. 더 이상의 지체 없이, 이제 그 결과를 공개합니다.

화자는 로스만즈 마켓에 대해 뭐라고 말하는가?
(A) 가족 소유이다.
(B) 행사를 후원한다.
(C) 50년간 운영하고 있다.
(D) 판촉 판매 행사를 열고 있다.

세부 사항 문제 단서 제시 방식

P4_12

세부 정보	질문	What is the company planning to do? 회사가 계획하고 있는 일은?
	단서	As you all know, our company is planning to relocate to San Francisco next month. 여러분 모두 아시다시피, 우리 회사는 다음 달에 샌프란시스코로 이전할 계획입니다.
	정답	Move to a new location 새로운 곳으로 이전하기

방법	질문	How can the listeners get a free gift ? 청자들은 어떻게 사은품을 받을 수 있는가?
	단서	If you fill out the survey, you will receive a complimentary bag of our carrot snacks . 설문조사를 완료하시면, 저희 당근 간식 제품 한 봉지를 무료로 받으시게 됩니다.
	정답	By completing a survey 설문조사를 완료함으로써

이유

① 이유를 나타내는 because, since, as 등

	질문	Why is the office currently closed ? 왜 사무실은 현재 문을 닫았는가?
	단서	Our office is closed this week because we're undergoing renovations. 저희 사무실은 수리 중이라 이번 주에 문을 닫습니다.
	정답	It is being renovated. 수리되는 중이다.

② 목적을 나타내는 to부정사 / so (that) 주어 + 동사 / 전치사 for

	질문	Why is the speaker travelling to Sydney ? 화자가 시드니에 가는 이유는?
	단서	I'm leaving for Sydney tomorrow to speak at the public health conference. 공공 보건 학회에서 연설을 하기 위해 내일 시드니로 떠날 거예요.
	정답	To participate in a conference 학회에 참가하기 위해

언급한 내용	질문	According to the speaker, what is special about the camera ? 화자에 따르면, 카메라의 특별한 점은 무엇인가?
	단서	What makes this camera unique is that it's the smallest on the market. 이 카메라를 특별하게 만드는 점은 시장에서 가장 작은 제품이라는 것입니다.
	정답	The size 크기

PART 4 | CHAPTER 01

ETS CHECK-UP

P4_13 정답 및 해설 p.204

1. What will the speaker help the listeners do?

(A) Set up a health program
(B) Attract qualified applicants
(C) Correct payroll errors
(D) Increase the number of customers

2. Why is the Gold Star package unavailable?

(A) Another customer has already booked it.
(B) Some software is malfunctioning.
(C) Some equipment is being replaced.
(D) A staff member is out of town.

❹ 문제점/걱정거리 문제

출제공식
1 화자가 언급한 문제점/걱정거리를 묻는 유형으로, 출제 빈도가 높지는 않은 편이다.
2 문제점/걱정거리를 자세히 설명하거나 이와 관련된 요청/제안하는 내용이 주로 출제된다.

문제유형
[문제점] What is the problem? 무엇이 문제인가?
 What problem does the speaker mention[report]? 화자는 어떤 문제를 언급[보고]하는가?
 What problem is the speaker discussing? 화자는 어떤 문제를 이야기하는가?

[걱정거리] What is the speaker concerned[worried] about? 화자는 무엇을 걱정하는가?
 What concern does the speaker mention? 화자는 어떤 우려를 언급하는가?
 Why does the speaker say she is concerned? 화자는 왜 걱정이 된다고 말하는가?

✎ **핵심 전략 | 우려를 나타내거나 부정적인 의미를 지닌 표현에 주목한다.** 🎧 P4_14

Hi, Michael. This is Sue Park. The other editors and I have finished checking the draft of the next issue of the magazine. We noticed a problem with the photo on page six. It looks a little blurry, and I don't think it will come out clear in print.

Can you try to improve the quality of the image? I'm surprised that a photograph like this was chosen in the first place, so I'm a little concerned about our selection process.

걱정거리를 나타내는 단서 표현: I'm a little concerned
화자의 걱정거리: 사진 선정 과정

I think we should review the steps in our work flow to help prevent this kind of problem in the future.

Q. What is the speaker worried about?
(A) An approaching deadline
(B) A customer complaint
(C) A work process
(D) A staffing shortage

단서 I'm a little concerned about our selection process.
정답 (C) 업무 처리 과정

안녕하세요, 마이클. 저 수 박이에요. 다른 편집자들과 제가 잡지의 다음 호 초안 확인을 마쳤는데요. 6페이지의 사진에 문제가 있는 것을 발견했습니다. 약간 흐릿해 보이고, 인쇄가 잘 안 될 것 같아요. **화질을 개선해봐 줄 수 있나요? 이런 사진이 애초에 선정됐다는 게 놀라울 따름이라, 우리의 선정 과정에 대한 우려가 약간 생기네요.** 앞으로 이런 문제가 발생하지 않도록 업무 흐름 단계를 검토해야 할 것 같습니다.

화자가 걱정하는 것은?
(A) 다가오는 마감 기한
(B) 고객의 불만
(C) 업무 처리 과정
(D) 인력 부족

업무	unclear / inefficient / hard[difficult] / complex[complicated] I know there have been some **complaints** about the complicated reimbursement process. 복잡한 환급 절차에 대한 불평이 있다는 점 알고 있습니다.
매출 / 예산	decrease / competitor[competition] / be short on / not sufficient **I'm worried** because our sales have decreased since our main competitor released a new model. 우리의 주요 경쟁사가 새 모델을 출시한 이래 우리 매출이 떨어지고 있어 걱정입니다.
재고	out of stock / unavailable / sold out / run out of / discontinue **I'm sorry** to say that the desk you ordered is out of stock at the moment. 죄송하지만 주문하신 책상은 현재 재고가 없습니다.
기기 / 설비	out of order / broken / malfunction / technical issue / undergoing repairs The elevator is still out of order, and it seems it will take at least three more hours to fix it. 엘리베이터가 여전히 고장이고 수리하는 데 적어도 세 시간은 더 걸릴 것 같아요.
일정	postpone / cancel / behind schedule / deadline **My biggest concern is that** we're behind schedule and might not be able to meet the deadline. 제 가장 큰 걱정은 우리가 일정에 뒤쳐져 있어 마감일을 맞추지 못할 수도 있다는 겁니다.
교통편	delay / run late / miss / suspended / closed / stuck in traffic Due to the heavy snow in the area, all northbound trains are experiencing delays. 해당 지역 내 폭설 때문에 모든 북행 열차가 지연되고 있습니다.

PART 4 | **CHAPTER 01**

ETS CHECK-UP　🎧 P4_16　정답 및 해설 p. 205

1. What problem is mentioned?

(A) A window is broken.
(B) A technician has not arrived.
(C) An e-mail address is not correct.
(D) A product is not available.

2. What problem does the speaker mention?

(A) Information is not conveyed clearly.
(B) Resources are limited.
(C) A manufacturing process takes too long.
(D) A project is understaffed.

P4_17 정답 및 해설 p.206

담화에 등장하는 단서가 알맞게 패러프레이징된 보기를 선택하세요.

W We are sorry to inform you that **today's final activity, which was supposed to take place from 5 to 6 P.M., has been delayed by an hour.** If you need to leave at six due to prior commitments, please let us know. We will give you a partial refund of the conference registration fee.

1. What does the speaker say about the final event?

(A) It will be held in a different building.

(B) It will begin later than scheduled.

M On our show today, I'll be interviewing **Mr. Padma Balani, the author of the best seller** *How to Communicate Effectively at Work*. **Since the book's release last month,** he has been on a tour to meet readers from all over the country.

2. What did Mr. Balani do last month?

(A) He published a book.

(B) He appeared on television.

W Hello, this is Jin-young Lee from Human Resources. I'm calling because **there seems to be something wrong with the air conditioner in our office. We turned it on about an hour ago, but it's not cooling the office at all.**

3. What problem does the speaker report?

(A) Some equipment is malfunctioning.

(B) Some documents are missing.

M We know you were all disappointed that **the premiere of Laura Kelly's film was canceled due to the power outage last night.** You'll be happy to hear it has been **rescheduled for 7 P.M. this Saturday** at the same venue, the Springfield Cinema House.

4. Why was the event postponed?

(A) The weather was bad.

(B) There was a power failure.

W We've got a huge project coming up, and we'll need to add more staff to our team to complete it on time. **But after speaking with management, I'm concerned that our budget won't allow for the number of people that we want.**

5. What is the speaker concerned about?

(A) A limited budget

(B) Inexperienced staff

M **If you would like to learn more about our lecture series and see the full schedule of the upcoming sessions, please visit our Web site, www.victoriastatelibrary. gov. au,** where you can also sign up for our newsletter to get regular e-mail updates.

6. How can the listeners get more information?

(A) By installing an application

(B) By visiting a Web site

LISTENING **PRACTICE**

ↁ ⴱ P4_18 정답 및 해설 p.208

담화를 들으면서 정답을 고르세요. 그리고 다시 들으면서 빈칸을 채우세요. (녹음은 두 번씩 들려줍니다.)

1. What has Patel Legal Services recently done?

(A) It has sponsored a fund-raiser.

(B) It has opened a new office.

2. Where can listeners find out more about Patel Legal Services?

(A) In a newspaper

(B) At a library

Patel Legal Services has been practicing _____. We specialize in representing nonprofit organizations that are working to make the world a greener place. _____ in Los Angeles, we are now better able to serve our clients on the West Coast who are _____ _____. For more information about our practice, _____ in the weekend edition of the *Southern California Times*.

3. How did the speaker learn about the company?

(A) She saw some work samples online.

(B) She got a recommendation from a friend.

4. What is the speaker mostly concerned about?

(A) The size of a space

(B) The location of a building

Hello. My name is Cynthia Haywood, and I'm the owner of a hair salon on West Main Street. I'm planning to have my salon redecorated this summer, and _____. She showed me how your designers decorated her boutique last year, and I hope you'll be able to do something similar for me. My biggest concern is that _____, and I'd like to find a way to _____. Maybe a brighter paint color would help? If you're interested in accepting the decorating project, please call me at 555-0178 so that we can _____.

5. What problem did Felipe Rashad have?

(A) Limited parking

(B) Decreasing sales

6. What does the speaker say about Johnny's Antique Shop?

(A) It will expand its location.

(B) It has won an award.

And in local business news, Felipe's Books _____. Felipe Rashad, the owner of the Rose Avenue shop, has announced his plans to retire after almost forty years serving Watertown residents. In an interview with our reporter, Mr. Rashad said that _____ _____ over the last ten years. However, the location won't be empty for long! Johnny's Antique Shop, which is right next door, _____ by the end of the year.

PART 4 | CHAPTER 01

1. Who most likely are the listeners?
   (A) Concert performers
   (B) Technical support staff
   (C) Conference attendees
   (D) Restaurant servers

2. What problem does the speaker mention?
   (A) A room has not been reserved.
   (B) Some tickets were not distributed.
   (C) A speaker is unavailable.
   (D) A microphone is not working.

3. According to the speaker, what will some listeners need to do?
   (A) Keep their receipts
   (B) Follow some signs
   (C) Wait in line
   (D) Show some identification

4. What has the listener agreed to do?
   (A) Speak at an event
   (B) Help plan a conference
   (C) Prepare a special tour
   (D) Teach a course

5. What did the speaker send in an e-mail?
   (A) An evaluation form
   (B) A detailed agenda
   (C) A list of names
   (D) A budget proposal

6. What does the speaker say about Ruby Weaver?
   (A) She needs to be trained.
   (B) She has changed jobs.
   (C) Her fees are too high.
   (D) Her availability is limited.

7. What products are being discussed?
   (A) Laptop computers
   (B) Medical equipment
   (C) Smartphone cases
   (D) Battery chargers

8. What problem is mentioned?
   (A) Incorrect results were reported.
   (B) Sales targets were not met.
   (C) Manufacturers recalled an item.
   (D) Customers complained about prices.

9. According to the speaker, what will Charles Han do today?
   (A) Prepare a presentation
   (B) Review a budget
   (C) Analyze a report
   (D) Form a team

10. What does the speaker say will open next month?
    (A) A museum
    (B) A train station
    (C) A shopping center
    (D) A university

11. According to the speaker, what is the last stage of a project?
    (A) A parking area will be paved.
    (B) A fund-raiser will take place.
    (C) Some roads will reopen.
    (D) Some artwork will be installed.

12. Who contributed to the project?
    (A) A charitable organization
    (B) A community bank
    (C) Local students
    (D) City officials

13. Where most likely is this announcement being made?
(A) At a construction site
(B) At a factory
(C) At a car dealership
(D) At an office supply store

14. What problem does the speaker mention?
(A) Some supplies are missing.
(B) A manager has not arrived.
(C) Bad weather is expected.
(D) Some equipment is not working.

15. What will employees be informed about this evening?
(A) Inspection results
(B) Safety policy changes
(C) Work schedule updates
(D) Road conditions

16. What does the speaker say the company is considering?
(A) Hiring a new vendor
(B) Extending the lunch hour
(C) Creating an intern program
(D) Refurbishing company kitchens

17. What can listeners receive for free tomorrow?
(A) A mug
(B) A T-shirt
(C) A notepad
(D) A beverage

18. Why should listeners visit Jeremy's office?
(A) To pick up training materials
(B) To sign up for a project
(C) To collect a prize
(D) To submit a form

19. What product is the speaker discussing?
(A) A computer program
(B) A home heating system
(C) A kitchen appliance
(D) A construction tool

20. How is the product better than previous versions?
(A) It is easier to use.
(B) It works more quickly.
(C) It has a compact design.
(D) It is more energy efficient.

21. What is the speaker concerned about?
(A) Manufacturing is behind schedule.
(B) The product will be more expensive.
(C) The product has technical problems.
(D) Competitors are releasing a similar product.

22. What is the speaker trying to sell?
(A) Packaging material
(B) Clothing fabrics
(C) Printing paper
(D) Recycling bins

23. According to the speaker, what is special about the product?
(A) It is lightweight.
(B) It is water-resistant.
(C) It is available in many colors.
(D) It is made from recycled material.

24. How can the listeners receive a discount?
(A) By making a purchase today
(B) By referring a friend
(C) By placing a large order
(D) By entering a number code

❺ 다음에 할 일/일어날 일 문제

출제공식
1 화자나 청자가 다음에 할 일, 담화 이후 이어질 일정, 청자가 다음에 듣게 될 방송 등을 묻는 질문은 보통 마지막 문제로 출제된다.
2 앞으로 일어날 일을 묻는 문제는 미래의 특정 시점이 단서로 언급된다.

문제유형
[할 일]　What does the speaker say she will do (next)? 화자는 (다음에) 무엇을 하겠다고 말하는가?
　　　　 What will the listeners most likely do (next)? 청자들은 (다음에) 무엇을 하겠는가?

[일어날 일]　What will happen[occur] in ~? ~에 어떤 일이 일어나겠는가?
　　　　　 What is going to take place in ~? ~에 어떤 일이 있을 예정인가?

✏ **핵심 전략** | 미래를 나타내는 표현이나 부탁/지시를 하는 부분에 주목한다.　🎧 P4_20

Hello, everyone. I'd like to start our warehouse staff meeting by discussing some upcoming changes to our safety routines. You'll still have to do a visual inspection of your forklift before you start working, but now you'll also be required to complete a checklist and have it signed by your supervisor. Your supervisors are aware of this update and will be available to sign your checklists before each shift. Please pass around these copies of the new inspection checklist. I'm going to review each point with you now.

다음에 할 일을 나타내는 단서 표현: I'm going to ~ now
화자가 할 일: 청자들과 점검표의 주요 사항 살펴보기

Q. What does the **speaker** say she will do next?
(A) Post work assignments
(B) Inspect some equipment
(C) Review a document
(D) Show a video

단서　new inspection checklist, I'm going to review each point ~ now
정답　(C) 문서 검토

안녕하세요, 여러분. 곧 있을 안전 수칙 변경 사항 몇 가지를 논의하는 것으로 창고 직원 회의를 시작하고자 합니다. 여러분은 작업을 시작하기 전에 여전히 지게차를 육안으로 점검해야 할 겁니다. 그런데 이제 점검표를 작성하고 관리자에게 서명도 받아야 합니다. 여러분의 관리자들은 금번 개정 사항을 알고 있으며 각 교대 근무 전에 시간을 내어 여러분의 점검표에 서명해 줄 겁니다. **이 새로운 점검표를 돌려 주시기 바랍니다. 제가 이제 여러분과 중요 사항을 하나씩 살펴보겠습니다.**

화자는 다음에 무엇을 하겠다고 말하는가?
(A) 업무 분장 공지
(B) 장비 검사
(C) 문서 검토
(D) 동영상 상영

✏️ 다음에 할 일 / 일어날 일을 나타내는 단서 표현　　　🎧 P4_21

전화 메시지	**I'll ~ / Let me ~** **I'll** try out the new projector in the boardroom later to make sure it works properly. 이사회실에 있는 새 프로젝터가 제대로 작동하는지 제가 이따가 확인해 볼게요.
회의 / 공지	**I'm going to ~ / Please ~ / I'd like you to ~** **I'm going to** pass out the sign-up sheet now. Please write your name and employee number on it clearly. 이제 제가 참가 신청서를 돌릴 건데요. 그곳에 이름과 사번을 깔끔하게 써주기 바랍니다.
관광 / 견학	**Now, let's ~ / Before we start, let's ~ / Now, we'll ~** **Now, let's** move to our showroom, where you can see the latest models of our electric cars. 자, 이제 전시장으로 이동하셔서 저희 전기 자동차의 최신 모델을 보시죠.
설명 / 발표	**And now, I'll ~ / OK, if you('ll) ~, I'll ~ / Let's start by ~** **OK, if you'll** look at the screen, **I'll** show you a video on the history of the company. 자, 이제 화면을 봐주시면 회사의 역사에 관한 영상을 보여드리겠습니다.
방송	**In a minute[few minutes] ~ / Now, let's welcome ~ / will be (-ing)** **In a minute**, the director of the museum will be joining us to talk about the upcoming exhibition. 곧 해당 미술관 관장님께서 출연하셔서 다가오는 전시회에 대해 말씀해 주실 겁니다.
광고	**be -ing / will be -ing / starting[beginning]** To celebrate our fifteenth anniversary, **we're having** a huge sale starting this Friday. 15주년을 기념하는 의미에서, 이번 금요일부터 폭탄 세일에 들어갑니다.

ETS CHECK-UP　　　🎧 P4_22　정답 및 해설 p.215

1. What will occur in Jefferson City in May?

(A) A sporting event
(B) A cooking competition
(C) A film festival
(D) An automobile show

2. What will the listeners do next?

(A) Draft a speech
(B) Tour a banquet hall
(C) Nominate award candidates
(D) Select menu options

❻ 요청/제안 사항 문제

출제공식 1 화자가 청자에게 요청/제안/추천하는 사항을 묻는 유형으로, 두 번째나 세 번째 문제로 자주 출제된다.

2 담화의 중·후반부에 단서가 등장할 확률이 높다.

문제유형 [요청] **What does the speaker ask listeners to do?** 화자는 청자들에게 무엇을 하라고 요청하는가?

What are the listeners asked[invited] to do? 청자들은 무엇을 하라고 요청 받는가?

What does the speaker request? 화자가 요청하는 것은 무엇인가?

[제안] **What does the speaker suggest[recommend]?** 화자는 무엇을 제안하는가?

What are the listeners advised to do? 청자들은 무엇을 하라고 권고 받는가?

What does the speaker encourage listeners to do?
화자는 청자들에게 무엇을 하라고 독려하는가?

What does the speaker offer to do? 화자는 무엇을 해 주겠다고 제안하는가?

✎ **핵심 전략** | 담화 중·후반부에 등장하는 요청/제안의 표현을 포착한다. 🎧 P4_23

Good news, team. Our application to participate in the annual Morristown Street Food Festival in July has been accepted! This will be a great opportunity for us to showcase our wonderful canned fruit products.

But… um, I'll need all of you to work this weekend. I'd like everyone to help carry boxes to the booth.

요청을 나타내는 단서 표현: **I'll need** ●━━━
청자들에게 요청하는 것: 이번 주말에 근무하기 ●━━━

And, I know our products are heavy, so I've asked for the booth closest to the parking area. That way, we'll just have to carry the boxes for a very short distance.

Q. What does the speaker **ask** the **listeners** to do?
(A) Send out invitations
● (B) Work over a weekend
(C) Recruit product testers
(D) Complete an inventory count

단서 I'll need all of you to work this weekend

정답 (B) 주말 근무

팀원 여러분, 좋은 소식이 있어요. 7월에 있을 연례 모리스타운 길거리 음식 축제 참가 신청이 승인됐어요! 우리 회사의 훌륭한 과일 통조림 제품을 선보일 절호의 기회가 될 거예요. 하지만, 음… **여러분이 이번 주말에 일을 해주어야 해요. 모두가 부스로 박스를 나르는 일을 도와줬으면 좋겠습니다.** 우리 제품은 무거워서 주차장에서 가장 가까운 부스로 요청해 뒀어요. 그러면 아주 짧은 거리만 박스를 옮기면 되니까요.

화자는 청자들에게 무엇을 해달라고 요청하는가?
(A) 초대장 발송
(B) 주말 근무
(C) 제품 테스터 모집
(D) 재고 수량 작성

Please (make sure to) ~ / I'd like you to ~ / I'm asking you to ~ / I'll need you to ~

요청

I'll be away on vacation next week, so **please** <u>confirm your attendance by tomorrow.</u>
제가 다음 주에 휴가 차 자리를 비우니, 내일까지 참석 여부를 확정해 주십시오.

Please make sure to <u>turn off your mobile phone</u> before the performance begins.
공연이 시작되기 전에 반드시 휴대 전화 전원을 꺼주십시오.

I'd like you all to take a few minutes to <u>look at the new logo design and tell me what you think.</u>
여러분 모두 잠깐 시간을 내어 새 로고 디자인을 보고 어떻게 생각하는지 말씀해 주셨으면 합니다.

① 제안 / 권유: I encourage you to ~ / I recommend[suggest] ~ / Feel free to ~

I encourage you to <u>visit our video channel and subscribe for more gardening tips!</u>
더 많은 정원 가꾸기 팁을 보시려면 저희의 비디오 채널을 방문해서 구독하시길 권해드려요!

As a first step, **I suggest** <u>identifying your competitors and evaluating their strengths.</u>
첫 번째 단계로, 여러분의 경쟁사를 찾아 그들의 강점을 평가해 볼 것을 권해드립니다.

If you have a question for Dr. Roland, **feel free to** <u>call us here at the station</u> at 555-0124.
롤랜드 박사님께 질문이 있으시면, 555-0124를 눌러 이곳 방송국으로 전화주세요.

제안

② 제안 / 제공: If you ~, I can[could] ~ / I'd be happy to ~ / We will ~ / We'd like to ~

If you're interested in that position, just let me know. **I can** <u>forward your résumé to him.</u>
그 자리에 관심이 있다면 알려주세요. 제가 그에게 당신의 이력서를 전달해 줄게요.

I'd be happy to <u>drop the prototype off at your office</u> later this afternoon.
이따 오후에 당신의 사무실로 기꺼이 견본품을 가져다 드리겠습니다.

If you purchase any of our new athletic shoes this month, **we'll** <u>ship them to your home for free.</u>
이번 달에 저희 신제품 운동화를 구매하시면, 댁까지 무료로 배송해 드립니다.

ETS CHECK-UP   🎧 P4_25   정답 및 해설 p.215

1. What does the speaker offer to do?

(A) Provide an estimate
(B) Notify a colleague
(C) Work over a weekend
(D) Visit a customer

2. What are the listeners advised to do?

(A) Pick up their luggage
(B) Take a shuttle bus
(C) Visit an information counter
(D) Check a flight timetable

담화에 등장하는 단서가 알맞게 패러프레이징된 보기를 선택하세요.

M The book you ordered was scheduled to arrive at our store this morning, but the supplier just informed us that it won't get here for another two or three days. **I'll send you a text message when it arrives so that you can come by and collect it.**	**1.** What does the speaker say he will do? (A) Send a notification later (B) Ship a replacement product
W Next year, **the hospital will add a wing on the west side of the main building.** The new wing will feature one hundred private patient rooms and three rehabilitation gyms for inpatients.	**2.** What will happen next year? (A) A local bridge will be closed. (B) Some construction will take place.
M Before I show you around the museum and assign each of you a task, **I'd like to invite you all to our on-site restaurant to enjoy a special lunch.** It's on the third floor, so you can either use the stairs or take the elevator next to the information desk.	**3.** What will the listeners most likely do next? (A) Have a meal (B) Watch a demonstration
W If you wish to participate in the skills development **workshop** next month, **I recommend signing up early**, as space is limited to 50 people. After this meeting, I'll send you a link to the online registration page.	**4.** What does the speaker recommend? (A) Checking a Web page regularly (B) Registering for an event in advance
M If you use our carts to carry your groceries to your car, **please drop them off at the cart corrals after unloading.** There are corrals installed across the parking area, so you'll be able to find one easily. Thanks for your cooperation.	**5.** What are the listeners asked to do? (A) Complete a customer survey (B) Leave carts in designated areas
W To celebrate the release of our new language learning app, we're giving you the opportunity to use it for a month at no cost. **This exceptional offer is only available during May, so visit www.linguas.com today to download the app and begin your free trial!**	**6.** What does the speaker encourage the listeners to do? (A) Take advantage of a special offer (B) Donate to an upcoming project

LISTENING **PRACTICE**

P4_27 정답 및 해설 p.218

담화를 들으면서 정답을 고르세요. 그리고 다시 들으면서 빈칸을 채우세요. (녹음은 두 번씩 들려줍니다.)

1. What does the speaker ask the listeners to do?

(A) Put on their uniforms
(B) Read some documents

2. What will the speaker do next?

(A) Answer some questions
(B) Hand out identification badges

Thanks, everyone, for coming in so early today. We want to make _____.
It's going to be a great first day. Thomas, I see that you've already placed flowers on all the tables, so
thank you for that. Theresa is _____—we just got them in, and
I think they look good. Please _____. And I see a few of you
already have your hands up, so before I give out your assignments, I'll _____
_____.

3. According to the speaker, what will happen tomorrow?

(A) A special offer will expire.
(B) A business will move to a new building.

4. What additional incentive does the speaker offer the listener?

(A) A gift certificate
(B) An extended warranty

Hi, this message is for Jun Tang. This is Hector from Affordable Home Kitchens. You were in our
showroom a few days ago _____. I know you wanted some
time to think it over, but I'm calling to remind you that _____.
If you do decide to buy it by tomorrow, we can also _____.
Please let me know by six o'clock tomorrow evening. My number is 555-0191.

5. What will the group Thunderbear do next month?

(A) Start a tour
(B) Release a new album

6. What will listeners hear next?

(A) A schedule of events
(B) A song

Good morning, Radio 82 listeners. On today's show we'll be joined by Adam Brennan, _____
_____ Thunderbear. This group, based right here in Toronto, _____
_____ after the release of their debut album, Room for Two, last year. And next month the group will
_____. Mr. Brennan will be joining us shortly to talk about the
upcoming tour. Until then, let's listen to _____.

1. What will the listeners learn about?
   (A) Creating strong passwords
   (B) Organizing e-mail folders
   (C) Obtaining identification badges
   (D) Protecting e-mail attachments

2. What does the speaker ask some of the listeners to do?
   (A) Upgrade their hardware
   (B) Assist their coworkers
   (C) E-mail multiple recipients
   (D) Sign up for a future workshop

3. What will the speaker do next?
   (A) Distribute some work sheets
   (B) Introduce a guest
   (C) Request feedback
   (D) Demonstrate a procedure

4. What does the speaker expect will soon happen at the store?
   (A) New merchandise will arrive.
   (B) The number of customers will increase.
   (C) A display will be redesigned.
   (D) Payment processes will change.

5. What are employees encouraged to do?
   (A) Volunteer to work late
   (B) Read a manual
   (C) Make some recommendations
   (D) Distribute free samples

6. According to the speaker, what will begin next Tuesday?
   (A) Job interviews
   (B) Extended store hours
   (C) A renovation project
   (D) A training seminar

7. Who is Ms. Brownstein's advice intended for?
   (A) Company managers
   (B) Book authors
   (C) Office receptionists
   (D) University professors

8. According to Ms. Brownstein, what is the best way to promote creativity?
   (A) Rewarding excellent performance
   (B) Decorating office spaces
   (C) Inviting inspirational speakers
   (D) Allowing flexible work schedules

9. What does the speaker suggest the listeners do?
   (A) Sign up for a workshop
   (B) Tour some offices
   (C) Watch a video
   (D) Download a book

10. What will happen in two weeks?
    (A) A ticket price will increase.
    (B) Some building renovations will begin.
    (C) Some products will be discounted.
    (D) A park will close for the season.

11. What task are the listeners asked to do?
    (A) Make additional signs
    (B) Train new employees
    (C) Cover some equipment
    (D) Stock some shelves

12. According to the speaker, what will be provided to the listeners?
    (A) Meals
    (B) Transportation
    (C) Uniforms
    (D) Mobile phones

13. What is the speaker mainly discussing?
(A) A marketing technique
(B) An upcoming retail sale
(C) A career opportunity
(D) A new product line

14. What customer benefit does the speaker mention?
(A) Improved technical support
(B) Reduced shipping time
(C) Flexible payment options
(D) Advance notice of special offers

15. What will the speaker do next?
(A) Complete a survey
(B) Give a demonstration
(C) Explain a policy change
(D) Distribute some brochures

16. What is the company doing next month?
(A) Reorganizing a department
(B) Sharing employee feedback results
(C) Working with a new client
(D) Upgrading its computers

17. Why is the speaker calling?
(A) To report an equipment malfunction
(B) To ask for feedback about a process
(C) To announce a work opportunity
(D) To schedule a performance evaluation

18. What does the speaker ask the listener to do?
(A) Work late
(B) Contact a client
(C) Write up a report
(D) Confirm availability

19. What is taking place in June?
(A) An equipment upgrade
(B) A series of seminars
(C) A company move
(D) A retirement party

20. What does the speaker request?
(A) Larger office spaces
(B) An updated filing system
(C) Increased security staff
(D) Volunteers for a position

21. What does the speaker indicate about the project?
(A) It will finish under budget.
(B) It will require a change in work hours.
(C) It will involve more research studies.
(D) It will be reviewed by the company president.

22. What is the speaker mainly discussing?
(A) A business reorganization
(B) A proposed budget
(C) Company policies
(D) Energy efficiency

23. What does the speaker recommend?
(A) Hiring additional staff
(B) Changing vendors
(C) Installing special equipment
(D) Rescheduling a meeting

24. What does the speaker provide to the listeners?
(A) Survey results
(B) Floor plans
(C) Product brochures
(D) Employee handbooks

❼ 화자의 의도 파악 문제

출제공식 **1** 문제에 제시된 문장의 숨은 의도를 묻는 문제로, 파트 4에서는 매회 3문항씩 출제된다.

2 결정적인 단서는 제시문 앞뒤에 있지만, 전체적인 맥락을 이해해야 적절한 답을 선택할 수 있다.

3 문제의 특성상 주로 두 번째나 세 번째 순서로 출제된다. 이전 문제의 답을 선택하자마자 이어지는 내용을 파악하며 제시문을 노려 듣도록 한다.

문제유형 Why does the speaker say, "~"? 화자가 "~"라고 말하는 이유는 무엇인가?

What does the speaker imply when she says, "~"? 화자가 "~"라고 말할 때 암시하는 바는 무엇인가?

What does the speaker mean when he says, "~"? 화자가 "~"라고 말할 때 의미하는 바는 무엇인가?

✏️ **핵심 전략 |** 질문 및 보기를 읽은 후 담화의 전체적인 흐름을 파악하며 청취한다. 🎧 P4_29

I've called this staff meeting today to talk about the upcoming improvements we're making to the hotel. First, electrical and plumbing repairs will be completed. Then the entire interior will be repainted, and all carpeting will be replaced. Many of you have asked about your work schedules during the renovation project. **We will remain open during construction.**

호텔 보수 공사 동안 근무 일정을 묻는 질문에 대한 답변: ●

영업 지속 = 업무 지속 ●

There will be some noise and dust throughout the building while the work is being done. If any guests have any complaints, please let me know right away.

Q. What does the speaker imply when she says, "We will remain open during construction"?
(A) She is not happy about a decision.
(B) The listeners' work hours will not change.
(C) The project will take a long time.
(D) The listeners have been misinformed.

단서 Many of you have asked about your work schedules during the renovation project.

정답 (B) 근무 시간에는 변동이 없을 것이다.

우리 호텔에 앞으로 진행할 개선 사항에 대해 이야기하려고 오늘 직원회의를 소집했습니다. 첫째로 전기 및 배관 수리가 완료될 겁니다. 그리고 나서 내부 전체를 다시 칠하고 카펫을 모두 교체할 예정입니다. **여러분 중 다수가 보수 공사 중의 업무 일정에 대해 문의했는데요. 우리 호텔은 공사 중에도 계속 영업할 겁니다.** 공사가 이뤄지는 동안 건물 전체에 소음과 먼지가 발생할 것입니다. 고객에게서 어떤 불만이라도 나오면 저에게 바로 알려주세요.

화자가 "공사 중에도 계속 문을 영업할 겁니다"라고 말할 때 암시하는 바는 무엇인가?
(A) 결정사항이 만족스럽지 않다.
(B) 청자들의 근무 시간에는 변동이 없을 것이다.
(C) 프로젝트는 시간이 오래 걸릴 것이다.
(D) 청자들은 잘못된 정보를 받았다.

맥락에 따른 화자의 의도 파악하기

의도 파악 문제는 문장의 표면적 의미가 아닌 문맥상 드러나는 화자의 의도를 묻기 때문에, 맥락 이해가 필수적이다.
같은 문장이 다른 맥락에서 어떤 의미를 갖는지 살펴보자.

담화문 1) P4_30

Q Why does the speaker say, "I had to read it twice"? (A) To make a complaint (B) To express surprise	**Q** 화자는 왜 '두 번이나 읽어야 했어요"라고 하는가? (A) 불평을 하려고 **(B) 놀라움을 표하려고**

I have some great news about the plans for the charity dinner we're organizing. We had asked Arc Airlines for a small donation. Well, they've decided to donate four plane tickets, and to any destination that they fly to. Yeah! I just got their e-mail. **I had to read it twice!**

우리가 준비하고 있는 자선 만찬회 계획에 관해 좋은 소식이 있어요. 아크 항공에 소정의 기부를 요청했었잖아요. **글쎄, 취항하는 목적지 중 어느 곳이든 갈 수 있는 비행기표 4장을 기부하기로 결정해 주셨어요! 그렇다니까요! 방금 이메일을 받았어요. 두 번이나 읽어야 했어요!**

→ 기대했던 것보다 큰 후원을 받게 된 것에 대해 놀라움 표현

담화문 2) P4_31

Q Why does the speaker say, "I had to read it twice"? (A) To make a complaint (B) To express surprise	**Q** 화자는 왜 '두 번이나 읽어야 했어요"라고 하는가? **(A) 불평을 하려고** (B) 놀라움을 표하려고

I'm calling about the training manual you wrote for the new interns who will be starting next week. I thought that all of the parts were well-written and clear—except for the one on their working hours. **I had to read it twice.** Do you think you can revise it by Friday?

다음 주에 근무를 시작할 신입 인턴들을 위해 당신이 작성한 교육 매뉴얼 관련해서 전화해요. **거의 모든 부분이 잘 작성되었고 명확한데, 근무시간과 관련된 부분은 그렇지 않더군요. 두 번이나 읽어야 했어요.** 금요일까지 수정할 수 있을까요?

→ 혼동을 줄 수 있는 내용에 대해 불평하며 수정 요청

ETS CHECK-UP 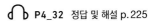 P4_32 정답 및 해설 p.225

1. Why does the speaker say, "I couldn't have done that"?

(A) To show gratitude
(B) To offer encouragement
(C) To avoid blame
(D) To correct a mistake

2. What does the speaker mean when she says, "I need to finish the kitchen inventory this morning"?

(A) She does not have enough ingredients.
(B) Nobody has offered to help her.
(C) She would like a response soon.
(D) A special event will take place this afternoon.

담화에 등장하는 단서를 보고 화자의 의도를 파악해 보세요.

W Your remodeling plan sounds quite intriguing, but I'm currently working on two projects at the same time. **I do know a couple of other reliable interior designers that might be available, though. Let me know if you would like their contact information.**

1. Why does the speaker say, "I'm currently working on two projects at the same time"?

(A) To reject a proposal
(B) To explain a delay

M Starting April second, our company will be running **a leadership program. Some of you might think it's intended for those who are in managerial positions, but actually**, it's open to everyone.

2. Why does the speaker say, "it's open to everyone"?

(A) To congratulate management on a decision
(B) To suggest that the listeners register

W As you know, I did some research this week to find the right contractor for our new project. Hammer Structure's name came up the most often, but I've worked with them before. **Let me present some other options.**

3. What does the speaker imply when she says, "I've worked with them before"?

(A) She was not pleased with a company's performance.
(B) She is well-qualified to manage a project.

M Has everyone got the procedure manuals? Please read them carefully before beginning your tasks. **If you have any inquiries about their contents,** I'll be in Seminar Room B the rest of the day.

4. Why does the speaker say, "I'll be in Seminar Room B the rest of the day"?

(A) To inform listeners of a scheduling change
(B) To tell listeners where to go to ask questions

W **Are you looking for a fun and exciting part-time job?** If so, you'll be happy to hear that party-supplies retailer Cybercat is expanding to London! We offer a lively atmosphere and competitive wages.

5. What does the speaker mean when she says, "Cybercat is expanding to London"?

(A) Some products are very popular.
(B) A business has open positions.

M **I've just reviewed the findings of our market survey.** About fifty percent of respondents indicated that they had not heard of our brand, nor had they ever purchased our products. We might have to change our marketing strategy.

6. What does the speaker imply when he says, "We might have to change our marketing strategy"?

(A) He wants to conduct a second survey.
(B) He is unhappy with some results.

LISTENING **PRACTICE**

🎧 P4_34 정답 및 해설 p. 227

담화를 들으면서 정답을 고르세요. 그리고 다시 들으면서 빈칸을 채우세요. (녹음은 두 번씩 들려줍니다.)

1. What is scheduled for Thursday?

(A) A job interview
(B) A product presentation

2. Why does the speaker say, "I know it's a long trip"?

(A) To advise the listener to get some rest
(B) To apologize for an inconvenience

Hi, Michelle. It's Cameron. I'm still waiting for _____ and the model of our new juice maker. Given the service I've had so far, I don't expect they'll find either _____ _____. And the presentation won't make much of an impression without a prototype. So, at this point, I think _____ with the backup model. I know it's a long trip, but _____.

---

3. What does the speaker mean when she says, "I have a meeting in Chicago"?

(A) She wants to reschedule a meeting.
(B) She is unable to meet in person.

4. What does the speaker recommend that the listener do?

(A) Try some software
(B) Contact some clients

Hi, Nancy, it's Insook. I'm happy to hear that we'll be working together to _____ _____. I've seen the other _____, and I think we'll be a great team. Anyway, I'm just calling about your invitation to meet next week. Thank you for _____ _____, but I have a meeting in Chicago. I've heard that the new _____ _____. I suggest we both _____. Looking forward to our meeting.

---

5. What does the speaker say is most important?

(A) Collecting feedback
(B) Deleting extra details

6. What does the speaker imply when he says, "there are more people here than were registered for the workshop"?

(A) He does not have enough copies of a document.
(B) He thinks a topic is interesting.

Thank you for attending this business-writing workshop. Many people underestimate _____ _____, but it can be the difference between signing a major account and losing one. When it comes to business writing, it's most important that you're concise. _____ _____, your writing is guaranteed to become much clearer. Now, I have _____ _____, but there are more people here than were registered for the workshop… so, um, I'll be right back. When I return, we'll _____.

---

1. What has happened recently?
   (A) Some expenses have increased.
   (B) Some sales have declined.
   (C) Some managers have left.
   (D) Some new shops have opened.

2. What does the speaker imply when he says, "there are many new products on the market"?
   (A) Consumers like the selection.
   (B) More employees are being hired.
   (C) The company has several competitors.
   (D) More refrigerators need to be ordered.

3. What will the listeners receive at the next meeting?
   (A) Some samples
   (B) Some calendars
   (C) An instruction manual
   (D) A list of assignments

4. Where does the speaker work?
   (A) At a recruiting agency
   (B) At a paper supply company
   (C) At a hospital
   (D) At a university

5. Why does the speaker say, "We already have a lot of volunteers signed up for this event"?
   (A) To make a request
   (B) To extend an invitation
   (C) To reassure an event planner
   (D) To decline an offer

6. What does the speaker ask the listener to do?
   (A) Pay a registration fee
   (B) Attend a meeting
   (C) Complete an online form
   (D) Pick a date and time

7. Who most likely are the listeners?
   (A) Customer service representatives
   (B) Software developers
   (C) Corporate attorneys
   (D) Financial advisers

8. What does the speaker mean when she says, "Yes, I know that's not enough"?
   (A) She acknowledges her own mistakes.
   (B) She is worried about a deadline.
   (C) She wants the listeners to volunteer.
   (D) She recognizes the listeners' concerns.

9. What task does the speaker assign to the listeners?
   (A) Updating a mailing list
   (B) Revising training materials
   (C) Mentoring new staff
   (D) Learning to use a software program

10. What does the speaker say is being planned?
    (A) A music festival
    (B) An awards banquet
    (C) A ribbon-cutting ceremony
    (D) A shareholders' meeting

11. What does the speaker imply when he says, "some new members were elected to the council this year"?
    (A) Some programs will be discontinued.
    (B) Some job positions need to be filled.
    (C) A policy could change.
    (D) A meeting room is too small.

12. What does the speaker ask about?
    (A) Some contract details
    (B) Some flyers
    (C) A location
    (D) A software program

13. Which department does the speaker most likely work in?
(A) Finance
(B) Advertising
(C) Human Resources
(D) Technology Support

14. What does the speaker say will happen at a meeting?
(A) A business merger will be approved.
(B) A presentation will be given.
(C) A new board member will be introduced.
(D) A salary raise will be discussed.

15. Why does the speaker say, "the meeting in Room B has been canceled"?
(A) To indicate that she has free time
(B) To correct an error in a schedule
(C) To apologize for a delay
(D) To suggest a different location

16. Why is a change being made to a production process?
(A) Because of government regulations
(B) Because of a problem with the supply chain
(C) Because of customer demands
(D) Because of technological innovations

17. What has Makoto done?
(A) He has written a user manual.
(B) He has completed a training course.
(C) He has secured a supply of materials.
(D) He has met the requirements for a promotion.

18. What does the speaker imply when she says, "I think the decision will be a simple one"?
(A) She is disappointed with the outcome of a project.
(B) The cheapest option will be chosen.
(C) A product has not been not selling well.
(D) The company makes the same decision every year.

19. Who most likely are the listeners?
(A) Museum visitors
(B) Art students
(C) Café workers
(D) Paint store employees

20. Why does the speaker say, "The event will be very small"?
(A) To reassure the listeners
(B) To express disappointment
(C) To describe a venue
(D) To negotiate a price

21. What are the listeners asked to bring to the event?
(A) Cleaning supplies
(B) Tickets
(C) Photo identification
(D) Snacks

22. According to the speaker, what is happening today?
(A) An ad campaign is being launched.
(B) A store is opening new branch.
(C) A product is being released in stores.
(D) A clearance sale is beginning.

23. What does the speaker mean when he says, "From the look of it, you'd think they were giving the phones away"?
(A) The store's advertising is misleading.
(B) Some products are no longer in stock.
(C) There are a lot of customers waiting at the store.
(D) There are many good bargains at the store.

24. According to the speaker, what feature of the Aria 7D is most attractive?
(A) Its water resistance
(B) Its affordable price
(C) Its colorful patterns
(D) Its slim design

PART 4 | CHAPTER 01

⑧ 시각 정보 연계 문제

출제공식
1. 목록, 평면도, 차트 등 다양한 시각 자료와 담화 내용을 연계해서 풀어야 하는 문제로, 파트 4에서는 매회 2문항씩 출제된다.
2. 시각 정보 상에서 보기와 상응하는 부분, 혹은 질문의 키워드가 담화 내에 그대로 등장할 가능성이 높다. 고난도 문제의 경우 패러프레이징되기도 하므로, 반드시 담화가 나오기 전에 문제와 시각 정보의 키워드를 파악해야 한다.

문제유형
Look at the graphic. What / Which / Where / Who / How ~?
시각 정보에 따르면, 무엇이 / 어떤 것이 / 어디에서 / 누가 / 어떻게 ~?

✏️ **핵심 전략 | 문제 및 시각 정보를 보고 담화 내 단서와 연계될 부분을 예상한다.** 🎧 P4_36

Hi, it's Sonya. I'm calling about tonight's journalism awards ceremony at the convention center. The event coordinator e-mailed me a seating chart so we know what table we're at. We're in the first row from the stage but furthest away from the buffet table…

시각 정보의 Stage와 Buffet Table이 단서로 등장 ●
테이블 위치: 무대에서 첫째 줄, 뷔페 테이블에서 가장 먼 곳 ●

I'm really excited, because I think we've got a good chance at winning. And I'd like to chat with some of the other nominees before dinner starts. So let's try to get to the event a little early.

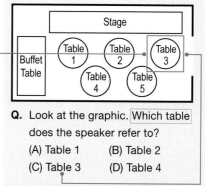

Q. Look at the graphic. Which table does the speaker refer to?
(A) Table 1   (B) Table 2
(C) Table 3   (D) Table 4

단서 first row from the stage, furthest away from the buffet table

정답 (C) 테이블 3

안녕하세요. 소냐예요. 오늘밤 컨벤션 센터에서 열리는 언론상 시상식 건으로 전화했어요. 우리가 어느 테이블에 앉는지 알 수 있게 행사 진행 담당자가 제게 이메일로 좌석 배치도를 보냈어요. **우리 자리는 무대로부터 첫째 줄이지만 뷔페 테이블에서는 가장 멀리 떨어져 있네요…** 우리가 수상할 가능성이 높은 것 같아 정말 신나요. 그리고 만찬이 시작되기 전에 다른 후보 몇 명과 이야기를 나누고 싶어요. 그러니 행사에 조금 일찍 가도록 하죠.

시각 정보에 따르면, 화자는 어떤 테이블을 언급하는가?
(A) 테이블 1
(B) 테이블 2
(C) 테이블 3
(D) 테이블 4

시각 정보 유형별 전략

1. 목록(List)

가장 많이 출제되는 유형으로, 사람/제품/서비스 등의 목록, 일정표, 가격표, 주문서, 회의 안건, 전화번호부 등이
나온다. 보기에 상응하는 정보를 키워드로 삼고 노려 들어야 한다.

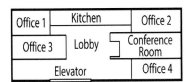

Workshops	Month
Creating Graphics	July 19
E-mail Policies	August 20
Managing Files and Data	September 22
Reading Financial Reports	October 18

Look at the graphic. Which session has been canceled ?
(A) Creating Graphics
(B) E-mail Policies
(C) Managing Files and Data
(D) Reading Financial Reports

취소된 강좌는?
질문의 키워드인 canceled와 각 강좌에
해당하는 날짜 노려 듣기

담화 내 단서

The October session's been canceled due to the staff meeting on the 18th.

18일에 열리는 10월 강좌 → Reading Financial Reports (재무 보고서 읽기)

2. 지도(Map)/평면도(Floor plan)

마을, 도로 등의 지도, 회사/사업장의 평면도, 공연장, 시상식 등의 좌석 배치도(layout)가 출제된다. 위치나 방향 관련
빈출 표현들(heading toward, closest to, across from 등)을 반드시 익혀 두어야 한다.

Look at the graphic. Which office belongs to the speaker?
(A) Office 1
(B) Office 2
(C) Office 3
(D) Office 4

화자의 사무실은?
각 사무실의 위치 확인 후 주변 장소(Kitchen,
Conference Room 등) 노려 듣기

담화 내 단서

My office is on the left, directly across from the conference room.

회의실 바로 맞은 편 → Office 3

3. 그래프(Graph)/차트(Chart)

막대 그래프, 원 그래프, 선 그래프 등의 형태로 출제되며, 수익, 시장 점유율, 점수, 선호도 등을 보여준다. 최고점이나
최저점, 순위, 또는 급락, 급등과 같이 특별히 눈에 띄는 변화나 대략적인 수치를 확인해 둔다.

Inspection Scores

Look at the graphic. When was the safety training session held?
(A) In March
(B) In April
(C) In May
(D) In June

안전 교육 시간이 열린 시기는?
최고점 및 최저점 확인 후 최상급,
수치 등의 관련 표현 노려 듣기

담화 내 단서

You can see that the factory received the highest inspection score in the
month we held a safety training session.

가장 높은 점수를 받은 달 → April

PART 4 | CHAPTER 01

215

4. 테이블(Table)

두 가지 이상의 대상을 서로 비교하는 차트나 테이블이 출제된다. 두 대상이 나올 경우 차이점/변별점을 눈여겨보고, 여러 대상이 있을 경우 순위를 파악해 둔다.

Project	Cost	Duration
Tennis court	$1.5 million	2 months
Pool	$2 million	1 month
Playground	$2.5 million	3 months
Recreational center	$3 million	4 months

Look at the graphic. How long will the selected project take?

(A) 1 month
(B) 2 months
(C) 3 months
(D) 4 months

선정된 프로젝트의 소요 기간은?
각 프로젝트의 비용 및 소요 기간 비교한 후 노려 듣기

담화 내 단서

We know that recreational center was the most popular choice, but we've decided to go with the project that costs the least.

가장 적은 비용이 드는 프로젝트: Tennis Court → 소요 기간: 2 months

---

5. 쿠폰(Coupon)/티켓(Ticket)/영수증(Receipt)

쿠폰이 출제되면 종류, 혜택, 만료일 등 특이 사항을 파악하고, 시설 입장권, 대중교통 티켓 등이 나오면 시간, 좌석 종류, 혜택 대상 등을 살펴보아야 한다. 영수증은 품목 및 금액, 특이 사항을 확인하면 된다.

Receipt

Sushi	$160
Rice and chicken	$140
Pasta	$135
Assorted fruit	$50

Look at the graphic. How much money will the speaker be refunded?

(A) $160
(B) $140
(C) $135
(D) $50

화자가 환불 받을 금액은?
각 금액에 상응하는 메뉴 확인 후 노려 듣기

담화 내 단서

I wanted to make sure we get a refund on the pasta.

파스타 금액 환불 → $135

---

6. 기타

각종 양식, 안내문, 일기 예보, 상품 정보 및 취급 가이드, 그림이 있는 광고/웹페이지/브로슈어 등 점점 더 다양한 시각 정보가 출제되고 있다. 문제의 보기로 제시되는 주제, 숫자, 요일, 이름 등과 연계되는 정보에 주목한다.

Work Order Form

Step 1	Employee Name
Step 2	Description
Step 3	Quantity
Step 4	Department Code

Look at the graphic. Which part of the form does the speaker remind employees to complete?

(A) Employee Name
(B) Description
(C) Quantity
(D) Department Code

화자가 작성하라고 상기시키는 부분은?
양식 각 칸에 해당하는 단계 노려 듣기

담화 내 단서

Don't forget to enter step 4, as I'll need that for budgeting purposes.

4번째 단계 잊지 말기 → Department Code (부서 코드)

담화를 들으면서 정답을 고르세요. 그리고 다시 들으면서 빈칸을 채우세요. (녹음은 두 번씩 들려줍니다.)

Floor	Department
4	Bedding and Mattresses
3	Kitchen and Bath
2	Tables and Chairs
1	Lamps and Lighting

1. Look at the graphic. On which floor are discounts available?

(A) Floor 4   (B) Floor 3
(C) Floor 2   (D) Floor 1

Attention, shoppers! The cash registers on the third floor are _____.
For purchases, please visit any of our other floors. And while you're here today, be sure to _____ _____, on sale for 25 percent off for one day only! Not sure _____ _____? Visit one of our computer kiosks to complete a short questionnaire about _____ _____. Our sales associates can then suggest the best mattress for you!

TO:	chase@firsttierdev.com
SUBJECT:	**FW: Ticket Confirmation**
Passenger	Evan Chase
Departing from	Saint Louis
Arriving in	Toledo
Seat number	22F

2. Look at the graphic. What value will probably be changed?

(A) Evan Chase   (B) Saint Louis
(C) Toledo   (D) 22F

Hi Carly, this is Evan Chase calling about _____ _____ in Toledo. Thank you for arranging that, but I noticed a problem with the, um, _____. Did you know I'm transferring to our Springfield office in June? Because of that I'll need _____.
After you change that, can you forward the confirmation to my personal e-mail address? It's evanchase@ mailexchange.com. Thanks.

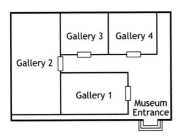

3. Look at the graphic. In which room is the Native American pottery exhibit?

(A) Gallery 1   (B) Gallery 2
(C) Gallery 3   (D) Gallery 4

And that concludes the tour of the _____ _____. If you'd like to learn more about the exhibit, we have an excellent book in the gift shop. I highly _____, titled *Watercolor Paintings*. Now that we're done with the tour, you're welcome to _____ _____. There's a map of the museum at the entrance for your convenience. You won't want to miss the exhibit of Native American pottery in our temporary exhibits gallery. It's the _____ _____. This exhibit will only be here for two more weeks.

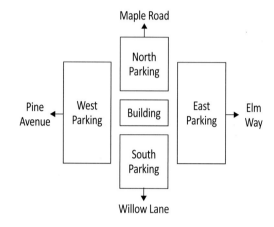

Survey Results
Larger pool–40%
Longer hours–20%
Better exercise equipment–10%
Different classes–30%

Maple Road
North Parking
Pine Avenue
West Parking
Building
East Parking
Elm Way
South Parking
Willow Lane

1. According to the speaker, what is the center's main concern?
   (A) Satisfying current members
   (B) Meeting industry standards
   (C) Reducing operating expenses
   (D) Creating effective advertising

2. Look at the graphic. What survey result does the speaker want to address?
   (A) Larger pool
   (B) Longer hours
   (C) Better exercise equipment
   (D) Different classes

3. What does the speaker ask the listeners to do?
   (A) Conduct safety inspections
   (B) Take a certification course
   (C) Refer potential employees
   (D) Tour a building site

4. What project will begin next week?
   (A) A building will be renovated.
   (B) A parking area will be repaved.
   (C) Some road signs will be installed.
   (D) Some outdoor areas will be landscaped.

5. What does the speaker emphasize about the project?
   (A) It will improve office safety.
   (B) It requires additional funding.
   (C) It will make a commute easier.
   (D) It supports an environmental initiative.

6. Look at the graphic. Which parking area will be closed?
   (A) North Parking
   (B) East Parking
   (C) South Parking
   (D) West Parking

Monday	Tuesday	Wednesday	Thursday

Tuesday Schedule

Tuesday Schedule	
9:00	
10:00	Conference Call
11:00	
Noon	
1:00	Staff Meeting
2:00	
3:00	Client Consultation
4:00	

7. Who most likely is the speaker?
(A) A radio broadcaster
(B) An event planner
(C) A restaurant owner
(D) A magazine editor

8. Look at the graphic. What day will the reception be held?
(A) Monday
(B) Tuesday
(C) Wednesday
(D) Thursday

9. What does the speaker ask the listener to do?
(A) Submit some diagrams
(B) Revise some fliers
(C) Prepare a budget
(D) Contact a vendor

10. Where most likely does the speaker work?
(A) At an interior design company
(B) At a staffing agency
(C) At an event planning service
(D) At an accounting firm

11. What would the speaker like to discuss with the listener?
(A) A hiring process
(B) An increase in rent
(C) A project budget
(D) A client complaint

12. Look at the graphic. What time does the speaker want to meet?
(A) At 9:00
(B) At 11:00
(C) At 2:00
(D) At 4:00

PART 4 | CHAPTER 01

Market Shares

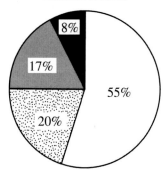

8%

17%

55%

20%

☐ Sylkview Studios
▨ DTQ and Co.
▨ Entertainable
■ Cube 9

Facilities Service Requests

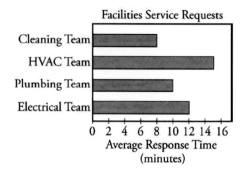

Cleaning Team
HVAC Team
Plumbing Team
Electrical Team

0 2 4 6 8 10 12 14 16
Average Response Time
(minutes)

13. What industry does the speaker work in?
(A) Game development
(B) Film production
(C) News reporting
(D) Interior design

14. Look at the graphic. What company does the speaker work for?
(A) Sylkview Studios
(B) DTQ and Co.
(C) Entertainable
(D) Cube 9

15. According to the speaker, what will the company do in the next quarter?
(A) Restructure a department
(B) Reduce production costs
(C) Negotiate a contract
(D) Try a different business model

16. What kind of system did the speaker's company change?
(A) Data storage
(B) Payroll
(C) Transportation
(D) Communication

17. Where do the listeners work?
(A) At a food processing plant
(B) At an automobile factory
(C) At a public swimming pool
(D) At a customer service call center

18. Look at the graphic. What is the average response time for Wataru's team?
(A) 8 minutes
(B) 15 minutes
(C) 10 minutes
(D) 12 minutes

Franklyn Supermarket

25% Discount This Weekend!

Sale Item	Store Location
Fresh fruit	Allendale
Dairy products	Kleinsburg
Beverages	Pine Valley
Baked goods	Yardville

Floor Plan

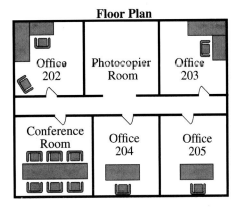

19. What is Franklyn Supermarket celebrating?
(A) An anniversary
(B) A new store opening
(C) A national holiday
(D) A profitable quarter

20. Look at the graphic. At which store location is the announcement being made?
(A) Allendale
(B) Kleinsburg
(C) Pine Valley
(D) Yardville

21. Why should listeners visit a Web site?
(A) To vote for the employee of the week
(B) To sign up for a membership program
(C) To check for job openings
(D) To write a customer review

22. What did the company recently do?
(A) Sponsor an athletic competition
(B) Sign a business contract
(C) Hold an employee health fair
(D) Publish a product review

23. What does the speaker ask the listeners to do?
(A) Collect participant feedback
(B) Work additional hours
(C) E-mail professional athletes
(D) Submit design ideas

24. Look at the graphic. Which office is the speaker's?
(A) Office 202
(B) Office 203
(C) Office 204
(D) Office 205

담화 유형별 전략

⑨ 전화 메시지

출제공식 1 발신자가 남기는 음성 메시지가 주로 출제되며, 회사나 공공기관의 녹음 메시지도 종종 나온다.

2 전화 메시지는 인사 및 소개 → 전화 용건 → 세부 내용 → 요청 사항/연락 방법 순으로, 녹음 메시지는 인사 및 소개 → 서비스/운영 관련 공지 → 추가 안내 순으로 전개되는 경우가 많다.

3 화자의 직업/근무지, 전화 목적, 요청/제안 사항을 묻는 문제, 전화가 연결된 업체와 안내 사항을 묻는 문제가 자주 출제된다.

✎ 담화 흐름 파악하기　　　　　🎧 P4_39

인사 및 소개	Hi, this message is for Selena. ① This is Roberto from Worldwide Carpets.	① 근무지: 월드와이드 카펫
전화 용건	② We were scheduled to deliver and install some carpeting in your hotel restaurant early tomorrow morning. But during the thunderstorm this afternoon a tree came down and it's blocking the road from our factory. I'm sorry for the inconvenience—I hope it doesn't affect your business.	② 화자의 의도: 예정대로 배송이 불가능한 이유 설명 및 사과
요청 사항	③ Please call me when you get this message, and we can make another arrangement.	③ 요청 사항: 회신 전화
연락 방법	I'm at 555-0102.	

화자 근무지	**1.** What type of business does the **speaker** work for? 화자는 어떤 업체에서 근무하는가?	A carpet manufacturer 카펫 제조사
의도 파악	**2.** What does the speaker imply when he says, "it's blocking the road from our factory"? 화자가 "그게 저희 공장에서 나오는 도로를 막고 있습니다"라고 말한 의도는 무엇인가?	A delivery will be delayed. 배송이 지연될 것이다.
요청 사항	**3.** What does the speaker ask the **listener** to do? 화자가 청자에게 요청하는 것은?	Return a phone call 회신 전화

안녕하세요, 이 메시지는 셀리나 님에게 남기는 것입니다. **저는 월드 와이드 카페츠의 로베르토입니다.** 저희가 내일 아침 일찍 고객님의 호텔 식당에 카펫을 시공할 예정이었습니다. 그러나 오늘 오후 뇌우가 쏟아지는 동안 나무 한 그루가 쓰러져 저희 공장에서 나오는 도로를 막고 있습니다. 불편을 끼치게 되어 죄송합니다. 이것이 고객님의 영업에 영향을 미치지 않기를 바랍니다. **이 메시지를 받고 제게 전화하시면** 약속을 다시 잡을 수 있습니다. 제 번호는 555-0102입니다.

✏️ **상황별 핵심 표현** 🎧 P4_40

발신자가 남기는 음성 메시지

– 일정 확인 및 변경 알림, 주문 확인 및 수정 알림, 환불 요청, 회신 전화 요청
– 축하/감사 메시지 전달, 동료에게 업무 관련 질문 또는 부탁 후 회신 전화 요청

수신자 언급 **발신자 소개**	Hello. This message is for Kate Jones. This is Ted calling from Vante Photo Studio. 안녕하세요. 이 메시지는 케이트 존스 씨에게 남기는 것입니다. 저는 반테 사진관의 테드입니다.
메시지 용건	I'm calling about the quarterly meeting scheduled for June thirtieth. 6월 30일로 예정된 분기별 회의에 관해 전화 드립니다.
요청/연락 방법	Please call me back at your earliest convenience. You can reach me at 555-0127. 가능한 한 빨리 제게 전화 주세요. 555-0127로 하시면 됩니다.

부재중 음성 메시지/회사 및 기관의 ARS 안내 메시지

– 휴무, 휴점, 담당자의 부재 등을 알리며 영업 시간을 안내하는 내용
– 주요 행사, 서비스, 직원 연결 방법 등을 알리는 내용

회사/기관 소개	Hello, you've reached Brenson Electronics' customer service center. 안녕하세요, 브렌슨 일렉트로닉스 고객 서비스 센터입니다.
휴무 이유	Our office is currently closed, as we're undergoing renovations from May first to May eleventh. 5월 1일부터 11일까지 보수 공사가 진행 중이라 현재 저희 사무소는 휴무입니다.
서비스 안내	If there's a problem with your gas service, please press one to be connected to a representative. 가스 서비스에 문제가 있다면, 1번을 누르세요. 상담원과 연결됩니다.

PART 4 | CHAPTER 02

ETS CHECK-UP 🎧 P4_41 정답 및 해설 p.242

1. What type of business has the listener reached?

(A) A bank
(B) A law firm
(C) A phone company
(D) A doctor's office

2. What does the speaker say will happen on Monday?

(A) Renovations will begin.
(B) A holiday will be observed.
(C) Staff will return phone calls.
(D) Business hours will be extended

3. Why should the listener press two?

(A) To speak with an assistant
(B) To hear a list of names
(C) To return to the main menu
(D) To leave a message

문의 및 회답 메시지

calling to see if ~인지 알아보려고 전화하는
returning your call 답신 전화를 하는
about your request to ~해달라는 요청에 관해
I wanted to ask about ~에 대해 문의하고 싶습니다.
I've just received your message about
~에 대한 메시지 방금 받았습니다.
I received your e-mail inquiry about
~에 관한 당신의 이메일 문의 받았습니다.

follow up on ~에 대해 추가로 알려주다, 후속 조치를 하다
change one's reservation ~의 예약을 변경하다
reschedule an appointment 예약 일정을 조정하다
You mentioned[reported] ~를 언급[보고]하셨죠.
Would you have time to ~할 시간 있으실까요?
Please give me a call back at ~로 회신 전화 주세요.
Let me know your decision as soon as
possible. 가능한 한 빨리 당신의 결정을 알려주세요.

업무 관련 메시지

with regard to ~에 관해 (= regarding)
calling with feedback on ~관련 피드백을 주려고 전화하는
remind you that ~라는 점을 상기시키기 위해
let you know that ~라는 점을 알려주기 위해
I've been thinking about ~에 대해 생각해 보고 있는데
set up a time 약속 시간을 잡다
make another arrangement 약속을 다시 잡다
be scheduled to ~할 예정이다

host a conference call 전화 회의를 열다
discuss ~ in person later 나중에 직접 만나 ~를 논의하다
look forward to the meeting 회의를 고대하다
check with A and confirm that
A와 확인한 후 ~라는 것을 확정하다
at your earliest convenience 가급적 빨리
extension 429 내선번호 429
Please remember to ~할 것을 기억해 주세요.

기업 / 기관 ARS 메시지

automated message 자동 응답 메시지
automatic recording service 자동 녹음 서비스
office[business] hours 영업 시간, 근무 시간
open from 8 A.M. to 6 P.M., Monday through Friday
월요일-금요일 오전 8시부터 오후 6시까지 영업하는
leave a message 메시지를 남기다
If you need immediate assistance
즉각적인 도움이 필요하면

to be transferred[connected] to ~로 연결되려면
by pressing two now 지금 2번을 누름으로써
stay on the line 전화를 끊지 않고 기다리다
You've reached ~로 전화하셨습니다.
Thank you for calling ~에 전화 주셔서 감사합니다.
For more information, please check our Web site.
더 많은 정보를 원하시면 저희 웹사이트를 확인해 주세요.
Your call may be recorded.
귀하의 전화는 녹음될 수 있습니다.

휴무 / 부재중 안내 메시지

away on vacation 휴가로 자리를 비운
out of town 도시를 떠나 있는, 타지에 있는
currently attending 현재 ~에 참석 중인
in observation of the national holiday 국경일을 기념하여
while we move[relocate] 이전하는 동안
in the meantime 그 동안, 그 사이에

will be closed until ~까지 문을 닫을 예정입니다.
We apologize for the inconvenience.
불편을 끼쳐드려 죄송합니다.
If anything comes up, you can call my
assistant. 무슨 일이 생기면 제 비서에게 전화하면 됩니다.

LISTENING **PRACTICE**

♩ ♭ P4_43 정답 및 해설 p.242

담화를 들으면서 정답을 고르세요. 그리고 다시 들으면서 빈칸을 채우세요. (녹음은 두 번씩 들려줍니다.)

1. What is the main purpose of the telephone message?
(A) To suggest a location for the book club meeting
(B) To inform a member of a schedule change

2. Who should be notified if a member is unable to attend?
(A) Valerie
(B) Monica

Hello, Emma. This is Valerie _____. It's Monday at one-thirty P.M.,
and I'm calling to _____. Rather than meeting on Tuesday,
we will be meeting at Monica's house on Thursday at eleven o'clock, our regular time. Just to remind
you, we are reading *The Lily in Mayberry Park* by Louise Evanston this week. If you _____
_____, _____ so that she will know how many members to expect at the
meeting. I hope to see you there. Goodbye.

3. What does the speaker remind the listener to do?
(A) Get a signature
(B) Enter a building pass code

4. Look at the graphic. Who is the package addressed to?
(A) Wei Li
(B) Hans Mayer

Stewart Office Building Directory
200 . . . . Robert Jenkins
201 . . . . Satoshi Ito
204 . . . . Wei Li
205 . . . . Hans Mayer

Hi Fatima, it's James. Thanks for _____
_____; I really appreciate it. I wanted to tell you that one of
the packages is a computer that's going to the Stewart Office
Building on Main Street. Just remember that _____
_____, so it has to be _____
_____. I don't remember the name of the recipient, but
_____. Thanks again!

5. According to the speaker, what has caused a problem?
(A) A computer malfunction
(B) A broken pipe

6. What does the speaker encourage the listeners to do?
(A) Make a new appointment
(B) Attend a local event

Hello and thank you for calling Miguel's Arts and Crafts. Because of _____
we'll be closed for repairs until next week. However, we _____ the
local Pottersville Winter Festival this Saturday _____. You can find a
list of the products we'll be selling at the festival on our Web site. We apologize for the inconvenience
and _____!

1. What does the speaker's business produce?
   (A) Pottery
   (B) Soap bars
   (C) Picture frames
   (D) Scented candles

2. Why does the speaker say, "what makes our products great is that everything's done by hand"?
   (A) To justify a product's high price
   (B) To reject the listener's suggestion
   (C) To explain a production delay
   (D) To request additional workers

3. What does the speaker say she will do tomorrow?
   (A) Host a workshop
   (B) Respond to a customer's inquiry
   (C) Pick up packaging materials
   (D) Attend a housewares show

4. Why is the speaker calling?
   (A) To schedule a pickup
   (B) To apologize for an error
   (C) To discuss a payment
   (D) To explain a policy

5. What does the speaker say happened last week?
   (A) A new facility was opened.
   (B) A product was launched.
   (C) Some inventory was misplaced.
   (D) Some data was recorded incorrectly.

6. What will the company provide at no cost?
   (A) Expedited shipping
   (B) An automatic billing plan
   (C) A lifetime warranty
   (D) Online assistance

7. What type of job is the listener being offered?
   (A) Tour guide
   (B) School receptionist
   (C) Personal trainer
   (D) Grocery store cashier

8. What job qualification does the speaker say is especially impressive?
   (A) Professional certification
   (B) Work experience
   (C) Language ability
   (D) Strong references

9. What does the speaker say the listener is required to do?
   (A) Be fitted for a uniform
   (B) Fill out an online survey
   (C) Have a physical examination
   (D) Watch a series of videos

10. Why does the speaker apologize?
    (A) A production has been canceled.
    (B) Some tickets are unavailable.
    (C) A schedule is incorrect.
    (D) Some actors have been replaced.

11. What will take place on Wednesday night?
    (A) A dance competition
    (B) An art lecture
    (C) A backstage tour
    (D) An outdoor play

12. How does the speaker say people can save money?
    (A) By purchasing tickets in advance
    (B) By becoming a member
    (C) By attending on a weekday
    (D) By participating in a group

13. Who is the speaker?
(A) A store manager
(B) A customer service representative
(C) An advertising executive
(D) An accountant

14. What does the speaker imply when he says, "none have been returned"?
(A) Additional employees are needed.
(B) The quality of a product has improved.
(C) A delivery address was correct.
(D) Some feedback forms are difficult to complete.

15. What is the speaker interested in hearing about at next month's meeting?
(A) The company's history
(B) The company's finances
(C) A colleague's retirement
(D) Some managers' experiences

16. What type of business has the caller reached?
(A) A bank
(B) An electronics store
(C) A delivery service
(D) A cable television company

17. What does the speaker apologize for?
(A) Incorrect instructions
(B) A damaged product
(C) Interrupted service
(D) An office closure

18. According to the speaker, why should listeners visit a Web site?
(A) To check account information
(B) To order new parts
(C) To get schedule updates
(D) To learn about new offers

CREATURES OF THE SEA

Submission deadline	June 10
Exhibition dates	July 11 – September 15
Opening reception	July 17
Lecture	August 20

19. Where does the speaker most likely work?
(A) At a post office
(B) At a catering company
(C) At a pet store
(D) At an art gallery

20. Look at the graphic. Which date on the flyer will be changed?
(A) June 10
(B) July 11
(C) July 17
(D) September 15

21. What will the speaker do this afternoon?
(A) Give a guided tour
(B) Review a document
(C) Take a client to a restaurant
(D) Bring materials to a print shop

⑩ 회의/업무 관련 공지

출제공식
1. 회사 및 업무 관련 공지 사항을 직원들에게 전달하거나, 회의 안건에 대해 논의하는 내용이 출제된다.
2. 회의 목적 및 주제/안건 → 본론/세부 내용 → 제안·요청사항/추가 내용 순으로 전개되는 경우가 많다. 최근에는 도입부의 인사말을 생략하고 바로 본론으로 시작하는 유형도 나오고 있으므로, 초반부터 집중하도록 한다.
3. 회의/공지의 주제나 목적, 화자가 언급한 내용, 청자들에 관한 문제가 주를 이룬다.

✏️ 담화 흐름 파악하기

🎧 P4_45

회의 목적 주제/안건	I called this meeting to officially announce that ① our bank will be uniting with Doylestown Bank at the beginning of next year.	① 화자의 근무지: 도일스타운 은행과 합병 예정인 은행
세부 내용	The merger of our two banks will have a positive impact on you as our employees. ② The biggest change is that we'll be moving to another building. The building's right by the bus line, so it'll be very convenient for those of you who commute from the city.	② 새 건물의 이점: 버스 노선과 가까워 통근하기 편리
추가 내용	Additionally, we will follow Doylestown Bank's vacation policy, so ③ all employees will now have three extra days of vacation each year.	③ 정책 변화: 추가 휴가 지급

화자 근무지	1. What kind of business does the **speaker** work in? 화자는 어떤 업체에서 근무하는가?	A bank 은행
세부 정보	2. According to the speaker, what advantage does the new location have? 화자에 따르면 새 장소의 이점은 무엇인가?	It is easily accessible by public transit. 대중 교통으로 쉽게 접근할 수 있다.
세부 언급	3. What policy change does the speaker mention? 화자가 언급하는 정책 변화는 무엇인가?	Employees will have more vacation time. 직원들이 휴가를 더 얻게 된다.

우리 은행이 내년 초에 도일스타운 은행과 합친다는 소식을 공식 발표하려고 이 회의를 소집했습니다. 우리 두 은행이 합병하면 직원 여러분께 긍정적인 영향을 미칠 것입니다. 가장 큰 변화는 우리가 다른 건물로 이전하게 된다는 것입니다. 건물이 버스 노선 바로 옆에 있기 때문에 시내에서 통근하는 분들께 매우 편리할 것입니다. 게다가, 우리가 도일스타운 은행의 휴가 정책을 따르게 되어 **모든 직원이 이제 해마다 휴가일수를 추가로 사흘 더 얻게 됩니다.**

✏️ **상황별 핵심 표현**   🎧 P4_46

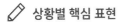

<u>회의 / 업무 관련 공지</u>

- 예산, 실적, 인사, 프로젝트, 내·외부 행사 등의 다양한 회의 안건에 대한 논의
- 회사 합병, 교육, 정책 등과 관련된 새로운 소식 알림
- 회의 내용을 바탕으로 직원들에게 업무를 지시하거나 협조를 구하는 내용, 직원들의 노고 치하

도입부	Thank you all for coming to this meeting on such short notice. 갑작스러운 공지에도 이 회의에 참석해 주셔서 감사합니다.
안건 / 주제 공지 / 알림	I called this meeting to discuss some feedback we recently received from our customers. 최근에 고객들로부터 받은 피드백에 대해 논의하고자 이 회의를 소집했습니다. The first item on the agenda is the new software we'll use for entering customer records. 첫 번째 안건은 우리가 고객 정보를 입력하는 데 사용하게 될 새로운 소프트웨어입니다. I'm happy to announce that our request to add more staff to our department has been approved. 우리 부서에 인력을 충원하자는 요청이 승인되었다는 소식을 알리게 되어 기쁩니다. I'd like to remind you that starting next week, we'll be implementing a new travel policy. 다음 주부터 새로운 출장 정책을 시행한다는 점을 다시 한 번 상기시켜 드리고 싶습니다. I have a brief update on the artificial intelligence conference we're attending next month. 우리가 다음 달에 참석할 인공 지능 회의에 관해 짤막한 새 소식이 있습니다.
제안·요청 사항 / 추가 내용	And please don't forget to bring your ID badge to the training session. 교육 시간 때 신분증 가져오는 것 잊지 마세요. If you need more information, the revised safety manual is available on our company intranet. 정보가 더 필요하다면, 수정된 안전 매뉴얼이 우리 회사 인트라넷에 있으니 확인해 보세요.

PART 4 | CHAPTER 02

ETS CHECK-UP   🎧 P4_47 정답 및 해설 p.248

1. What is the topic of the upcoming workshop?
- (A) How to negotiate more effectively
- (B) How to develop a marketing strategy
- (C) How to recruit qualified employees
- (D) How to use social media

2. What does the speaker say about registration?
- (A) It needs to be done in person.
- (B) It is free of charge.
- (C) It includes workshop materials.
- (D) It will close soon.

3. What will workshop participants be asked to do?
- (A) Join an online discussion
- (B) Read a book
- (C) Bring a client list
- (D) Complete a questionnaire

회의

board of directors 이사회

management meeting 경영진 회의

bimonthly sales meeting 격월 영업 회의

shareholder(s') meeting 주주 회의

staff meeting agenda 직원 회의 안건

discuss the results of a survey
설문조사 결과에 대해 논의하다

give a quick overview 간략하게 설명하다

review an updated manual 업데이트된 설명서를 검토하다

share customer feedback 고객 피드백을 공유하다

go over our company's plan 회사의 계획을 점검하다

familiarize our team with changes
팀에게 변경사항을 숙지시키다

talk about this year's financial goals
올해의 재정 목표에 대해 이야기하다

tell you about the upcoming improvements
앞으로 있을 개선 사항에 대해 이야기해 주다

new initiative 새로운 계획

unite[merge] with ~와 병합[합병]하다

partner with ~와 제휴하다

employee satisfaction 직원 만족도

sales fluctuations 매출 변동

budget surplus 예산 흑자

operating expenses 운영비

increase business 거래를 늘리다

boost sales 판매를 증진시키다

attract customers[guests] 고객[손님]을 유치하다

grow one's clientele 고객을 늘리다

expand one's customer base 고객층을 넓히다

keep up with competitors 경쟁사들을 따라잡다

deal with clients 고객[의뢰인]을 대하다

negotiation skills 협상 기술

marketing strategies 마케팅 전략

decision-making process 의사 결정 과정

업무 관련 공지

Before we begin tonight's shift
오늘 밤 근무를 시작하기 전에

remind you of a few things 몇 가지 사안을 상기시키다

officially announce that ~라는 것을 공식적으로 발표하다

make an important announcement 중요 발표를 하다

share some good news 몇 가지 좋은 소식을 나누다

update you on ~에 대해 새 소식을 알려주다

have some urgent business to attend to
급히 처리해야 할 일들이 있다

adopt a new policy 새로운 정책을 채택하다

implement some changes
몇 가지 변경 사항을 시행하다

try out a change to ~에 변화를 시도하다

roll out some changes 몇 가지 변화를 시작하다

new addition to ~에 새로운 추가 사항

in preparation for the event 행사를 준비하며

assign a task 업무를 배정하다

speed up the process 공정의 속도를 높이다

improve efficiency 효율성을 높이다

make a visit to the company 회사에 방문하다

address a problem 문제를 처리하다

identify the errors 오류를 찾다

provide training 교육을 제공하다

pass around a sign-up sheet 등록 신청서를 돌리다

postpone a seminar 세미나를 연기하다

update[upgrade] the software 소프트웨어를 업데이트하다

install an automated system 자동화 시스템을 설치하다

work extra hours 초과 근무를 하다

receive overtime pay 초과 근무 수당을 받다

keep in mind that ~라는 점을 염두에 두세요.

All employees will be given training.
모든 직원이 교육을 받게 될 것입니다.

This new regulation will go into effect next week.
이 새로운 규정은 다음 주부터 시행될 것입니다.

LISTENING **PRACTICE**

P4_49 정답 및 해설 p. 249

담화를 들으면서 정답을 고르세요. 그리고 다시 들으면서 빈칸을 채우세요. (녹음은 두 번씩 들려줍니다.)

1. What is the purpose of the announcement?
(A) To explain safety procedures
(B) To describe a new printer

2. What benefit does the speaker mention?
(A) Reduced harm to the environment
(B) Greater output capacity

I'm happy to announce that Keyton Advertising will be _____.

We'll now be able to offer our clients the best possible quality and _____

_____. This printer is the latest model and uses soy-based ink, which won't _____

_____ – and the chemicals we'll need to clean it are safer as well. All employees will be

given training on _____ on Friday. And to be sure that workers

on all shifts will be able to attend, _____—one in the morning

and one in the evening.

---

3. What does the speaker say recently happened?
(A) An award ceremony took place.
(B) A business opened.

4. What is the purpose of the meeting?
(A) To outline a new regulation
(B) To discuss ways of increasing business

So, our gym _____ now and we've been relatively successful.

Thank you for your hard work. I've been _____. We could do

cross-marketing, like advertising with another business. There's a café down the street _____

_____, and I've already talked to the manager there. She'd be willing to _____

_____ when they stop by after working out. I like this café because it has lots

of online reviews, and they're all very positive.

---

5. Who most likely are the listeners?
(A) Store employees
(B) Restaurant servers

6. According to the speaker, what have customers complained about?
(A) A lack of parking
(B) Long wait times

Good afternoon, everyone. Before we finish off today's staff meeting, I'd like to announce _____

_____. Many customers have complained about _____

when making their purchases. Even when every checkout station is open, _____

_____. So, the store owner has agreed to _____. They'll be

installed on Friday.

---

1. Who most likely are the listeners?
   (A) Board members
   (B) News reporters
   (C) Civil engineers
   (D) Career counselors

2. What does the speaker imply when he says, "there are plans to build a new hotel across the street"?
   (A) He hopes there will be more job opportunities.
   (B) He is afraid construction noise will bother guests.
   (C) He anticipates an increase in local tourism.
   (D) He is concerned about competition in business.

3. What does the speaker propose?
   (A) Renovating a facility
   (B) Moving a business to another location
   (C) Launching an advertising campaign
   (D) Redesigning staff uniforms

4. What is the main topic of the announcement?
   (A) Redesigning the company Web site
   (B) Giving new employees more time off
   (C) Providing managers with advanced training
   (D) Making work schedules more flexible

5. According to the speaker, why is a change being made?
   (A) To retain current employees
   (B) To follow a company regulation
   (C) To improve communication
   (D) To introduce better safety procedures

6. What are the listeners reminded to do?
   (A) Update their client contact information
   (B) Consult their department handbook
   (C) Inform their employees of company policies
   (D) Change their passwords frequently

7. What does the speaker have good news about?
   (A) A promotion
   (B) A schedule
   (C) A contract
   (D) A budget

8. According to the speaker, what is wrong with the current software?
   (A) It is not secure.
   (B) It is difficult to learn to use.
   (C) It does not work with some applications.
   (D) Its processing time is very slow.

9. What will the listeners most likely do next?
   (A) Greet their clients
   (B) Share their suggestions
   (C) Review a policy
   (D) Watch a video

10. What is the company offering for the first time?
    (A) Free furniture removal
    (B) Lifetime warranties
    (C) Next-day delivery
    (D) Interior decorating services

11. What will be available at the customer service desk?
    (A) A catalog
    (B) A sign-up sheet
    (C) Some fabric samples
    (D) Some product coupons

12. What does the speaker mean when she says, "this will be our biggest sale of the year"?
    (A) More commercials will be on television.
    (B) The store's inventory will be expanded.
    (C) Additional work will be available.
    (D) The sale will happen at several stores.

13. What is the main topic of the talk?
(A) Software for teaching work skills
(B) Suppliers of raw materials
(C) Plans for a company merger
(D) Directions for fixing broken machinery

14. According to the speaker, what can the company expect to see?
(A) Changes in meeting times
(B) Increased productivity
(C) Extensive renovations
(D) Improved client relations

15. What does the speaker recommend doing?
(A) Comparing prices for textbooks
(B) Extending contracts for employees
(C) Beginning a program with new recruits
(D) Remodeling workstations

16. Who is the speaker addressing?
(A) International journalists
(B) Sales representatives
(C) Product designers
(D) Business investors

17. What makes the shoes special?
(A) They are made from recycled materials.
(B) They come in a wide variety of colors.
(C) They were created by a famous designer.
(D) They were the first product the company produced.

18. Where does the speaker say the shoes will be sold initially?
(A) At sports events
(B) Through a catalog
(C) In department stores
(D) On an athlete's Web site

Expected Delivery Dates

Forklifts, June 15
Shelving, June 18
HVAC Fans, June 23
Safety Mirrors, June 28

19. According to the speaker, what happened last week?
(A) A construction project was finished.
(B) A safety inspection was conducted.
(C) Some batteries were replaced.
(D) Some tasks were reassigned.

20. Why was a purchase request approved?
(A) To improve organization
(B) To improve comfort
(C) To save time
(D) To save money

21. Look at the graphic. When will a training session be held?
(A) On June 15
(B) On June 18
(C) On June 23
(D) On June 28

⑪ 발표/설명/소개

출제공식

1 워크숍, 컨벤션, 기자회견 등 각종 행사에서 다양한 주제나 제품에 대해 발표하거나, 오리엔테이션 및 교육 시간에 직원들을 대상으로 강연 및 설명하는 내용이 자주 출제된다. 본인 소개 → 주제 언급 → 상세 설명 → 요청/당부 사항 순으로 전개되는 경우가 많다.

2 연회, 시상식 등에서 특정 인물을 소개하는 담화에는 이력 및 업적 소개, 환영/감사의 말이 주를 이룬다.

3 소개/설명 대상에 관한 문제, 화자의 요청 사항이나 다음에 할 일/일어날 일을 묻는 문제가 자주 출제된다.

✏️ 담화 흐름 파악하기

🎧 P4_51

본인 소개	Hello, I'm Salma Samir—your instructor for this professional-development workshop.	
주제 설명	Today, ① I'll be teaching you the newest 3-D Design software program. During this session, ② we'll be creating high-quality, 3-D models of architectural structures. My goal is for you to improve your skills, so you can offer your clients better models of their buildings.	① 워크숍에서 배울 내용: 최신 3D 디자인 소프트웨어 ② 청자의 업계: 건축물과 관련된 분야
요청 사항	Before we get started, ③ please tell me which computer programs you already know—use the survey sheet in your packet. When you're finished, I'll collect them.	③ 요청 사항: 설문지에 알고 있는 컴퓨터 프로그램 적어내기

세부 정보	**1.** What will the **listeners** learn during a workshop? 청자들이 워크숍 동안 배울 것은?	How to use a software program 소프트웨어 사용 방법
청자 업계	**2.** What industry do the **listeners** most likely work in? 청자들이 종사할 것 같은 업계는?	Architecture 건축
요청 사항	**3.** What does the speaker ask the **listeners** to do? 화자가 청자들에게 요청하는 것은?	Complete a survey 설문조사 완료하기

안녕하세요. 저는 이번 직무능력 개발 워크숍의 강사를 맡은 살마 사미르입니다. **오늘 여러분께 최신 3D 디자인 소프트웨어 프로그램에 대해 가르쳐 드릴 예정입니다. 이 시간 동안 건축물의 고품질 3D 모델들을 만들어 볼 것입니다.** 제 목표는 여러분이 역량을 향상시켜서 고객들의 건물을 더 나은 모델로 만들어 제공할 수 있게 되는 겁니다. **시작하기에 앞서, 어떤 컴퓨터 프로그램을 이미 알고 있는지 알려 주세요. 서류 꾸러미에 있는 설문조사지를 활용해 주세요.** 다 마치면 제가 걷겠습니다.

✏️ 상황별 핵심 표현　　　　　　　　　　　　🎧 P4_52

발표 / 설명

- 기술, 건축, 의학, 마케팅 등 다양한 내용이나 회사 제품에 관한 발표 및 연설, 행사 일정 관련 안내
- 신입사원 오리엔테이션, 인턴이나 직원 대상 교육에서 특정 주제와 관련해 설명하는 내용

행사 소개	I'd like to thank everyone for attending today's marketing conference. 오늘 마케팅 회의에 오신 모든 여러분들께 감사 드립니다.
주제 / 대상 언급	Welcome to our first photographers' workshop here at the Silverdale Community Center. 여기 실버데일 주민센터에서 열리는 제1회 사진작가 워크숍에 오신 것을 환영합니다. I'm honored to be presenting our new product to you all at this fair today. 오늘 이 박람회에서 저희의 신제품을 선보이게 되어 굉장히 영광스럽습니다.
일정 안내	We will first watch a short video about our company. When it's over, I'll take you on a tour of the building. 우선 우리는 회사 관련 짧은 영상을 볼 겁니다. 끝나면 여러분에게 건물을 구경시켜 주겠습니다.

소개

- 회사에 새로 들어오거나 승진, 은퇴하는 직원의 이력 및 업적 소개
- 워크숍, 시상식, 프레젠테이션 등의 각종 행사나 모임에서 연설자 / 수상자 발표 및 소개

소개 대상 언급	I'm very excited to introduce our keynote speaker, Professor Everett Paterson. 우리의 기조 연설자, 에버렛 패터슨 교수님을 소개하게 되어 굉장히 기쁩니다.
경력 / 업적	Ms. Robinson has been leading our sales team for the past seven years, and under her leadership, our sales have doubled. 로빈슨 씨는 지난 7년간 영업팀을 이끌어 왔고, 그녀의 리더십 하에 우리의 매출이 두 배로 뛰었습니다.
환영 / 감사 인사	Now please join me in welcoming Dr. Amal Halim to the stage. 이제 저와 함께 아말 할림 박사를 무대로 환영해 주십시오.

ETS CHECK-UP　　　　　　　　　　🎧 P4_53　정답 및 해설 p.256

PART 4 | CHAPTER 02

1. Where is the talk taking place?

(A) At a science museum
(B) At a department store
(C) At a publishing company
(D) At a mayor's office

2. What will the listeners do in the afternoon?

(A) Participate in team-building activities
(B) Watch a documentary
(C) Meet with a mentor
(D) Fill out a membership application

3. Why does the speaker say, "many of our staff members started off as interns"?

(A) To explain a decision
(B) To offer encouragement
(C) To introduce some guests
(D) To correct a mistaken assumption

ETS X-FILE | 발표 / 설명 / 소개 빈출 표현

발표 / 설명

instructor 강사 (= lecturer)

visiting consultant 객원 컨설턴트

financial planner 재무 설계사

conference organizer 회의 기획자 / 주관자

panel (전문) 위원단, 패널

training session 직원 연수, 교육 (과정)

management training seminar 관리(자) 교육 세미나

assembly training 조립 교육

new-employee orientation 신입 사원 오리엔테이션

professional-development workshop
직무 개발 워크숍

press conference 기자회견

attend 참석하다

turnout 참가자 수

subject 주제 (= topic)

cover 다루다

marketing tool 마케팅 도구

advanced technology 첨단 기술

smart device 스마트 기기

product demonstration 제품 시연

expert advice on ~에 대한 전문가 조언

give[make, deliver] a speech 연설하다

present one's product 제품을 소개하다

turn one's attention to ~에 주의를 돌리다

give you a firsthand look 직접 보여주다

give you a rundown[overview] 개요를 알려주다

take you through the process 과정을 익히게끔 도와주다

pioneer a technique 기술을 개척하다

make a difference 변화[차이]를 가져오다

explore the basics 기본기를 알아보다

be assigned to ~에 배정되다

hold a question and answer session
질의 응답 시간을 갖다

continue[proceed] with the workshop 워크숍을 계속하다

discussion on ~에 대한 논의[토론]

be split into small groups 소규모 그룹으로 나뉘어지다

소개

award(s) ceremony 시상식

present an award to ~에게 시상하다

accept an award 상을 받다

the prestigious award 권위 있는 상

employee of the year 올해의 직원

keynote speaker 기조 연설자

appoint A (as) B A를 B로 임명하다

renowned 유명한 (= famous, known)

contribute 공헌하다, 기여하다

inspire 격려하다, 고무하다, 영감을 주다

instrumental in ~에 도움이 되는, ~에 중요한 역할을 하는

most notable achievement 가장 주목할 만한 업적

do an outstanding job 뛰어난 업적을 이루다

distinguished work as an economist
경제학자로서의 뛰어난 업적

leading expert on ~분야의 뛰어난 전문가

talented author 재능 있는 작가

hard work and commitment 노고와 헌신

as head of the education center 교육 센터장으로서

in the field of international business
국제 비즈니스 분야에서

begin one's position as ~로서 직책을 시작하다

begin one's career as ~로서 경력을 쌓기 시작하다

have been with us for + 기간
~의 기간 동안 우리와 함께해 왔다

leave one's position 현직에서 물러나다

retire after thirty-five years with + 회사
~에서 35년간 근무한 후 퇴직하다

a token of appreciation 감사의 표시

a 200-dollar gift certificate 200달러 상당의 상품권

give a round of applause 박수를 보내다

be honored to introduce ~을 소개하게 되어 영광이다

be delighted to be here 이 자리에서 있게 되어 기쁘다

on behalf of my company 저희 회사를 대표하여

This award recognizes an employee who ~.
이 상은 ~한 직원의 공로를 치하하는 상입니다.

LISTENING **PRACTICE**

◁ ▷ P4_55 정답 및 해설 p.256

담화를 들으면서 정답을 고르세요. 그리고 다시 들으면서 빈칸을 채우세요. (녹음은 두 번씩 들려줍니다.)

1. What is the subject of the workshop?
(A) Workplace safety
(B) Business presentations

2. What will listeners probably do next?
(A) Work in small groups
(B) Listen to audio files

> OK everyone, let's continue with the workshop. We've had a _____
> _____. Another important point to consider is _____. Some
> people speak at a faster or slower rate than others. I recommend _____
> _____ before you present, so that you can monitor your speed. And now, I'm going to _____
> _____ so you can see how the speed of a presenter's speech impacts communication.

3. What industry does the speaker most likely work in?
(A) Technology
(B) Accounting

4. What does the speaker say tablet computers can be used for?
(A) Facilitating meetings
(B) Showing advertisements

> Good morning, everyone. My partner, Rajesh, and I are honored to be _____
> today. The ride-sharing mobile application that you developed enables people without cars to get around
> cities easily. _____ for your app. When installed in your drivers'
> cars, it will _____ near their destination. We've prepared _____
> _____ for you to look at. Let me see—Rajesh, the handouts are in your briefcase.

5. Who is Linda McKenna?
(A) A radio announcer
(B) A writer

6. What will happen in July?
(A) A book will become available.
(B) A contest will be held.

> As part of this year's awards banquet, I would like to _____ to
> Ms. Linda McKenna. Ms. McKenna is best known for her in-depth personality profiles and for _____
> _____. In addition to her popular weekly newspaper column, Ms. McKenna
> is also the author of *Twenty Years of Women in Sports*, which will _____
> _____. Please help me in welcoming Linda McKenna.

1. What is the speaker announcing?
(A) A contest
(B) A partnership
(C) A retirement
(D) A promotion

2. According to the speaker, what did Natalia do for the company last year?
(A) She developed an online presence.
(B) She doubled investments.
(C) She lowered costs.
(D) She expanded the staff.

3. What does Natalia do in her spare time?
(A) She makes short films.
(B) She writes novels.
(C) She plays sports.
(D) She designs jewelry.

4. What product has the speaker's company developed?
(A) An exercise machine
(B) A bicycle helmet
(C) An inflatable mattress
(D) A sports shoe

5. What does the speaker say was important to him?
(A) Affordability
(B) Attractiveness
(C) Comfort
(D) Durability

6. What will the speaker do next?
(A) Show a video
(B) Introduce a colleague
(C) Answer some questions
(D) Pass around a sample

7. What is the workshop mainly about?
(A) Reducing company spending
(B) Expanding global markets
(C) Learning data entry skills
(D) Improving client relationships

8. What are the listeners instructed to do first?
(A) Put on a name tag
(B) Check an identification number
(C) Open a user manual
(D) Sign some security forms

9. According to the speaker, what should the listeners have with them?
(A) A meal voucher
(B) A business card
(C) A mobile phone
(D) A power cord

10. What event is taking place?
(A) A retirement party
(B) A fund-raising banquet
(C) A sales convention
(D) A career fair

11. According to the speaker, what has been Anthony Lee's greatest achievement?
(A) He started a charitable foundation.
(B) He oversaw a company merger.
(C) He developed a best-selling product.
(D) He expanded a client base.

12. What does the speaker ask Anthony Lee to do?
(A) Give a speech
(B) Lead a committee
(C) Accept a gift
(D) Pose for a picture

13. Who are the listeners?
   (A) Board members
   (B) Recent retirees
   (C) New employees
   (D) Potential investors

14. What does the speaker say has recently changed?
   (A) A class time
   (B) A meeting location
   (C) A hiring process
   (D) A work-site regulation

15. What does the speaker imply when she says, "People like to walk on the roads during their breaks"?
   (A) Drivers should be careful.
   (B) Cars are forbidden during specific hours.
   (C) A work site cannot be reached by car.
   (D) The company encourages staff to be physically active.

16. What type of event is taking place?
   (A) An awards ceremony
   (B) A retirement party
   (C) A shareholder meeting
   (D) A grand opening

17. What product does the speaker highlight?
   (A) A wireless security system
   (B) An innovative automobile
   (C) An efficient appliance
   (D) An illuminated keyboard

18. Who is Bradley Lipinski?
   (A) A graphic designer
   (B) A journalist
   (C) A sales director
   (D) A corporate executive

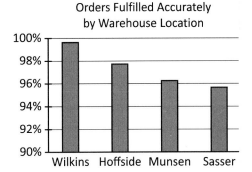

Orders Fulfilled Accurately by Warehouse Location

19. What has the company decided to change?
   (A) A warehouse facility layout
   (B) A delivery tracking system
   (C) A performance evaluation practice
   (D) An online scheduling platform

20. What has been an unexpected result of the change?
   (A) Less damaged merchandise
   (B) Substantial energy savings
   (C) Reduced shipping times
   (D) Higher employee satisfaction

21. Look at the graphic. Where is the talk most likely taking place?
   (A) In Wilkins
   (B) In Hoffside
   (C) In Munsen
   (D) In Sasser

출제공식 1 상점, 공연장, 도서관 등에서 이용객을 대상으로 하는 안내 방송이 주로 출제되며, 간혹 직원들에게 하는 사내 방송이나 시민에게 공지하는 방송도 나온다. 안내가 나오는 장소, 요청/당부 사항을 묻는 경우가 많다.

2 공항, 기차역 등의 장소나 비행기, 열차와 같은 교통 수단에서 들을 수 있는 안내 방송도 자주 출제된다. 문제점이나 변경 사항에 관련된 문제가 나올 가능성이 높다.

✏️ 담화 흐름 파악하기   🎧 P4_57

시작 멘트	① Attention Noguchi Grocery shoppers!	① 안내 방송 장소: 식료품점
안내 사항	Be sure to stop by our newly expanded freezer section. ② You'll find a wider variety of prepared foods that you can enjoy in the comfort of your home—including frozen meals that can be heated up in minutes.	② 업체가 제공하는 것: 냉동식을 포함해 더 다양해진 즉석식품
요청 사항	And ③ please give us your feedback on how we can improve your grocery shopping experience. You can fill in a form with your suggestions at the customer service desk by the main entrance.	③ 양식 작성을 권유받는 이유: 쇼핑 경험 개선을 위한 의견 공유

담화 장소	1. Where is the announcement most likely being made? 안내 방송이 나오는 장소는 어디겠는가?	At a grocery store 식료품점에서
세부 정보	2. What is the business now offering? 업체가 이제부터 제공하는 것은?	Frozen meals 냉동식
세부 이유	3. Why are customers asked to fill in a form? 고객들이 양식을 작성하도록 권유 받는 이유는?	To provide feedback 의견을 제공하라고

노구치 식료품점 고객들께 알려드립니다! 저희 매장의 새로 확장된 냉동 코너에 꼭 들러 보시기 바랍니다. **몇 분이면 데워지는 냉동식을 포함하여, 여러분의 가정에서 편히 즐길 수 있는 더욱 다양해진 즉석식품들을 발견하실 수 있습니다.** 그리고 여러분의 식료품 구매 경험을 어떻게 개선할 수 있을지 저희에게 의견을 주시기 바랍니다. 정문 옆에 있는 고객 서비스 창구에서 여러분의 제안을 양식에 기입하실 수 있습니다.

✏️ 상황별 핵심 표현

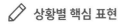 P4_58

시설 관련 안내 방송

– 상점, 공연장, 도서관 등의 운영 시간, 특징 및 특별 행사, 서비스 관련 변경 사항, 이용 시 주의 사항 알림
– 공공장소 이용객, 주민, 사원들을 대상으로 주요 행사 안내, 참여 요청, 공사/보수 작업 등 공지

특별 행사 안내	All of our office supplies are now on sale for thirty percent off, so be sure to check them out today! 저희의 모든 사무 용품이 현재 30퍼센트 세일 중이니, 오늘 반드시 둘러 보세요!
공연 지연 알림	We're having a problem with the sound system. Our technician is working on it, so we should be able to begin shortly. 음향 시스템에 문제가 있습니다. 기술자가 수리 중이니, 곧 시작할 수 있을 겁니다.
보수 작업 공지	Please be advised that from May tenth to thirtieth, the Hamilton Library will be closed for repairs. 5월 10일부터 30일까지 해밀튼 도서관이 보수 작업으로 휴관할 예정임을 일러드립니다.
요청/당부 사항	If you're purchasing five items or fewer, please use the self-checkout kiosks near the exit. 5개 이하의 물품을 구매하신다면, 출구 근처의 셀프 계산대를 이용해 주십시오.

교통 수단 관련 안내 방송

– 공항, 터미널 등에서 날씨, 연착, 수리 등으로 인한 출발 지연이나 취소, 탑승 장소 변경 등 공지
– 비행기, 기차, 버스 안에서 운행 시간, 목적지 및 경유지 정보, 새로운 서비스, 주의 사항 등을 알리는 내용

운행 취소	Attention, passengers on Flight 910 to London. That flight has been canceled due to heavy rain. 런던행 910 항공편 승객 여러분께 안내 말씀 드립니다. 해당 항공편이 폭우로 인해 취소되었습니다.
탑승 장소 변경	The three P.M. bus to Madrid will now leave from Platform A, rather than from Platform B. 마드리드행 3시 버스가 플랫폼 B가 아닌 플랫폼 A에서 출발할 예정입니다.
주의 사항	This train is fully booked, so please do not put your belongings on the seat next to you. 이 열차는 만석이오니, 옆 좌석에 소지품을 두지 말아 주십시오.

ETS CHECK-UP

 P4_59 정답 및 해설 p. 262

1. Who is the speaker?

(A) A theater director
(B) An audience member
(C) A cast member
(D) A ticket salesperson

2. What does the speaker say is special about the play?

(A) It has won several awards.
(B) It was written by a local playwright.
(C) A famous actor has the lead role.
(D) All shows have sold out.

3. How will proceeds from the evening's sales be used?

(A) To purchase computers
(B) To fund an awards ceremony
(C) To support school programs
(D) To repair the theater

PART 4 | CHAPTER 02

시설 관련 안내 방송

상점 / 도서관

patron 고객, 이용객

shopper 쇼핑객

loyal[regular] customer 단골 손님

sales associate 판매 직원

customer service representative 고객 서비스 직원

a variety of 다양한 (= a wide selection of)

purchase 구매하다; 구매(품)

grocery 식료품, 잡화

preferences and needs 선호하는 것과 필요한 것

express lane 신속 처리 계산대

cash register 금전등록기, 계산대 (= checkout counter)

self-checkout kiosk 셀프 계산대[대출대]

check out 확인하다, 계산하다, 대출하다

voucher 쿠폰, 상품권

annual sale 연례 할인 행사

special deal 특가 혜택, 특별 할인 행사

drawing 추첨 행사

main entrance 중앙 출입구

전시장 / 공연장 / 극장

exhibition 전시회

performance 공연, 연주

audience 관객

cast 출연진

appearance 출연, 외관

technical difficulties 기술적 문제[어려움]

sound system 음향 시스템

audio[sound] equipment 음향 기기

resolve the issue 문제를 해결하다

turn off mobile phones 휴대폰 전원을 끄다

recording device 녹음[녹화] 기기

strictly prohibited 엄격히 제한되어 있는

extend hours of operation 운영 시간을 늘리다

begin shortly 곧 시작하다

during the intermission 중간 휴식 시간에

proceeds from ticket sales 티켓 판매 수익금

support local arts groups 지역 예술가 그룹을 후원하다

proceed to ~로 가다

교통 수단 관련 안내 방송

flight attendant 승무원

conductor 차장

train station 기차역

ferry terminal 여객선 터미널

major bus routes 주요 버스 노선들

ticket counter 매표소

automated ticketing system 자동 티켓 판매 시스템

boarding pass 탑승권

cabin 객실, 선실

in-flight service 기내 서비스

accommodate passengers 승객을 수용하다

overbook 정원 이상의 예약을 받다

inclement weather 악천후

weather conditions 기상 상태

heavy fog / rain 짙은 안개 / 폭우

snowstorm 눈보라

personal belongings 개인 소지품

baggage claim area 수하물 찾는 곳

transfer 환승하다, 갈아타다

leave[depart] from Gate 8 8번 게이트에서 출발하다

anticipate a smooth flight 순조로운 비행을 예상하다

expect to arrive on time 제시간에 도착할 것으로 예상하다

delayed until ~까지 지연되는

engine trouble 엔진 문제

call a mechanic[technician] 기술자를 부르다

investigate a problem 문제를 조사하다

get tires replaced 타이어를 교체시키다

repaving work 도로 재포장 작업

water pipe installation 수도관 설치

track maintenance 선로 수리

temporarily closed 일시적으로 폐쇄된

be back to normal 정상으로 돌아가다

Welcome aboard ~ 탑승을 환영합니다

My apologies for the inconvenience. 불편을 끼쳐드려 죄송합니다.

Thank you for your patience / cooperation. 양해해 / 협조해 주셔서 감사합니다.

🎧 P4_61 정답 및 해설 p.263

담화를 들으면서 정답을 고르세요. 그리고 다시 들으면서 빈칸을 채우세요. (녹음은 두 번씩 들려줍니다.)

1. When will Main Street close to automobile traffic?
(A) On August 8
(B) On August 11

2. What should people do if they have questions?
(A) Send an e-mail
(B) Make a phone call

The city of Dover would like to inform residents of the _____.
Beginning Monday, August 8, Main Street will be closed for water pipe installation. _____
_____ on Main Street between Sixteenth Street and Twentieth Street. Pedestrians will be able to
access all stores in the area _____. We expect to reopen Main Street by
August 11. We apologize for any inconvenience this closure may cause. If you have any _____
_____ on Main Street, please call the City Planning Office at 555-3701.

3. What has caused a cancellation?
(A) Bad weather
(B) Mechanical problems

4. Look at the graphic. What time will the ferry leave?
(A) 6:30 P.M.
(B) 8:30 P.M.

Saint Marshall's Island Ferry

Departures	Arrivals
9:00 A.M.	9:30 A.M.
11:00 A.M.	11:30 A.M.
6:30 P.M.	7:00 P.M.
8:30 P.M.	9:00 P.M.

Attention all passengers waiting for the 6:30 P.M. ferry to Saint
Marshall's Island. _____,
this ferry has been canceled. However, the storm is moving
quickly, so it should be out of the area _____
_____. To accommodate all the _____
_____, we'll be opening the upper deck of the boat. It
can get pretty chilly up there, so you'll want to _____
_____ if you have one with you. Thanks for
your patience, and we apologize for any inconvenience.

5. What will happen next week?
(A) A parking area will be repaved.
(B) Hours of operation will be extended.

6. Where can the sign-up sheet be found?
(A) In the lobby
(B) In the cafeteria

Attention, employees. This is a reminder that _____ in the west
parking area. Because of the reduced number of available parking spaces, employees are encouraged to
_____. A sign-up sheet for carpooling _____
_____. If you'd like to arrange to share a ride, _____
to the list.

1. Why is the performance delayed?
   (A) Some equipment is not working.
   (B) Some instruments are being set up.
   (C) A performer is running late.
   (D) The theater is being cleaned.

2. According to the speaker, what can be purchased in the lobby?
   (A) Food and beverages
   (B) Event tickets
   (C) A band's recordings
   (D) Autographed photos of a band

3. What is being advertised at the theater?
   (A) Acting classes
   (B) Upcoming performances
   (C) Guided tours
   (D) Local restaurants

4. Who most likely is the speaker?
   (A) A bus driver
   (B) A tour guide
   (C) A flight attendant
   (D) A train conductor

5. What does the speaker remind the listeners about?
   (A) The number of travel stops
   (B) The weather conditions
   (C) The regulations for storing luggage
   (D) The availability of wireless Internet

6. What will the listeners most likely do soon?
   (A) Choose their seats
   (B) Order food
   (C) Depart from a vehicle
   (D) Show their tickets

7. Where is the announcement taking place?
   (A) At a train station
   (B) At a grocery store
   (C) At a restaurant
   (D) At a furniture store

8. Why does the speaker say, "It'll only take a minute"?
   (A) To correct a misunderstanding
   (B) To encourage participation
   (C) To ask for permission
   (D) To explain a delay

9. What does the speaker offer customers?
   (A) A discount coupon
   (B) Home delivery
   (C) Upgraded seating
   (D) A free dessert

10. What is the purpose of the announcement?
    (A) To introduce a lecture series
    (B) To promote a volunteer opportunity
    (C) To explain parking regulations
    (D) To publicize new business hours

11. What will happen on April 21 ?
    (A) A community fair will be held.
    (B) Parking will be restricted.
    (C) Some gardening work will be done.
    (D) Some books will be delivered.

12. What does the speaker say will be distributed?
    (A) Some flowers
    (B) A newsletter
    (C) A T-shirt
    (D) Some food

13. Where most likely is this announcement being made?
(A) At an airport
(B) At a train station
(C) At a shopping center
(D) At an amusement park

14. What does the speaker say is now available?
(A) An expanded cafeteria
(B) A renovated waiting area
(C) Complimentary Internet access
(D) Automated ticketing machines

15. What is mentioned about the user instructions?
(A) They are available on the Web site.
(B) They are offered in different languages.
(C) They are written on each ticket.
(D) They can be found inside the merchandise packaging.

---

16. What does the speaker say is prohibited?
(A) Smoking
(B) Walking on stage
(C) Making recordings
(D) Talking

17. Why does the speaker say, "we only need to raise two thousand dollars to reach our goal"?
(A) To apologize for interrupting
(B) To correct a mistake
(C) To ask for donations
(D) To explain a delay

18. What can the listeners find in the lobby?
(A) A coat closet
(B) Some programs
(C) A ticket-sales counter
(D) Some refreshments

Departures		
Destination	**Time**	**Platform**
Webster	10:30 A.M.	B
Burgess	10:37 A.M.	C
Patterton	10:44 A.M.	A
Cody Springs	10:52 A.M.	F

19. Look at the graphic. Which platform does the announcement concern?
(A) Platform B
(B) Platform C
(C) Platform A
(D) Platform F

20. What has caused the problem?
(A) Poor weather
(B) A vehicle malfunction
(C) A scheduling mistake
(D) Heavy road traffic

21. What are some travelers asked to do?
(A) Wait for a display to be updated
(B) Speak to a ticketing agent
(C) Use a different platform
(D) Form a line near a door

⑬ 광고

1 제품/서비스/업체 광고가 주를 이루며, 구인 광고나 시설 견학, 행사 참여를 권하는 광고도 등장한다. 광고 대상, 특징 및 장점, 혜택, 추가 정보 관련 내용을 묻는 문제가 자주 출제된다.

2 주의를 끄는 광고성 멘트/광고 대상 → 특징 및 장점 → 혜택 → 추가 정보/연락 방법 순으로 전개되는 경우가 많다.

담화 흐름 파악하기

P4_63

광고성 멘트	① Are you a busy professional always flying off on business trips?	① 광고의 타깃: 항상 출장을 급히 떠나는 직장인
광고 대상	② If so, then Davidson's clothing is right for you. Davidson's just launched its new collection of anti-wrinkle clothing for business travel.	② 광고 대상: 새롭게 출시한 구김 방지 의류
특징/장점	Each piece in this collection of suits, skirts, and blazers is made with a special kind of fabric that'll come out of your suitcase wrinkle-free and ready-to-wear.	
구매 혜택	③ And for a limited time only, shop Davidson's online and get free shipping with every order.	③ 한시적으로 제공하는 것: 온라인 구매 시 무료 배송

청자 신분	**1.** Who is the intended audience for the advertisement? 누구를 겨냥한 광고이겠는가?	Business travelers 출장자
광고 대상	**2.** What is being advertised ? 광고되고 있는 것은?	Clothing 의류
세부 정보	**3.** What can customers who shop online get for a limited time ? 온라인으로 구매하는 고객들이 한시적으로 받을 수 있는 것은?	Free shipping 무료 배송

항상 출장을 급히 떠나는 바쁜 직장인인가요? 그렇다면, 데이비슨즈 의류가 당신에게 딱 맞을 겁니다. 데이비슨즈에서 최근 출장용 구김 방지 의류의 새 컬렉션을 출시했습니다. 정장, 스커트, 블레이저 컬렉션에 있는 모든 의상은 여러분의 여행 가방에서 구김 없이 바로 입을 수 있는 상태로 나오게끔 특별한 종류의 천으로 만들어집니다. 한정된 기간 동안, 데이비슨즈에서 온라인으로 구매하고 모든 주문을 무료로 배송 받으세요.

✏️ **상황별 핵심 표현** 🎧 P4_64

광고

- 제품 / 서비스 광고: 식품, 장비, 소프트웨어 등의 제품 광고, 신제품 출시 홍보, 유지·보수 / 법률 자문 등의 서비스 광고, 관광 / 견학 상품 광고, 교육 기관이 제공하는 프로그램 광고
- 업체 / 시설 광고: 병원, 식당, 상점, 운동 시설 등의 업체 홍보, 업체의 구인 광고, 행사를 위한 시설이나 부동산 광고

광고성 멘트 광고 대상	Are you planning to renovate your house? If so, Conwell Construction can help. 주택을 개조하려고 계획 중이신가요? 그렇다면, 콘웰 건설이 도와드릴 수 있습니다. Are you looking for a place to host your dinner party? Well, look no further than Eden's! 저녁 파티를 열 장소를 찾고 계신가요? 자, 다른 곳 볼 필요 없이 이든스만 알아보시면 됩니다!
특징 및 장점	We specialize in authentic Italian dishes that you won't find anywhere else in the city. 저희는 이 도시 어디에서도 찾아볼 수 없는 정통 이탈리안 요리를 전문으로 하고 있습니다. We've been providing top-quality repair services to Greenville car owners for over thirty years. 저희는 30년 넘게 그린빌의 차량 소유주들에게 최고의 수리 서비스를 제공해 오고 있습니다. Springdale Shopping Center is conveniently located in the heart of the commercial district. 스프링데일 쇼핑 센터는 상업 지구 중심의 편리한 곳에 위치해 있습니다.
할인 및 특별 혜택	If you register before the end of this month, you'll receive a complimentary sports bag. 이번 달 말까지 등록하시면, 무료 스포츠 가방을 받게 되실 겁니다. For this week only, we're offering a thirty percent discount on all of our online courses. 이번 주만 저희의 모든 온라인 코스를 30퍼센트 할인해 드립니다.
추가 정보	For more details about the position or to apply, please visit our Web site at www.sanfashion.com. 해당 직책에 대한 더 자세한 정보를 원하거나 지원하고 싶다면, 당사 웹사이트 www.sanfashion.com을 방문해 주세요. To take advantage of this special offer, enter the promotional code FREESHIPPING when you check out. 이 특별 혜택을 이용하시려면, 계산 시 쿠폰 번호 FREESHIPPING을 입력하세요.

PART 4 | CHAPTER 02

ETS CHECK-UP 🎧 P4_65 정답 및 해설 p.269

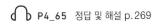

1. What kind of product does the store sell?

(A) Clothing
(B) Hand tools
(C) Computers
(D) Books

2. Why does the speaker suggest visiting the store today?

(A) A shipment is expected.
(B) A business is closing.
(C) A discount will end soon.
(D) A product will sell out quickly.

3. What additional service does the store provide?

(A) Repairs
(B) International shipping
(C) Gift wrapping
(D) Delayed payment options

광고 대상

beverage 음료
athletic equipment 운동 장비
appliance 가전제품
electronic goods 전자 제품
office furniture 사무용 가구
art supplies 미술용품
event hall 이벤트 홀

cleaning/maintenance service 청소/유지보수 서비스
security company 보안 업체
plumbing company 배관 업체
apartment complex 아파트 단지
clothing manufacturer 의류 제조사
career opportunity 취업 기회
training program 교육 프로그램

제품/서비스

feature 특징, 기능; ~을 특징으로 하다
functional 기능적인
easy to use/follow 사용하기/따라하기 쉬운
authentic 정통의, 진짜의
unique 유일무이한, 유일한
revolutionary 혁신적인, 획기적인
newest model 최신 모델
compact 소형의
portable 휴대용의, 휴대가 쉬운
lightweight 가벼운, 경량의
long-lasting 오래 지속되는 (= durable, sustainable)

environmentally friendly 친환경적인
fuel-efficient 연료 효율적인, 연비가 좋은
affordable[reasonable] price 적당한 가격
especially designed to부정사 ~하기 위해 특별히 고안된
customized 맞춤화된, 맞춤 제작의
excellent[quality] service 훌륭한[양질의] 서비스
perfect for ~에 안성맞춤인, 완벽한
economic choice 경제적인 선택
the smartest decision 가장 현명한 결정
maximize efficiency 효율성을 극대화하다
endorse (유명인 등이) 특정 상품을 보증하다

업체/시설/행사

leading 선도하는, 일류의
dependable[reliable] company 믿을 수 있는 회사
be the top name in (특정 분야에서) 일류이다
recognize us as 우리를 ~로 선정[인정]하다
specialize in ~를 전문으로 하다
serve clients[customers] 고객에게 서비스를 제공하다
offer a new attraction 새 명물을 제공하다
suit one's needs 필요[요구]에 들어맞다
equipped 장비를 갖춘
ideal location 이상적인 장소
convenient parking area 편리한 주차 공간
be located in the heart of ~의 중심부에 위치해 있다

easy access to public transportation
대중교통에 대한 접근성
breathtaking[stunning] view 숨막힐 정도로 멋진 전망
have an enjoyable experience 즐거운 경험을 하다
celebrate special occasions 특별한 행사를 기념하다
fill up quickly 자리가 빨리 차다
There's no better place than ~.
~보다 더 좋은 장소는 없습니다.
Schedule your visit now. 지금 바로 방문 예약을 하세요.
That's not the only reason to choose ~.
그것이 ~를 선택할 유일한 이유는 아닙니다.
Come and celebrate ~. 와서 ~를 축하해 주세요.

할인 및 특별 혜택

special promotion 특별 판촉 행사
for a limited time only 한시적으로, 한정된 기간 동안만
expire 종료[만료]되다
for half the price 절반 가격에
save up to 20 percent 20프로까지 절약하다
coupon[voucher] for 50 percent off 50프로 할인 쿠폰
available for your next purchase 다음 번 구매 때 쓸 수 있는

at no extra charge 무료로
free shipping 무료 배송
complimentary consultation 무료 상담
extended warranty 연장된 보증기간
trial period 무료 체험 기간
take advantage of 이용하다, 혜택을 받다
earn/redeem points 포인트를 얻다/(다른 것으로) 교환하다

담화를 들으면서 정답을 고르세요. 그리고 다시 들으면서 빈칸을 채우세요. (녹음은 두 번씩 들려줍니다.)

1. What is being advertised?
(A) A party-supply shop
(B) An event hall

2. What is mentioned about the facility?
(A) It can accommodate many group sizes.
(B) It has been expanded recently.

Are you planning a special event? _____ to celebrate weddings, birthdays—any special occasion. Our facility features spacious dining rooms and party halls that can be easily arranged for _____. We have reception rooms that are just right for small groups, while our largest hall will accommodate up to 300 people. Catering is available on-site, and for a limited time, we're offering _____. So make your reservation now! Call 555-0100 today.

---

3. According to the advertisement, what is special about Peterson's?
(A) It has been in business for 30 years.
(B) It has been featured in a magazine.

4. What is offered to the first 50 callers?
(A) A merchandise discount
(B) A complimentary service

When you _____ with Peterson's Heating and Cooling, you get more than a repair service. You get peace of mind from knowing your heating and cooling systems will be maintained correctly. _____, as the oldest heating and cooling contractor—_____. So, what are you waiting for? Call Peterson's today and put your worries behind you. The first fifty callers will _____ _____!

---

5. What type of business is being advertised?
(A) An interior design firm
(B) A home improvement store

6. What is the topic of this Saturday's workshop?
(A) Choosing a decorating style
(B) Installing carpet

Do you wish you could _____, but don't know where to start? Garcia's Home Center can help. Every Saturday morning, we offer free instruction on everything from building a shed to tiling your bathroom. This Saturday's workshop will focus on _____ _____. Come and learn about buying the right carpeting and using the best tools. Anyone who attends the workshop will also _____—our step-by-step guides are sure to make your project a success. So stop by the store to register today!

---

1. What is being advertised?
   (A) An event venue
   (B) A cleaning service
   (C) A seasonal sale
   (D) A career opportunity

2. What does the speaker mention about a showroom?
   (A) It has been renovated.
   (B) It is close to public transportation.
   (C) It has parking nearby.
   (D) It has recently moved.

3. How can listeners get more information?
   (A) By going to a showroom
   (B) By visiting a Web site
   (C) By calling customer service
   (D) By sending an e-mail

4. Why is the restaurant having a celebration?
   (A) The head chef won an award.
   (B) The service was favorably reviewed.
   (C) It has served 10,000 customers.
   (D) It is opening a new location.

5. What does the restaurant specialize in?
   (A) Steak
   (B) Seafood
   (C) Spicy meals
   (D) Pasta dishes

6. What will customers receive if they mention the advertisement?
   (A) A 20 percent discount
   (B) A cooking class
   (C) A free dessert
   (D) A coupon

7. Who is the advertisement intended for?
   (A) Financial news reporters
   (B) Small business owners
   (C) Administrative assistants
   (D) Bank tellers

8. What is being described?
   (A) An instructional video
   (B) A laptop computer
   (C) A security system
   (D) A software program

9. What are listeners encouraged to do?
   (A) Purchase new electronic devices
   (B) Open a savings account
   (C) Make a phone call
   (D) Read some reviews

10. What new attraction is open to visitors?
    (A) Water slides
    (B) Ancient cave art
    (C) Hiking trails
    (D) Observation platforms

11. What safety measure does the speaker mention?
    (A) More trail signs
    (B) Tall railings
    (C) Lighted pathways
    (D) Small group sizes

12. How can visitors receive a discount?
    (A) By presenting a coupon
    (B) By arriving early
    (C) By joining an association
    (D) By making a reservation online

13. What is being advertised?
(A) Home-repair services
(B) Monthly commuter passes
(C) An apartment complex
(D) An office-supply store

14. What does the speaker say will happen next month?
(A) A city park will be renovated.
(B) An office branch will be moved.
(C) A bus route will change.
(D) A train station will open.

15. What special offer does the speaker mention?
(A) Short-term contracts
(B) An extended warranty
(C) Holiday rates
(D) Free transportation

16. What is the mobile phone application for?
(A) Buying movie tickets
(B) Completing bank transactions
(C) Placing food orders
(D) Getting driving directions

17. What do customers say they like about the mobile phone application?
(A) It allows them to give feedback.
(B) It saves them time.
(C) It provides a variety of choices.
(D) It is free to use.

18. According to the speaker, what will be added to the mobile phone application next month?
(A) Parking information
(B) Links to social media
(C) A delivery service
(D) A reward point program

Cleaning Solution
$15

Travel Mug
$20

Water Filters
$25

Pod Holder
$30

19. What does the speaker emphasize about Selby coffeemakers?
(A) Their brewing speed
(B) Their relatively low prices
(C) Their ease of use
(D) Their stylish design

20. How can listeners take advantage of a special deal?
(A) By placing orders regularly
(B) By using a coupon code
(C) By attending a grand opening
(D) By purchasing a new product

21. Look at the graphic. What is the regular price of the free item being offered?
(A) $15
(B) $20
(C) $25
(D) $30

⑭ 방송

1 경제, 문화, 과학 기술 등의 다양한 분야와 지역 관련 소식을 전하는 뉴스 및 라디오 프로그램이 주로 출제된다. 교통방송, 일기예보나 프로그램/게스트를 소개하는 내용도 등장한다.

2 프로그램/진행자 소개 → 주제 언급 → 세부 내용 → 마무리 순으로 전개되는 경우가 많다. 객관적인 정보를 전달할 뿐만 아니라 행사 소식을 알리며 청취자의 참여를 독려하기도 한다.

3 방송 주제나 내용 관련 세부 정보를 묻는 문제가 자주 나온다.

🖊 담화 흐름 파악하기
🎧 P4_69

	And now, for business news...
프로그램 주제 언급	① Are you ready to start a career in technology? Join hundreds of recent college graduates for the fourth annual Science and Technology Career Expo on Saturday, May twenty-second.
세부 내용	This event will take place at the Groves Convention Center. Many companies are hiring this year... ② so be sure to go online to see which companies will be attending.
추가 내용/ 참여 독려	③ And this year there's something special: one of the corporate sponsors is offering five computers as door prizes. Register by May first, and you'll automatically be entered into a drawing to win one of these computers.

① 안내 중인 행사: 과학 기술 취업 박람회

② 온라인으로 확인할 것: 박람회에 참석하는 회사들

③ 올해 특별한 점: 경품으로 컴퓨터 제공

주제	**1.** What event is being announced? 어떤 행사가 안내되고 있는가?	A career fair 취업 박람회
세부 정보	**2.** What does the speaker say the **listeners** can do online? 화자는 청자들이 온라인에서 무엇을 할 수 있다고 하는가?	Find a list of companies 회사 목록 확인
세부 정보	**3.** According to the speaker, what will be different at this year's event? 화자에 따르면, 올해 행사에서 다른 점은 무엇인가?	Computers will be offered as prizes. 컴퓨터가 상품으로 제공된다.

그럼 이제, 비즈니스 소식입니다… 기술 분야에서 직장 생활을 시작할 준비가 되셨나요? 최근 대학을 졸업한 수백 명과 함께 5월 22일 토요일, 제4회 연례 과학 기술 취업 박람회에 참여해 보십시오. 이 행사는 그로브즈 컨벤션 센터에서 열릴 예정입니다. 올해 많은 기업이 직원을 채용합니다… 그러니 어떤 회사들이 참여하는지 온라인으로 꼭 확인해 보시기 바랍니다. 올해에는 특별한 일도 있습니다. 기업 후원자들 중 한 곳이 추첨을 통해 컴퓨터 다섯 대를 제공합니다. 5월 1일까지 등록하시면 자동으로 이 컴퓨터 중 한 대를 받을 수 있는 추첨 대상이 됩니다.

상황별 핵심 표현　　　🎧 P4_70

방송 프로그램 및 뉴스

- 기업 합병, 시장 변화, 매출 증감, 신제품 출시, 고용 계획 등의 경제 뉴스나 지역 행사 및 프로젝트 소식
- 음악, 영화, 과학 기술, 건강, 경제 등 다양한 주제나 프로그램 게스트를 소개하는 내용

프로그램 및 진행자 소개	Thanks for tuning in to *Movies Today* on TBC Radio 1. I'm your host, Marlee Sandoval. TBC 라디오 1의 〈오늘의 영화〉를 들어주셔서 감사합니다. 저는 진행자 말리 산도발입니다.
프로그램 주제	On today's episode, we'll talk about how to protect your personal data in this digital world. 오늘 회차에서는 이 디지털 환경에서 어떻게 개인 정보를 보호해야 할지에 대해 이야기해 보겠습니다.
경제 뉴스	Patel Enterprises, a leading car manufacturer, announced that its sales have gone up by twenty-two percent this quarter. 일류 자동차 제조업체인 파델 사가 이번 분기 매출이 22퍼센트 올랐다고 발표했습니다.
지역 소식	In local news, the city council approved the plans for the expansion of Bailey Park. 지역 소식입니다. 시의회가 베일리 공원 확장 계획을 승인했습니다.

교통 방송 / 일기 예보

- 사고, 공사, 행사, 날씨 등의 이유로 인한 교통 정체나 도로 폐쇄를 알리며 우회로 안내
- 현재 또는 특정일의 날씨 상황과 이에 따른 주의 사항 전달

교통 방송	Crews are currently making emergency repairs to the bridge, so it's closed to all traffic. 작업반이 현재 대교를 긴급 수리하고 있어 모든 차량 통행이 금지되고 있습니다.
일기 예보	Right now it's clear and dry, but there will be heavy showers across the region later this evening. 현재는 맑고 건조하지만, 이따 저녁에는 전 지역에 강한 소나기가 내릴 것으로 보입니다.
제안 / 요청 사항	Until the construction work is done, drivers are advised to take a detour along Wilson Road. 공사 작업이 완료될 때까지 운전자들은 윌슨 로로 우회하시는 것이 좋겠습니다.

PART 4 | CHAPTER 02

ETS CHECK-UP　　　🎧 P4_71　정답 및 해설 p.276

1. Who is Fatima Ali?

　(A) A medical researcher
　(B) A radio show host
　(C) A memory expert
　(D) A video game designer

2. What are some listeners invited to do?

　(A) Apply for a job
　(B) Enter a competition
　(C) Take part in a study
　(D) Try out a new game

3. What will the speaker do after a break?

　(A) Make a special announcement
　(B) Report local news
　(C) Answer questions
　(D) Interview a guest

ETS X-FILE | 방송 빈출 표현

P4_72

방송 프로그램

radio station 라디오 방송국
host (TV / 라디오 프로그램의) 사회자, 진행자
viewer / listener 시청자 / 청취자
an important reminder 중요한 정보[알림]
call in to the station 방송국으로 전화하다
take a deep dive into ~를 심도 있게 다루다
have ~ on the show 프로그램에 ~을 초대하다
previously aired episodes 기존에 방송된 회차들

exclusive interview with ~와의 독점 인터뷰
innovations in ~ 분야의 획기적인 것들
award-winning actor 수상 배우
community bulletin board 커뮤니티 게시판
commercial break (프로그램 중간의) 광고 방송
Stay tuned for ~. ~를 위해 주파수를 고정하세요.
With[Joining] me in the studio is ~.
저와 함께 스튜디오에 나와 계신 분은 ~입니다.

뉴스

local news 지역 뉴스
regional business news 지역 비즈니스 뉴스
reporting live from ~에서 생중계하고 있는
city council 시의회
city[town] official 시 공무원
authority 당국
mayor 시장
election 선거
citizen / resident 시민 / 거주민
community member 지역사회 구성원
institute 기관
corporate sponsor 후원사

approve funding 자금 지원을 승인하다
reveal / announce a plan 계획을 공개 / 발표하다
take action on ~에 대한 조치를 취하다
go on the market 시판되다
create jobs 일자리를 창출하다
generate revenue[profits] 이윤을 창출하다
dominate the global market 세계 시장을 장악하다
meet growing demand 늘어나는 수요에 부응하다
According to a spokesperson 대변인에 따르면
almost complete 거의 완성[완공]된
just around the corner (행사 등이) 임박한
open to the public 대중에게 공개되다

교통 방송

commuter 통근자
latest traffic report 최신 교통 정보
lane 차선
expressway 고속도로
traffic light 신호등
heavy traffic 극심한 교통량
bottleneck 병목 지역
metropolitan area 수도권, 대도시권

be closed for ~로 인해 폐쇄되다
traffic congestion[jam] 교통 혼잡[정체]
expect delays 정체가 예상되다
be backed up (차·도로 등이) 막혀 있다, 정체되어 있다
be stuck[held up] in traffic 교통 체증에 걸리다
make[take] a detour 우회도로를 이용하다
take an alternate[alternative] route 다른 길로 가다
take public transportation 대중교통을 이용하다

일기 예보

weather forecast[report] 일기예보
inclement[bad] weather 악천후
favorable (날씨가) 좋은
temperature 온도, 기온
degree (온도 단위인) 도
precipitation 강수량 (= amount of rain)
with no chance of rain 비가 올 확률이 없는
typical for this time of year 연중 이맘때에 늘 그렇듯이

extremely hot 극도로 더운
humid 습기가 많은 (= damp)
heat wave 폭염
snowstorm 눈보라
strong wind 강풍
shower 소나기
thunderstorm (강풍이 따르는) 뇌우
hail 우박

LISTENING **PRACTICE**

♩ ♭ P4_73 정답 및 해설 p.277

담화를 들으면서 정답을 고르세요. 그리고 다시 들으면서 빈칸을 채우세요. (녹음은 두 번씩 들려줍니다.)

1. What will listeners hear at eight o'clock?
(A) An interview with a local official
(B) Details about upcoming events

2. What does the speaker remind listeners to do?
(A) Call the station with questions
(B) Get a mobile app

Thank you for listening to WDKT103 Radio. In the eight o'clock hour, we'll be bringing you _____ _____ Frank Walters. But first, here's the traffic report for the metropolitan area. _____ in the city center. However, there are delays in the area around the Riverdale Bridge _____. Remember, for the most up-to-date traffic conditions, be sure to _____.

3. What is Dougherty Films looking for?
(A) A lead actor
(B) A filming location

4. What does the speaker imply when she says, "But this is Santiago Diaz we're talking about"?
(A) She has never heard of Santiago Diaz.
(B) Santiago Diaz is very famous.

And for today's _____... Renowned film company, Dougherty Films, recently announced they'll be shooting a movie right here in Brayville. In fact, the crew is looking to _____ to film some of their main scenes in. In the movie, the apartment that is chosen will be owned by the award-winning actor Santiago Diaz's character. Now, if it were someone else, you _____ to let a film crew into your home for several weeks. But this is Santiago Diaz we're talking about. To have your apartment considered for the film, fill out an application on the Dougherty Films Web site.

5. What is the main topic of the broadcast?
(A) Business news
(B) The weather

6. What recommendation is made in the broadcast?
(A) Visiting a new store
(B) Remaining indoors

This is Jeff Johnson at Radio 2SY, Sydney's number-one music and information station. And now, _____. It will continue to be _____ today and air quality remains poor. Because of these unhealthy conditions, medical professionals _____ as much as possible until this heat wave breaks. I'll have _____ _____. Next up is Marc Hernandez, who will be _____ _____.

1. What did the city council approve funding for?
   (A) Recycling services for the community
   (B) Additional bus routes in town
   (C) Lighting along a trail
   (D) Construction of a school

2. According to the speaker, what did some community members do last month?
   (A) They gave a presentation at a meeting.
   (B) They held a fund-raising event.
   (C) They collected signatures from residents.
   (D) They filled out a questionnaire.

3. What will the city council do next week?
   (A) Take a break
   (B) Make a hiring decision
   (C) Visit a local business
   (D) Look for a new meeting location

4. Who is Lucy Harper?
   (A) A science fiction author
   (B) A museum director
   (C) A television weather reporter
   (D) An environmental engineer

5. What did Lucy Harper recently receive?
   (A) A promotion
   (B) An award
   (C) An invitation
   (D) A degree

6. What does the speaker say is on display?
   (A) A design model
   (B) A rare manuscript
   (C) A traveling exhibit
   (D) A competition trophy

7. What does the speaker say is reopening?
   (A) Some sports fields
   (B) Some city offices
   (C) A shopping mall
   (D) A pedestrian bridge

8. What caused a delay in repairs?
   (A) A change in design
   (B) A shortage of supplies
   (C) Budget cuts
   (D) Bad weather

9. According to the speaker, what kind of event will take place on Sunday?
   (A) An election
   (B) A parade
   (C) A celebrity appearance
   (D) A community picnic

10. What item is being featured on the show?
    (A) A set of gardening tools
    (B) A floral arrangement
    (C) A self-help book
    (D) A plant container

11. What is Ms. Russell going to do?
    (A) Read an excerpt from a book
    (B) Show a short video
    (C) Demonstrate the use of a product
    (D) Answer questions from viewers

12. What is offered to the first 25 callers?
    (A) A ticket to the show
    (B) Free shipping on an order
    (C) A club membership
    (D) A magazine subscription

13. What has the Wilson Dance Company recently done?
(A) It went on an international tour.
(B) It added some more performers.
(C) It hired a new advertising firm.
(D) It made some videos.

14. What does the speaker imply when she says, "tickets for the first three shows have sold out"?
(A) An opinion is surprising.
(B) A promotion has been successful.
(C) A change cannot be made.
(D) A performer should not worry.

15. What are the listeners encouraged to do?
(A) Visit a museum
(B) Register for a class
(C) Make a purchase
(D) Consult a calendar

16. What type of event is being announced?
(A) A film festival
(B) A lecture series
(C) A music competition
(D) A concert tour

17. According to the speaker, what has changed?
(A) The start time
(B) The registration cost
(C) The age requirement
(D) The event location

18. According to the speaker, what should interested listeners do?
(A) Submit a proposal
(B) Register online
(C) Reserve tickets
(D) Complete a survey

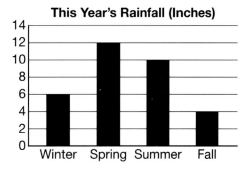

This Year's Rainfall (Inches)

19. What industry is the broadcast mainly about?
(A) Agriculture
(B) Tourism
(C) Construction
(D) Transportation

20. Look at the graphic. Which amount of seasonal rain was unusual?
(A) 6 inches
(B) 12 inches
(C) 10 inches
(D) 4 inches

21. According to the speaker, what can consumers expect?
(A) Traffic delays
(B) Higher prices
(C) Property damage
(D) Power disruptions

⑮ 관광/견학

출제공식 1 공원, 박물관, 공장, 시설 등을 관광/견학하는 사람들을 대상으로 가이드가 안내하는 내용이 주를 이룬다.

2 인사말/자기 소개 → 일정 안내/특징 설명 → 당부/주의사항 전달 순으로 전개되는 경우가 많다. 또한 견학 중간에 지금까지 본 것을 정리한 후 다음에 갈 곳을 소개하거나, 견학을 마무리하며 추후 진행될 행사 등을 공지하는 상황도 자주 나온다.

3 청자들이 참여하는 행사, 담화가 이루어지는 장소, 주의/당부 사항, 다음에 할 일을 묻는 문제가 자주 출제된다.

✏️ 담화 흐름 파악하기 🎧 P4_75

견학 내용 중간 정리	① At this stop of the tour, you saw how designs are printed onto the fabric that we make. We saw the different processes that are used to print simple and complex designs.	① 청자들이 하고 있는 것: 직물 공장 견학
특징 설명	② As you may assume, the simple designs are more economical. They don't cost much to make because they take fewer steps and require less ink.	② 화자가 말하는 단순한 디자인의 특징: 비용이 많이 들지 않음
장소 이동	③ Now, let's move into the next room, where you'll see several samples of fabric with different designs on them.	③ 다음에 할 일: 다양한 디자인의 직물 샘플 살펴 보기

참여 행사	1. What are the **listeners** doing? 청자들이 하고 있는 것?	Taking a factory tour 공장 견학
세부 언급	2. What does the speaker say about fabrics with simple designs? 화자는 단순한 디자인의 직물에 대해 뭐라고 말하는가?	They are inexpensive to make. 만드는 데 비용이 많이 들지 않는다.
할 일	3. What will the **listeners** do next? 청자들은 다음에 무엇을 할 것인가?	Look at some samples 샘플 보기

본 견학의 이번 장소에서는 저희가 제작한 직물에 디자인이 어떻게 프린트되는지 보셨습니다. 단순하고 복잡한 디자인을 프린트하는 데 이용되는 다양한 공정을 알아봤는데요. 추측하시는 대로 간단한 디자인이 더 경제적입니다. 단계가 더 적고 잉크가 덜 들기 때문에 만드는 데 비용이 많이 들지 않거든요. 이제 다음 방으로 이동하셔서 다양한 디자인이 프린트된 몇 가지 샘플을 보시겠습니다.

✏️ 상황별 핵심 표현 🎧 P4_76

관광 / 견학

- 관광 / 관람: 국립공원, 미술관, 박물관, 유적지, 마을 등의 관광지나 목적지로 이동하는 차량 안에서 일정, 명소 및 전시품 등의 특징, 주의 사항 등을 설명하는 내용
- 견학: 공장 등의 시설에서 제작 상품, 작업 절차 및 공정, 기타 주의 사항을 안내하는 내용

환영 인사	Thank you for joining this tour of our glass manufacturing plant. 저희 유리 제조 공장 견학에 참가해 주셔서 감사합니다.
일정 안내	Today you'll have the opportunity to see how we produce our ceramic tiles. 오늘 여러분은 저희가 어떻게 도자기 타일을 만드는 지 볼 기회를 갖게 됩니다. We'll start in the Interactive Art exhibit, which features different sculptures that can be touched and played with. After that, we'll go to the museum café and have lunch. 쌍방향 예술 전시회장에서 시작할 텐데요, 이곳은 만지면서 놀 수 있는 다양한 조각품들을 선보입니다. 그 이후에 박물관 식당에 가서 점심 식사를 할 겁니다. At the end of the tour, everyone will receive a free box of our gourmet chocolates. 견학이 끝날 때 모든 분들이 저희의 고급 초콜릿 한 상자를 무료로 받게 됩니다.
특징 소개	This town is notable for its open-air market, where you can find unique handicrafts. 이 마을은 야외 시장으로 유명한데요, 이곳에서 여러분은 독특한 수공예품을 만나볼 수 있습니다.
장소 이동	So far we've seen how the juice is extracted from the oranges. Now, let's move into the filtration room. 지금까지 오렌지에서 즙이 추출되는 모습을 보셨습니다. 이제 여과실로 이동하시죠.
주의 사항	While walking through the forest, make sure you stay with your group and remain on the path. 숲 속을 걷는 동안, 반드시 일행과 함께 있고 길에서 벗어나지 말아주세요.

PART 4 | CHAPTER 02

ETS CHECK-UP 🎧 P4_77 정답 및 해설 p.283

1. What event is ending?
   (A) A community picnic
   (B) A gardening demonstration
   (C) A sports match
   (D) A nature tour

2. What must participants in the competition do?
   (A) Run in a race
   (B) Prepare a special dish
   (C) Identify trees correctly
   (D) Draw a picture

3. What are listeners cautioned about?
   (A) Drinking enough water
   (B) Making noise
   (C) Leaving trash
   (D) Walking on plants

관광/관람

guided tour 안내원이 딸린 여행/견학
courtesy[free] bus (손님용) 무료 버스
complimentary breakfast 무료 아침식사
next destination 다음 목적지
tourist attraction 관광 명소
landmark 랜드마크, 주요 지형 지물
historic structure 역사적인 구조물
observatory 전망대
setting for a famous movie 유명 영화의 촬영지
nature reserve 자연 보호 구역
breathtaking/spectacular scenery 숨 멎는 듯한/멋진 풍경
nature trail 자연 탐방로
walkway 보도 (= path)
within walking distance 도보로 갈 수 있는 거리에
explore 둘러보다, 탐험하다
stroll around ~ 주변을 산책하다/거닐다
be popular with ~에게 인기가 있다
be crowded with ~로 붐비다

exhibit 전시회, 전시장, 전시품; 전시하다
admission fee 입장료
feature 선보이다, 특별히 포함하다
temporary exhibition 임시전, 단기전
showroom 전시실 (= display area)
modern[contemporary] art 현대 미술
ancient era 고대 시대
interactive art 쌍방형 예술, 참여형 예술
artifact/handicraft 공예품/수공예품
sculpture 조각품
pottery 도예, 도자기
replica 복제품, 모형
souvenir 기념품
amazing invention 놀라운 발명품
collection of classical paintings 고전미술 작품들
masterpiece 명작, 걸작
impressive 인상적인, 감명 깊은
fascinating story 흥미로운 이야기

공장/시설 견학

be in operation 가동 중이다
factory/facility 공장/시설
manufacturing plant 제조 공장
assembly line 조립 라인
production area[floor] 생산 구역
distribution center 배송 센터
fabric 직물
raw material 원료, 원자재
ingredient 재료
mixture 혼합물
texture 질감
blend together 같이 섞다
add flavors 맛을 더하다
extraction 추출
aging 숙성
filtration 여과
packaging 포장
chemical process 화학 처리 공정
milling/grinding/weaving machine 공작기/분쇄기/직기

plant[factory] manager 공장장
maintenance team 관리팀
skilled artisan[craftsman] 숙련된 장인
demonstrate some techniques 일부 기술을 시연하다
take precautions 주의하다, 예방 조치를 취하다
prevent accidents 사고를 예방하다
follow safety rules 안전 규정을 따르다
safety gear 안전 장비
safety glasses 보안경
protective shoes 보호용 신발
move on to ~로 이동하다
go straight to ~로 바로 가다
head back to ~로 다시 돌아가다
refrain from ~을 삼가다
be required to부정사 ~하도록 요청되다
be prohibited to부정사 ~하는 것이 금지되어 있다
be not allowed to부정사 ~이 허용되지 않다
If you direct your attention to ~를 보시면
Remain[Stay] with your group. 일행과 함께 있으세요.

LISTENING **PRACTICE**

P4_79 정답 및 해설 p.284

담화를 들으면서 정답을 고르세요. 그리고 다시 들으면서 빈칸을 채우세요. (녹음은 두 번씩 들려줍니다.)

1. What does the speaker say about the village?
(A) It was recently renovated.
(B) It has over one hundred shops.

2. What is available in the gift shop?
(A) A map of the village
(B) A book about the area

Welcome to Mountain Creek Historical Village. My name is Jane, and I'll be your guide for the next hour. During this tour I will show you _____. As you may know, this town has been here for nearly one hundred and twenty years. The historical society purchased the property three years ago and _____. If you'd like to learn more about the history of this fascinating area, _____, *Beautiful Mountain Creek*. It is available in the gift shop, which will be the last stop on our tour today.

3. Where most likely is the speaker?
(A) In a pottery studio
(B) In an art museum

4. What will the tour members probably do next?
(A) Line up for tickets
(B) Look at art work

Welcome to _____. Our tour today will last about thirty minutes, and it will focus on the _____. These works cover thousands of years and a large geographic territory, so we will catch _____.
After the tour, be sure to visit the museum gift shop, where you can find posters of some of the pieces in the collection. The gift shop is across from the ticket desks. Now let's get started, since we have a lot to see in only half an hour. Let's _____ that stands in the center of the room.

5. Who most likely is the speaker?
(A) A factory representative
(B) An auto mechanic

6. Why will questions be answered in the distribution center?
(A) It is close to the lobby.
(B) It is quiet there.

Welcome to Bartlett Rubber Surfaces. On today's tour, I'll show you _____. Our surfaces are long-lasting and used in playgrounds and sports fields. Let me explain the basics before we go in, because _____. First we'll see the cleaning station, which washes and prepares the old tires for their new use. From there, we'll watch _____. We'll end the tour in the distribution center, which packages the finished product. _____, so I'll be able to answer any questions that you might have while we're there.

1. Where does the talk take place?
   (A) At a factory
   (B) At a restaurant
   (C) At a grocery store
   (D) At an orchard

2. What is being demonstrated?
   (A) Where to seat guests
   (B) Where to display products
   (C) How to add flavors
   (D) How to pick fruit

3. What will the speaker talk about next?
   (A) Storage instructions
   (B) Seasonal products
   (C) Greeting techniques
   (D) Cooling methods

4. What is the purpose of the talk?
   (A) To ask for donations
   (B) To publicize an art book
   (C) To introduce an exhibit
   (D) To discuss a renovation

5. What will the speaker distribute?
   (A) Entrance tickets
   (B) A list of activities
   (C) A map of the museum
   (D) Audio devices

6. According to the speaker, what will begin at 3 o'clock?
   (A) An auction
   (B) A lecture
   (C) A concert
   (D) A reception

7. Where is the tour most likely taking place?
   (A) At a recording studio
   (B) At a concert hall
   (C) At a musician's home
   (D) A musical instrument factory

8. What does the speaker mention about the tour?
   (A) It does not include access to certain spaces.
   (B) It must finish by a certain time.
   (C) Participants must be over a certain age.
   (D) Tour groups are limited to a certain size.

9. What should the listeners avoid doing?
   (A) Touching some equipment
   (B) Making loud noises
   (C) Leaving belongings behind
   (D) Becoming separated from each other

10. Where is the tour taking place?
    (A) At a nature park
    (B) At an art museum
    (C) At an aquarium
    (D) At a university

11. What does the speaker remind listeners to do?
    (A) Check their belongings
    (B) Wear comfortable shoes
    (C) Stay in marked areas
    (D) Keep a receipt

12. What will the listeners receive?
    (A) Maps
    (B) Booklets
    (C) Badges
    (D) Headsets

13. According to the speaker, what is distinctive about the factory?
(A) It was the first in the city.
(B) It is the largest in the area.
(C) It has recently been updated.
(D) It operates 24 hours a day.

14. What will be distributed to the visitors?
(A) Product samples
(B) Tour schedules
(C) Floor plans
(D) Headphones

15. What are visitors asked to do?
(A) Speak quietly
(B) Fill out a survey
(C) Remain with the group
(D) Wear protective clothing

16. What will the listeners do at 2:00 ?
(A) Go to a museum
(B) Attend a performance
(C) Eat lunch
(D) Board a bus

17. Why does the speaker say, "Hartford Sweet Shop's ice cream is delicious"?
(A) To recommend that listeners go there
(B) To tell listeners why a business is so popular
(C) To explain why the number of customers has increased
(D) To compare two businesses

18. What does the speaker say she will do next?
(A) Check a guidebook
(B) Make a reservation
(C) Hand out some tickets
(D) Find a parking space

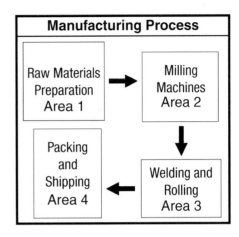

19. According to the speaker, what is the company proud of?
(A) It uses locally-sourced materials.
(B) It is a family-run operation.
(C) It has won an award for excellence.
(D) It is the largest supplier for the automobile industry.

20. Look at the graphic. Which area will the listeners go to next?
(A) Area 1
(B) Area 2
(C) Area 3
(D) Area 4

21. Who most likely is Stefan Schmidt?
(A) A company executive
(B) A customer
(C) A technician
(D) A salesperson

PART 4
기출

PARAPHRASING
LIST

PARAPHRASING LIST

1. **e-mail you a copy**
   사본을 이메일로 보내다

   ▶ **send a manuscript**
   원고를 보내다

2. **put up a sign**
   표지판을 설치하다

   ▶ **hanging a sign**
   표지판 걸기

3. **gain of nearly 10 percent in sales**
   거의 10퍼센트의 매출 증가

   ▶ **an increase in sales**
   매출 증가

4. **need your final manuscript**
   최종 원고가 필요하다

   ▶ **request a new version of a manuscript**
   원고의 새 버전을 요청하다

5. **a drop in profits**
   수익 감소

   ▶ **a decrease in a company's profits**
   회사 수익 감소

6. **send someone out to take care of the problem**
   문제를 해결할 사람을 보내다

   ▶ **send a repair person**
   수리 기사를 보내다

7. **experiencing problems with our sound equipment**
   음향 장비에 문제가 있는

   ▶ **Some equipment is not working.**
   어떤 장비가 작동하지 않는다.

8. **collaborated**
   공동 작업을 했다

   ▶ **worked together**
   함께 작업했다

9. **patronage**
   후원

   ▶ **support**
   지원

10. **send to the wrong individuals**
    엉뚱한 사람에게 보내다

    ▶ **send incorrectly**
    잘못 보내다

11. **less expensive**
    덜 비싼

    ▶ **lower costs**
    더 적은 비용

12. **collect your pool passes**
    수영장 출입증을 받다

    ▶ **pick up passes**
    출입증을 찾아가다

13. **gets in tomorrow**
    내일 도착한다

    ▶ **has not arrived**
    도착하지 않았다

14. **give you another call**
    다시 전화를 하다

    ▶ **make a phone call**
    전화를 하다

15. **if you add your name to our mailing list**
    저희 우편물 수신자 명단에 이름을 올리시면

    ▶ **by joining a mailing list**
    우편물 수신자 명단에 가입해서

16. **become an effective public speaker**
    효과적인 대중 연설자가 되다

    ▶ **improving public speaking skills**
    대중 연설 능력 향상시키기

17. **be short on chairs**
    의자가 부족하다

    ▶ **not be enough seats**
    좌석이 충분하지 않다

18. **the head of maintenance**
    관리 책임자

    ▶ **the maintenance supervisor**
    유지보수 관리자

19. **let you know that city workers will be making some repairs** 시 작업자들이 수리할 예정임을 알려 주다

    ▶ **give notice about a repair**
    보수 공사에 대해 공지하다

20. **pianist Rhonda Phelps will be performing**
    피아니스트 론다 펠프스 씨가 공연할 것이다

    ▶ **A musician will perform.**
    음악가가 연주할 것이다.

PARAPHRASING LIST

21. The rent is quite affordable.
임대료가 적당하다.
▸ The rent is not expensive.
임대료가 비싸지 않다.

22. new-associates
신입 직원들
▸ new employees
신입 직원들

23. Our annual earnings are the highest in the industry.
우리의 연간 수익은 이 업계 최고이다.
▸ It earns a lot of money.
돈을 많이 번다.

24. Premium-quality desserts are selling very well.
고급 디저트가 매우 잘 팔리고 있다.
▸ Sales are good for high-quality desserts.
고급 디저트의 매출이 좋다.

25. share some pastry samples with you
페이스트리 샘플을 제공하다
▸ pass out dessert samples
디저트 샘플을 나누어주다

26. reach
연락하다
▸ call
전화하다

27. open an office abroad
해외에 지점을 열다
▸ open an international office
해외 지점을 개장하다

28. temperatures will drop
기온이 떨어질 것이다
▸ It will get colder.
추워질 것이다.

29. how well we take care of these goods
우리가 이 물건들을 얼마나 잘 다루는지
▸ handle equipment carefully
장비를 조심스럽게 다루다

30. has lived in our town
우리 시에서 살았다
▸ local resident
지역 주민

31. a new service we're offering on the library's Web site
도서관 웹사이트에서 제공하고 있는 새로운 서비스
▸ Online services have been added.
온라인 서비스가 추가되었다.

32. coffee and desert
커피와 디저트
▸ refreshments
다과

33. Your flight will be leaving from gate five instead of gate sixteen. 여러분의 항공기는 16번 게이트가 아닌 5번 게이트에서 출발합니다.
▸ a change in the departure gate
출발 게이트의 변경

34. vacation destinations that both adults and children will enjoy 어른들과 아이들 모두 즐길 수 있는 휴가지
▸ family vacations
가족 휴가 여행

35. the company's security policy for visitors
방문객들에 대한 회사의 보안 정책
▸ the procedures for office visitors
사무실 방문객들을 위한 절차

36. renovations
수리
▸ a construction project
공사

37. use the rear doors to the building
후문을 이용하다
▸ use a different entrance
다른 출입구를 이용하다

38. unseasonably warm
때 아니게 따뜻한
▸ unusually warm
이례적으로 따뜻한

39. Temperatures should drop.
기온이 떨어질 것이다.
▸ Temperatures will decrease.
기온이 내려갈 것이다.

40. haven't been compensated for the overtime hours
시간 외 근무수당을 지급받지 못했다
▸ was not paid for extra work
시간 외 근무 수당을 받지 못했다

41.	my floor manager 저희 공장장	▶ a supervisor 관리자
42.	look over the new Sector TX 신형 섹터 TX를 살펴보다	▶ view a car model 자동차 모델을 살펴보다
43.	do not go too far 너무 멀리 가지 않다	▶ staying in the area 그 구역에 머무르는 것
44.	be reading a chapter and discussing her amazing discovery 한 장을 낭독하고 그녀의 놀라운 발견에 대해 이야기하다	▶ share part of her book 자신의 책 일부를 공유하다
45.	contract an overseas firm 해외 업체와 계약하다	▶ hire an overseas company 해외 업체를 고용하다
46.	water-protective coating 방수 코팅	▶ water resistance 방수
47.	moved into our new headquarters 새 본부로 이전했다	▶ relocated its head office 본사를 이전했다
48.	see and talk about our open office layout 우리의 열린 사무실 배치 형식을 취재하다	▶ describe an office's design 사무실 디자인에 관해 서술하다
49.	answer any questions you might have or just to say hello 질문에 답변하거나 인사하다	▶ meet an audience 관객을 만나다
50.	not normally open to the public 보통은 일반인에게 공개하지 않는	▶ a normally closed room 보통은 폐쇄된 방
51.	cost-saving 비용을 절감하는	▶ save money 돈을 절약하다
52.	make sure that the information you entered is correct 입력한 정보가 맞는지 확인하다	▶ confirm the size of an order 주문의 규모를 확인하다
53.	the sounds of wildlife, wind, and running water in the mountains 산에서 들리는 야생동물과 바람, 흐르는 물의 소리	▶ sounds in nature 자연의 소리
54.	the president of the Air Traffic Controllers' Association 항공 관제사 협회 회장	▶ a leader of a professional group 전문가 단체의 지도자
55.	you can't make it 당신은 시간을 낼 수 없다	▶ a member is unable to attend 회원이 참석할 수 없다
56.	get in touch with a moving company 이사업체에 연락하다	▶ contact a moving company 이사업체에 연락하다
57.	we ran out 다 떨어졌다	▶ A product is not available. 상품을 구입할 수 없다.
58.	relocate 이전하다	▶ moving 이전하는
59.	voice-mail system 음성 메일	▶ telephone messages 전화 메시지
60.	scratched 긁힌	▶ damaged 파손된

61. our corporate luncheon
회사 오찬

▶ a company lunch
회사 오찬

62. We're missing the pasta.
파스타가 없다.

▶ An item is missing.
한 가지 품목이 빠졌다.

63. put a new logo
새 로고를 넣다

▶ feature a new logo
새 로고를 특징으로 하다

64. a bonus
보너스

▶ some extra money
부수입

65. take a look at the notice board
게시판을 참고하다

▶ check a notice board
게시판을 확인하다

66. familiarize oneself with their Web site
그들의 웹사이트를 익히다

▶ review some information online
온라인상에서 몇 가지 정보를 검토하다

67. let your supervisor know
감독관에게 알려주다

▶ speaking to a supervisor
감독관에게 이야기하는 것

68. still closed
아직도 폐쇄되어 있는

▶ currently closed
현재 폐쇄된

69. increase the volume of vegetables that we purchase
우리가 구입하는 채소의 양을 늘리다

▶ buying more vegetables
더 많은 채소 구입하기

70. introduce our new software program
새 소프트웨어 프로그램을 소개하다

▶ launch a new product
신제품을 출시하다

71. non-polluting
오염시키지 않는

▶ environmentally friendly
친환경적인

72. our company's expansion
회사 확장

▶ the growth of a company
회사의 성장

73. pick up your gift bag
선물 봉투를 가져가다

▶ collect a gift
선물을 받아 가다

74. the president of National Science University
국립과학대학의 총장

▶ a university official
대학 관계자

75. research firm
연구 기업

▶ research company
연구 회사

76. present you with this small token of our appreciation
이 작은 감사의 징표를 증정하다

▶ An award will be given.
상이 수여될 것이다.

77. mayor
시장

▶ a city official
시 공무원

78. put your cell phones on mute
휴대전화를 무음으로 하다

▶ silence their mobile devices
휴대 기기를 무음으로 하다

79. alert you to some fantastic deals
놀라운 가격의 할인 상품에 대해 알려주다

▶ tell people about special offers
사람들에게 특별 행사에 대해 말하다

80. complimentary
무료의

▶ for free, free of charge
무료로

81.	a minor difficulty with the sound system 음향 시스템의 경미한 문제	▶ A sound system is not working. 음향 시스템이 고장 났다.
82.	the electricity will be off 전기가 차단될 것이다	▶ A building will be without power. 건물에 전력이 들어오지 않을 것이다.
83.	inform residents of the upcoming construction work 예정된 건설 공사에 대해 주민들에게 알려주다	▶ inform people of a city project 사람들에게 도시 프로젝트에 대해 알리다
84.	We've extended our hours of operation. 영업 시간을 연장했다.	▶ The store will stay open longer. 상점 문을 더 오래 열 것이다.
85.	commitment to the environment 환경에 대한 헌신	▶ environmentally friendly 친환경적인
86.	be arranged for gatherings of all sizes 모든 규모의 행사를 위해 마련되어 있다	▶ accommodate many group sizes 여러 규모의 단체를 수용하다
87.	laying carpet 카펫 깔기	▶ installing carpet 카펫 깔기
88.	basketball legend 농구계의 전설	▶ a professional athlete 프로 운동선수
89.	complete a practice interview 면접 실습을 마치다	▶ practice a skill 기술을 연습하다
90.	comprehensive resource book 종합적인 정보가 담긴 교재	▶ reference guide 안내서
91.	the first 100 customers in line 선착순 고객 100명	▶ customers who shop early 일찍 쇼핑하는 (가게에 온) 고객들
92.	the annual Millwood County Fair 연례 밀우드 카운티 박람회	▶ an annual celebration 연례 축하행사
93.	bring an umbrella 우산을 지참하다	▶ prepare for rain 비가 올 것에 대비하다
94.	Medical Center 메디컬 센터	▶ hospital 병원
95.	The location is easily accessible by public transportation. 위치가 대중 교통으로 접근하기 쉽다.	▶ the convenient location 편리한 위치
96.	a furnished apartment to film some of their main scenes 몇 가지 주요 장면을 찍기 위해 가구가 비치된 아파트	▶ a filming location 영화 촬영지
97.	staying away from the city center 도심을 피하는 것	▶ avoid the city center 도심을 피하다
98.	stay inside 실내에 머무르다	▶ remaining indoors 실내에 머무르기
99.	handle or lean against anything 어떤 것에든 만지거나 기대다	▶ touching the furnishings 가구를 만지는 것
100.	a lot less noisy 훨씬 소음이 적은	▶ quiet 조용한

PARAPHRASING LIST

101. distinctive architecture
멋진 건축물

▶ **unusual old buildings**
특이한 옛 건물들

102. take pictures
사진을 찍다

▶ **the use of cameras**
카메라의 사용

103. put on some sunscreen
자외선 차단제를 바르다

▶ **use sun protection**
자외선 차단제를 사용하다

104. fabrics
직물, 섬유

▶ **materials**
재료

105. move their cars
차량을 옮기다

▶ **move their vehicles**
차량을 옮기다

106. get tickets
티켓을 사다

▶ **purchase tickets**
티켓을 구입하다

107. bags and personal items
가방과 개인 물품

▶ **luggage**
수화물

108. storms
폭풍우

▶ **bad weather**
나쁜 날씨

109. give an address
연설하다

▶ **give a speech**
연설하다

110. temporary help
임시 지원

▶ **temporary workers**
임시 직원

111. request forms
요청서

▶ **some paperwork**
서류

112. add your e-mail address
이메일 주소를 추가하다

▶ **provide additional contact information**
추가 연락정보를 제공하다

113. city council president
시의회 의장

▶ **a local official**
지역 관료

114. repair work on the bridge
교량 보수 작업

▶ **A bridge is being fixed.**
다리가 보수되고 있다.

115. download the app on your mobile device
휴대폰에 앱을 다운받다

▶ **get a mobile app**
휴대폰 앱을 받다

116. purchase shares of stock
주식을 매입하다

▶ **invest**
투자하다

117. shoe
신발

▶ **footwear**
신발

118. run 24 hours a day, 7 days a week
하루 24시간 1주일 내내 작동되다

▶ **operate continuously**
계속 가동하다

119. reduce the amount of paper we use
종이 사용량을 줄이다

▶ **conserve paper**
종이를 절약하다

120. give you the chance to try the latest version of our product 제품의 최신 버전을 사용할 수 있는 기회를 제공하다

▶ **offer an updated product**
업데이트된 제품을 제공하다

121. show you all how the new machines work
새로운 기계의 작동법을 보여 주다

▶ demonstrate equipment
장비를 시연하다

122. fill in items one through twelve
항목을 1번부터 12번까지 기입하다

▶ fill out a form
양식을 작성하다

123. stay for an extra day
하루 더 머무르다

▶ extend her stay
숙박을 연장하다

124. go on sale
판매에 들어가다

▶ become available
구입할 수 있다

125. in-flight
기내의

▶ on an airplane
기내에서

126. social events
친목 행사

▶ social functions
친목 행사

127. brainstorm designs
디자인에 대한 아이디어 회의를 하다

▶ propose design ideas
디자인 아이디어를 제안하다

128. tune in to
~에 채널을 맞추다

▶ listen to
~을 듣다

129. a comprehensive folder full of information
정보가 가득한 종합 폴더

▶ information packet
자료집

130. gas and electric company
가스 전기 공사

▶ utility company
(전기·가스·상하수도 등의) 공익 기업

131. found/establish/install
설립하다; 설치하다

▶ set up
세우다; 설치하다

132. make a better place to live
더 살기 좋은 곳으로 만들다

▶ improvements to the community
지역사회 개선

133. what our customers have written about our service
고객들이 우리 서비스에 대해 작성한 것

▶ customer reviews
고객 의견

134. make your workspace more efficient
작업 공간을 더 효율적으로 만들다

▶ organize a workplace
작업장을 정돈하다

135. see the timetables for our new expanded service
새로 확대된 운행 시간표를 보다

▶ view revised schedules
수정된 시간표를 보다

136. The classes are very popular, with a long waiting list.
그 수업들은 매우 인기 있어 수강 대기자 명단이 길다.

▶ The classes are in high demand.
그 수업들을 들으려는 사람들이 많다.

137. We no longer carry that particular item.
그 상품을 더 이상 취급하지 않는다.

▶ An item is unavailable.
한 가지 물품이 없다.

138. It's within walking distance of many shops and restaurants. 걸어갈 만한 거리에 많은 상점과 식당이 있다.

▶ It is in a convenient location.
편리한 곳에 위치해 있다.

139. The factory will be adding a Saturday shift to the schedule. 공장 측이 일정에 토요일 교대 근무를 추가할 것이다.

▶ Hours of operation will be extended.
조업 시간이 연장될 것이다.

140. It was revolutionary for Thompson's time.
그것은 톰슨의 시대에 혁명적이었다.

▶ It was not a typical design for its time.
그것은 당시에 일반적인 디자인이 아니었다.

PART 4

Directions: You will hear some talks given by a single speaker. You will be asked to answer three questions about what the speaker says in each talk. Select the best response to each question and mark the letter (A), (B), (C), or (D) on your answer sheet. The talks will not be printed in your test book and will be spoken only one time.

71. What product is being advertised?
(A) A fitness watch
(B) A tablet computer
(C) A mobile phone
(D) A digital camera

72. How does the speaker say a model has changed?
(A) It is user-friendly.
(B) It is more accurate.
(C) It has a larger screen.
(D) It is now customizable.

73. According to the speaker, how can the listeners receive a discount?
(A) By recommending a product to a friend
(B) By using a discount code
(C) By purchasing a second item
(D) By posting a photograph on social media

74. What event is taking place?
(A) An anniversary celebration
(B) A staff meeting
(C) A company picnic
(D) A grand opening

75. What does the business manufacture?
(A) Tiles
(B) Art prints
(C) Eyeglasses
(D) Paint

76. What will the listeners most likely do next?
(A) Watch a video
(B) Move some patio furniture
(C) Eat some snacks
(D) View some samples

77. Who most likely is the speaker?
(A) A delivery driver
(B) A sales associate
(C) A repair person
(D) A production manager

78. What does the speaker recommend the listener do?
(A) Buy a new machine
(B) Check a calendar
(C) Update a company logo
(D) Expand a storage area

79. What does the speaker say he has e-mailed the listener?
(A) A project timeline
(B) An itemized invoice
(C) Results from a focus group
(D) Budget information

80. What will happen around noon?
(A) Some staff will arrive to help harvest vegetables.
(B) Customers will pick up some orders.
(C) The company will hand out samples.
(D) Some new shelving will be delivered.

81. Why does the speaker say to wait to pack the lettuce?
(A) He wants to put it in bags.
(B) He wants it to stay fresh.
(C) He needs to confirm a price.
(D) He needs to weigh it.

82. Why does the speaker say, "I doubt that will happen often"?
(A) To question a policy
(B) To provide some reassurance
(C) To justify investing in an appliance
(D) To explain why a schedule was revised

83. Where does the speaker most likely work?
(A) At a museum
(B) At a library
(C) At a publishing house
(D) At a bookstore

84. What is the topic of the workshop?
(A) Organizing archives
(B) Planning special events
(C) Selling antiques
(D) Restoring old books

85. What will the listeners most likely do next?
(A) Take a tour
(B) Complete a questionnaire
(C) Pay for some materials
(D) Form discussion groups

86. Who most likely are the listeners?
(A) Actors
(B) Musicians
(C) Dancers
(D) Fashion models

87. What does the speaker say Martina will do?
(A) Collect forms
(B) Provide a demonstration
(C) Take photographs
(D) Set up a sound system

88. What does the speaker imply when she says, "there are more people here than we expected"?
(A) More food should be ordered.
(B) Not everyone will be able to participate.
(C) A larger space is needed.
(D) A process will take longer than expected.

Go on to the next page

89. How can farmers benefit from using the business?
(A) They can increase profits.
(B) They can qualify for a government loan.
(C) They can save time.
(D) They can improve infrastructure.

90. What does the business provide advice about?
(A) Purchasing new equipment
(B) Hiring temporary workers
(C) Using eco-friendly practices
(D) Choosing crops to grow

91. According to the speaker, what can the listeners do on a Web site?
(A) Find a mailing address
(B) See customer reviews
(C) Access a discount coupon
(D) Request a brochure

92. Why is the speaker congratulating the listener?
(A) She received a promotion.
(B) She celebrated a work anniversary.
(C) She won an award.
(D) She was a keynote speaker at a conference.

93. Why does the speaker say, "I've been working with this client for three years"?
(A) To express regret about leaving a position
(B) To explain why there are so many documents
(C) To emphasize a good relationship with a client
(D) To clarify a misunderstanding about a timeline

94. Why does the speaker suggest that the listener wait to review some materials?
(A) He wants to correct some errors.
(B) He needs a supervisor's signature.
(C) The folder is incomplete.
(D) The folder is not yet protected with a password.

Category	Rating
Durability	★★★★★
Water resistance	★★
Weight	★★★★
Appearance	★★★

95. What type of product is the speaker discussing?
(A) Footwear
(B) Furniture
(C) Luggage
(D) Outerwear

96. Why does the speaker suggest not changing a price?
(A) The material used is expensive.
(B) Similar products have the same price.
(C) The price was already increased recently.
(D) Customers are satisfied with the current price.

97. Look at the graphic. Which category did Anya's idea have an impact on?
(A) Durability
(B) Water resistance
(C) Weight
(D) Appearance

Flight Information

1. Departure City
London ⌄

2. Destination
Jakarta ⌄

3. Departure Date
May 9 ⌄

4. Return Date
May 22 ⌄

98. Look at the graphic. Which field did the speaker change?
(A) 1
(B) 2
(C) 3
(D) 4

99. What does the speaker offer to do?
(A) Find a hotel
(B) E-mail a receipt
(C) Make a restaurant reservation
(D) Arrange an airport shuttle

100. Why is the listener going to Jakarta?
(A) To meet clients
(B) To attend a trade show
(C) To visit family
(D) To buy some supplies

ETS

FINAL

TEST

LISTENING TEST

In the Listening test, you will be asked to demonstrate how well you understand spoken English. The entire Listening test will last approximately 45 minutes. There are four parts, and directions are given for each part. You must mark your answers on the separate answer sheet. Do not write your answers in your test book.

PART 1

Directions: For each question in this part, you will hear four statements about a picture in your test book. When you hear the statements, you must select the one statement that best describes what you see in the picture. Then find the number of the question on your answer sheet and mark your answer. The statements will not be printed in your test book and will be spoken only one time.

Statement (C), "They're sitting at a table," is the best description of the picture, so you should select answer (C) and mark it on your answer sheet.

1.

2.

Go on to the next page →

3.

4.

5.

6.

Go on to the next page

PART 2

Directions: You will hear a question or statement and three responses spoken in English. They will not be printed in your test book and will be spoken only one time. Select the best response to the question or statement and mark the letter (A), (B), or (C) on your answer sheet.

7. Mark your answer on your answer sheet.

8. Mark your answer on your answer sheet.

9. Mark your answer on your answer sheet.

10. Mark your answer on your answer sheet.

11. Mark your answer on your answer sheet.

12. Mark your answer on your answer sheet.

13. Mark your answer on your answer sheet.

14. Mark your answer on your answer sheet.

15. Mark your answer on your answer sheet.

16. Mark your answer on your answer sheet.

17. Mark your answer on your answer sheet.

18. Mark your answer on your answer sheet.

19. Mark your answer on your answer sheet.

20. Mark your answer on your answer sheet.

21. Mark your answer on your answer sheet.

22. Mark your answer on your answer sheet.

23. Mark your answer on your answer sheet.

24. Mark your answer on your answer sheet.

25. Mark your answer on your answer sheet.

26. Mark your answer on your answer sheet.

27. Mark your answer on your answer sheet.

28. Mark your answer on your answer sheet.

29. Mark your answer on your answer sheet.

30. Mark your answer on your answer sheet.

31. Mark your answer on your answer sheet.

Directions: You will hear some conversations between two or more people. You will be asked to answer three questions about what the speakers say in each conversation. Select the best response to each question and mark the letter (A), (B), (C), or (D) on your answer sheet. The conversations will not be printed in your test book and will be spoken only one time.

32. Who is the woman?
    (A) An event planner
    (B) A music producer
    (C) A radio host
    (D) A film director

33. What incentive does the woman offer?
    (A) Celebrity endorsement
    (B) Higher pay
    (C) A flexible work schedule
    (D) Access to a recording studio

34. What will the man most likely do next?
    (A) Call his bandmates
    (B) Pack his equipment
    (C) Practice for an audition
    (D) Finish writing a song

35. Where do the speakers most likely work?
    (A) At an airport
    (B) At a bus station
    (C) At a luggage store
    (D) At a shipping warehouse

36. What does the woman say is causing extra work?
    (A) Bad weather
    (B) A scheduled inspection
    (C) Untrained employees
    (D) The holiday season

37. What does the man say he will locate before starting a task?
    (A) Packaging supplies
    (B) Safety equipment
    (C) An office key
    (D) A customer list

38. What are the men concerned about?
    (A) Meeting a deadline
    (B) Fixing a product defect
    (C) Increasing sales targets
    (D) Expanding their customer base

39. What types of products do the men sell?
    (A) Children's toys
    (B) Computer monitors
    (C) Office chairs
    (D) Bicycle accessories

40. What does the woman ask the men to provide?
    (A) Business references
    (B) Product specifications
    (C) Employee qualifications
    (D) Customer survey results

41. Where most likely are the speakers?
    (A) At a supermarket
    (B) At a clothing store
    (C) At a restaurant
    (D) At a home-goods store

42. How did the woman learn about the business?
    (A) From a flyer
    (B) From a colleague
    (C) From a magazine
    (D) From a television commercial

43. Why does the man say, "it's a seasonal item"?
    (A) To indicate why an item is unavailable
    (B) To explain where an item is located
    (C) To justify an item's high price
    (D) To recommend an item

Go on to the next page

44. Where do the speakers work?

(A) At a mobile phone store
(B) At a recording studio
(C) At an event venue
(D) At an investment bank

45. What does the woman say is causing a problem?

(A) Some software is malfunctioning.
(B) A payment was not received.
(C) A banquet hall is not big enough.
(D) Some schedules were not distributed.

46. What does the man say he will do?

(A) Issue a payment refund
(B) Investigate some alternatives
(C) Talk to a colleague
(D) Return a product

47. Where does the conversation most likely take place?

(A) At a department store
(B) At a television studio
(C) At a fashion school
(D) At a textile factory

48. What does the man suggest?

(A) Setting up a display
(B) Offering a class
(C) Changing a clothing design
(D) Training a new employee

49. What does the man say he has on file?

(A) Some application forms
(B) Some sample photos
(C) Some expense reports
(D) Some measurements

50. What service does the man's business provide?

(A) Industrial equipment cleaning
(B) Shared office space
(C) Property inspections
(D) Corporate training

51. What does the woman say she is concerned about?

(A) Payment schedules
(B) Parking availability
(C) Internet speed
(D) Noise levels

52. Why does the man suggest that the woman visit a Web site?

(A) To receive a discount
(B) To get driving directions
(C) To view membership information
(D) To read customer reviews

53. What department do the speakers work in?

(A) Human resources
(B) Data analysis
(C) Accounting
(D) Production

54. What does the man say he will send?

(A) A link to a Web site
(B) An invitation to a meeting
(C) A registration form
(D) An expense report

55. What does the woman imply when she says, "I don't complete my training until next week"?

(A) She can adjust a schedule.
(B) She is behind on some work.
(C) She thinks a training is too long.
(D) She is unsure about an assignment.

56. Where do the speakers most likely work?

(A) At a paper factory
(B) At a candy company
(C) At a publishing company
(D) At an advertising firm

57. What was the woman concerned about?

(A) Whether some equipment will have to be replaced
(B) Where a new office will be located
(C) How much some materials will cost
(D) How many employees are available

58. What is causing a delay?

(A) Limited supplies
(B) A mechanical issue
(C) A contract negotiation
(D) Bad weather

---

59. What would the man like to become?

(A) A private pilot
(B) An air traffic controller
(C) A flight attendant
(D) An airplane mechanic

60. What feature of a training program does the woman emphasize?

(A) The convenient location
(B) The short duration
(C) The knowledgeable instructors
(D) The well-established history

61. What does the woman offer to give to the man?

(A) A detailed bill
(B) A study manual
(C) A certificate of completion
(D) A recommendation for a doctor

https://www.bridgelaneflorists.com

Floral Centerpieces

Birdcage – $12   Potted Plants – $15

Flower Bucket – $20   Grand Vase – $22

62. What kind of event is the woman planning?

(A) A conference
(B) An awards banquet
(C) A company retreat
(D) A product launch

63. Look at the graphic. What is the price of the product the woman selects?

(A) $12
(B) $15
(C) $20
(D) $22

64. What will the woman do to save money?

(A) Use a coupon
(B) Order in bulk
(C) Pick up an order
(D) Shorten a guest list

Go on to the next page

Name	Product Number
Strawberry Splash	Z28
Meadow Rush	X59
Python Green	W63
Rainbow Fun	F97

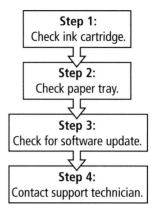

Step 1:
Check ink cartridge.

Step 2:
Check paper tray.

Step 3:
Check for software update.

Step 4:
Contact support technician.

65. Where do the speakers most likely work?

(A) At an ice cream shop
(B) At a cosmetics store
(C) At a toy shop
(D) At an art supply store

66. According to the woman, why is a product popular?

(A) It is affordable.
(B) It recently won an award.
(C) It appeared in a celebrity's photo.
(D) It is easy to use.

67. Look at the graphic. Which product number will the woman order?

(A) Z28
(B) X59
(C) W63
(D) F97

68. Why do the speakers need to leave?

(A) To pick up an order
(B) To meet with a client
(C) To attend a workshop
(D) To allow workers to do repairs

69. Look at the graphic. Which step does the woman tell the man to complete?

(A) Step 1
(B) Step 2
(C) Step 3
(D) Step 4

70. What does the man ask the woman about?

(A) The location of some supplies
(B) The start time of an event
(C) A warranty
(D) A time estimate

Directions: You will hear some talks given by a single speaker. You will be asked to answer three questions about what the speaker says in each talk. Select the best response to each question and mark the letter (A), (B), (C), or (D) on your answer sheet. The talks will not be printed in your test book and will be spoken only one time.

---

71. What does the speaker say is a priority for the company?

(A) Customer service
(B) Environmental responsibility
(C) Community involvement
(D) Employee satisfaction

72. What was a budget approved for?

(A) Beginning a renovation project
(B) Modifying a company logo
(C) Purchasing equipment
(D) Hiring temporary staff

73. What does the speaker encourage some listeners to do?

(A) Collaborate with their coworkers
(B) Talk to their managers
(C) Sign up for an additional shift
(D) Take public transportation

---

74. What event will be held this weekend?

(A) An art festival
(B) A business's grand opening
(C) A cooking competition
(D) An outdoor concert

75. Who most likely is Christopher Vogel?

(A) A town official
(B) A writer
(C) A talent scout
(D) A chef

76. What gift will some of the guests receive?

(A) A tote bag
(B) An autographed book
(C) A basket of snacks
(D) A pair of headphones

---

77. Who is Axel Schmidt?

(A) An athlete
(B) A physical therapist
(C) A sports coach
(D) A fitness center manager

78. What topic will the interview focus on?

(A) A successful career
(B) A new sports facility
(C) A youth athletic program
(D) A recent book

79. How can the listeners participate in the show?

(A) By making a phone call
(B) By sending an e-mail
(C) By posting on social media
(D) By attending a live recording

---

80. Where does the speaker most likely work?

(A) At an accounting firm
(B) A publishing agency
(C) At a bookstore
(D) At a technology company

81. What will be different about future meetings?

(A) They will be recorded.
(B) They will be held virtually.
(C) They will be held daily.
(D) They will be catered.

82. Why does the speaker say, "we're working on so many projects at once"?

(A) To apologize for forgetting a task
(B) To complain about a workload
(C) To request some assistance with a project
(D) To justify the use of a document

Go on to the next page

83. Where are the listeners?

(A) At a farm
(B) At a factory
(C) At a recording studio
(D) At a sports complex

84. What are the listeners asked to keep in lockers?

(A) Large bags
(B) Beverage containers
(C) Personal electronics
(D) Jackets

85. According to the speaker, what is available at an information desk?

(A) Discount coupons
(B) An employee directory
(C) Hard hats
(D) Shoe covers

86. What most likely is the speaker's job?

(A) Interior designer
(B) Real estate agent
(C) Furniture maker
(D) Construction worker

87. According to the speaker, what is an advantage of using paint?

(A) It is inexpensive.
(B) It lasts a long time.
(C) It is readily available.
(D) It is easy to change.

88. What will the speaker do next?

(A) Present some survey results
(B) Show some photographs
(C) Introduce a guest speaker
(D) Provide a promotional code

89. What is the focus of the certification program?

(A) Tunnel construction
(B) Security services
(C) Bridge inspection
(D) Food safety

90. What does the speaker say the listeners will do first?

(A) Introduce themselves
(B) Watch a video
(C) Complete some paperwork
(D) Change a password

91. What does the speaker imply when he says, "my e-mail address is on the handout"?

(A) The speaker's e-mail address has changed.
(B) A written assignment can be submitted electronically.
(C) The listeners should supply contact information.
(D) The listeners can send questions.

92. What does the speaker say is new at the hospital?

(A) A hiring process
(B) A lobby area for visitors
(C) A fund-raising procedure
(D) A check-in system for patients

93. Why does the speaker say, "that's only six months from now"?

(A) To express concern
(B) To correct some information
(C) To decline an offer
(D) To disagree with a decision

94. What does the speaker invite the listener to do?

(A) Tour a facility
(B) Submit a résumé
(C) Give a demonstration
(D) Join a research project

	Estimated Cost per Phase
Phase 1	$50 million
Phase 2	$40 million
Phase 3	$60 million
Phase 4	$35 million

Cabbage Field 1	Carrots Field 2
Lettuce Field 3	Potatoes Field 4

95. What problem does the speaker mention?

(A) A tractor has broken down.
(B) An insect has caused damage.
(C) Demand for vegetables has decreased.
(D) Government regulations have changed.

96. Look at the graphic. Which field will have a new crop?

(A) Field 1
(B) Field 2
(C) Field 3
(D) Field 4

97. According to the speaker, what will happen next week?

(A) A contract will be signed.
(B) A specialist will visit.
(C) An outdoor market will open.
(D) Some equipment will arrive.

98. Who most likely are the listeners?

(A) News reporters
(B) Government officials
(C) Travel agents
(D) Railway executives

99. What project is the city working on?

(A) Renovating some buildings
(B) Repairing some underground pipes
(C) Building a new park
(D) Extending some power lines

100. Look at the graphic. What phase of the project has just been completed?

(A) Phase 1
(B) Phase 2
(C) Phase 3
(D) Phase 4

ANSWER SHEET

Final Test

수험번호

응시일자 : 20   년   월   일

성명   한글
       한자
       영자

LISTENING (Part I ~ IV)

READING (Part V ~ VII)